Trinity CertTESOL Companion

Jason Anderson

Published by
DELTA PUBLISHING
Quince Cottage
Hoe Lane
Peaslake
Surrey GU5 9SW
England

www.deltapublishing.co.uk

© Jason Anderson 2017

ISBN 978-1-909783-24-9

Edited by Fiona McGarry
Designed by Peter Bushell
Illustrations by Jason Anderson
Printed in China by RR Donnelley

Author's Acknowledgements

I'd like to begin by sincerely thanking Ben Beaumont, Christine
Barker and Tom Lee at Trinity College London, and Nick Boisseau
at Delta Publishing for their shared vision in bringing the Trinity
CertTESOL Companion to fruition; without this teamwork, the
book would never have happened. No less important was my
patient editor, Fiona McGarry, whose extensive knowledge,
insightful suggestions and balanced opinions helped to improve
the text and its organisation greatly. Thanks also to the designer,
Peter Bushell, and the whole team at Delta Publishing for their
hard work and support.

Many thanks to the early reviewers of the material for opening
our eyes to the diversity of CertTESOL courses out there, including
Dylan Gates, Alice Oxholm, Anna Stubbs and Will Tichener.
Thanks also to the many trainers who contributed quotes for the
book, including: Stephanie Armstrong, Dylan Gates, Charlotte
Giller, Sinéad Laffan, Emma Meade-Flynn, Christa Mundin, Shaun
Sweeney, Ross Thorburn, Will Tichener and Samantha Tring.
Thanks to Shirley Norton, Ben Butler, Adam Bandstra, Helen Eames
and Lucy Pereira for help with job interview questions for After the
Course, and to Varinder Unlu and IH London for permission to take
classroom photographs.

Special thanks to all the respondents to my academic research on
pre-service teacher training courses, but especially to the non-
native English-speaking teachers (NNESTs) and teacher educators,
whose stories of challenges, discrimination and success against
the odds have informed my understanding of contexts, Englishes
and our complex identities as teachers and teacher educators.
Although ethical concerns prevent me from naming names, this
book is dedicated to you and to future NNESTs who face similar
challenges.

As always, the wisdom herein is shared, but any shortcomings are
mine alone.

Publisher's acknowledgements

The publisher would like to acknowledge the following sources of
copyright material:

p. 86 Phonemic Chart based on the Phonemic Chart designed by
Adrian Underhill, copyright © Adrian Underhill 1994. Published in
Sound Foundations: Chart and Guide (Macmillan Education, 1994)

p. 151 Coursebook extract by Hugh Dellar and Andrew Walkley,
copyright © Heinle Cengage ELT, 2010. Published in Outcomes
Intermediate (Heinle Cengage ELT, 2010)

pp. 98, 127, 158 images are from Shutterstock.

Contents

Introduction

The Trinity CertTESOL is one of the most popular qualifications for prospective English language teachers, awarded to thousands of candidates worldwide every year. It provides an opportunity for trainees to learn the fundamental skills to enable them to start teaching English as a foreign/second language anywhere in the world. It is taken both by those who have no prior teaching experience and those with teaching experience who require certification. As well as important theory and hands-on teaching practice, graduates of CertTESOL courses also gain useful reflective practice skills that enable them to continue developing as teachers after the course.

While the qualification is certified by Trinity College London, the courses that lead to it are offered by independent organisations called 'course providers' (e.g. language schools, universities, colleges, etc.). Each course provider develops their own unique course that covers the core components of the Trinity CertTESOL syllabus, and meets Trinity requirements regarding total hours of tuition, teaching practice and guided observation of experienced teachers. Course providers tailor their courses to the needs of their typical course members, whether these are in Anglophone countries (e.g. UK, USA, etc.) or countries where English is a second or foreign language. Many course providers offer intensive full-time courses (often four weeks in duration), and some also offer part-time courses run over several months.

The Trinity CertTESOL syllabus consists of five units which shape the structure of all validated courses. They are as follows:

Unit 1: Teaching Skills

Your own teaching practice, including six hours of assessed teaching of *real* English language learners. This is assessed through your lesson planning, your teaching and your reflection on your teaching after each lesson. There's also a *Guided Observation Journal* to complete with your reflections on four hours of observations of experienced teachers.

Unit 2: Language Awareness and Skills

Your understanding and practical application of the content knowledge that all language teachers need. This includes your understanding of the grammar, lexis and phonology of English, and your understanding of the four skills (speaking, listening, reading and writing), their composite sub-skills, and how these are practised in language learning classrooms.

Unit 3: Learner Profile

A written course assignment for which you interview and then describe the background, needs and linguistic profile of a real English language learner. You also teach a one-to-one lesson to this learner and provide recommendations for her/his further study in the future.

Unit 4: Materials Assignment

A course assignment for which you prepare and present one piece of teaching material and complete a written pro forma providing a rationale for, and evaluation of, the material. You will also present this material in an assessment interview with an external course moderator towards the end of your course.

Unit 5: Unknown Language

A written course assignment for which you participate as a learner in four hours of lessons in a foreign language at beginner level. You describe your experience in an *Unknown Language Journal* and also provide a summary of the overall experience.

What's in the CertTESOL Companion?

The five units of the CertTESOL syllabus form the core of this book, which is designed to support your learning throughout the course, firstly by explaining and unpacking the sometimes technical syllabus content, secondly by describing in detail what is required of you from each unit of the syllabus, and thirdly by providing guidance as you complete the assignments and teaching practice on the course itself.

Two additional units go beyond the CertTESOL syllabus to provide advice when preparing for your course, and guidance for your career and professional development after it. There's also an invaluable reference unit in the book called *The Knowledge* that includes, among other things, information on important aspects of the qualification itself, an overview of English language teaching exams and a useful grammar reference section.

Throughout the book you'll find extracts and examples from CertTESOL assignments, language teaching materials and lesson plans. These will provide useful support, showing one possible way of doing it, but always bear in mind that each course provider has their own requirements with regards to assignment rubric and lesson plan pro formas that you will need to follow. The exception to this is the Unit 4 *Materials Assignment*, for which the rubric and pro forma are specified by Trinity, so the completed example and advice for the interview provided gives clear, detailed guidance on how to get through this part of the course successfully.

The CertTESOL companion includes detailed *Contents* and an *Index* so you can find what you need quickly. There's also a *Glossary* at the back of the book which covers key terminology relating to language teaching and language analysis. Within the text itself, glossary terms are indicated in bold when first mentioned in a unit for your convenience and any unusual idioms or expressions are explained in the margin. CertTESOL courses are often intensive experiences, so it makes sense to have all the key information you need to complete your course successfully in one easy-to-use book. Where you may require further detail, or wish to do further reading, suggestions are provided in the text.

How to use this book

The Trinity CertTESOL Companion can be used in a number of ways to support your learning on your CertTESOL course. Where opportunity provides, you may begin using the CertTESOL companion before the start of your course, and read through it as part of your pre-course preparation, thereby enabling you to be ready for the demands and challenges you are likely to face. In such situations, this preparation will enable you to be aware of what's coming, how and why it's important, and how the different elements of the course link to the CertTESOL syllabus. Alternatively, you may begin using the book at the start of your course, or just after it. As mentioned above, the detailed *Contents* and *Index* will make it easy for you to find what you need quickly whenever you need support.

Texts, tasks and activities within the Trinity CertTESOL Companion may also be integrated into 'inputs' delivered by course providers. As such, the book may be used in the training room to facilitate discussion, support planning, and encourage reflection on the practice of English language teaching.

Each unit of the book (excluding *The Knowledge*) includes several key features to support your learning, and can be used either for self-study or for input activities during the course:

Learning opportunities

Learning opportunities are identified at the beginning of each unit to describe the intended learning within the unit. Unlike learning 'outcomes' or 'aims', the choice of the term 'learning opportunities' is intentional, recognising that learning cannot be forced, and that each reader always takes away something slightly different from other readers. You may find that you learn much more than what is described in the *Learning opportunities*!

Unit review

There's a review at the end of each unit in the form of a task with a number of questions or prompts for you to respond to. This helps you to self-evaluate whether you have learnt the most important content within the unit. It should also serve as a useful revision activity, helping you to process the learning more deeply. You'll find the answers to the unit review at the back of the book.

Pause for
thought

Pause for thought activities

Pause for thought activities are integrated throughout each unit whenever there is an opportunity for you to benefit from thinking for a moment about what you are reading. This helps to make the reading process less passive, leading to more application, deeper understanding and more learning as a result. We can sometimes be tempted to gloss over such activities, especially when time is limited, yet it is a self-evident truth that if we read something and forget it soon after, we have wasted our time. So as the activity title suggests, pause for a moment and think about the question or task. You may want to take a few rough notes, scan back over what you've just read, or even discuss appropriate questions with those around you – it all helps to take in what you are reading. You'll find answers/suggested answers in the *Pause for thought Key* at the back of the book.

Pre-course preparation tasks

Trainees who are reading the book before the start of their CertTESOL course may also find it useful to complete the *Pre-course preparation tasks* provided at the back of the book. These tasks usually require personalised, often reflective responses that do not have a single correct answer, so no answer key is possible. They are useful because they require you to process and interpret what you are reading, and therefore hopefully to remember it as a result. Some course providers may ask you to complete some or all of these tasks as part of your mandatory pre-course preparation.

Whatever your preferred way of using the book, it is hoped that it will provide the support you need and serve as a useful companion to make your CertTESOL course a more memorable, enjoyable and rewarding experience. Wishing you the best of luck on your CertTESOL journey!

Before the course

It's really important to prepare for your CertTESOL course carefully. Make sure you do the required pre-course preparation and try to familiarise yourself with the basics of grammar.
Samantha, CertTESOL trainer

Learning opportunities

This unit will help you to...

- understand the many terms and abbreviations used in English language teaching
- gain a clear idea of your own future career path
- identify key factors to consider when choosing a course provider
- become familiar with the basic procedure for CertTESOL interviews
- find out what happens on a CertTESOL course
- prepare yourself for the workload of the course

Before the course starts, make changes to your daily schedule to allow time for writing up assignments and lesson planning outside the course hours. Block out a couple of hours per day and regard this as a commitment rather than an option.
Christa, CertTESOL trainer

Introduction

Every year thousands of people of different ages, backgrounds and nationalities decide to embark on a new career as an English language teacher, joining an industry that offers a wide range of career paths and the opportunity to work in almost any part of the world. The choices you make at this stage will affect your future and ultimately your chances of success. Yet with so many options and so much advice available, making the right decisions can be quite a challenge. In this chapter we will explore commonly asked questions such as What types of course are available? What's the difference between them? What does the interview procedure involve? What usually happens on such a course? How can I prepare for it? Before we answer any of these questions though, let's begin by clarifying some of the abbreviations and acronyms used to describe English language teaching. There are quite a lot of them!

Abbreviation/ acronym	Pronunciation	Stands for...
TESOL	/tiːsɒl/	Teaching English to Speakers of Other Languages
ESOL	/iːsɒl/	English for Speakers of Other Languages
TEFL / EFL	/tefəl/ /iː ef el/	(Teaching) English as a Foreign Language
TESL / ESL	/tesəl/ /iː es el/	(Teaching) English as a Second Language
ELT	/iː el tiː/	English Language Teaching

The most important thing to note about these abbreviations is that they all often refer to pretty much the same thing: teaching English to people who did not learn it as their **first language**, but because they all evolved in slightly different contexts, they are sometimes used to contrast these contexts with one another. The CertTESOL ('Cert' stands for 'certificate', in case you weren't sure) is a general qualification suitable for all these contexts. ESOL, when contrasted with EFL, is often used to refer to courses for learners who now live permanently in an English-speaking country. For example, we can describe immigrants and refugees in the UK as 'ESOL learners'. EFL learners are often defined as students of English who do not live permanently in an English-speaking country and are studying English either in their home country or visiting an English-speaking country. Thus, Japanese learners in a **business English** class in Japan or Spanish teenagers in a summer school in the UK can all be classed as EFL learners, and their teachers as TEFL teachers. Courses of lessons that take place in private language schools are generally referred to as EFL courses, while classes in community colleges that are often part or fully government funded are normally referred to as ESOL courses. The terms TESL and ESL evolved in the USA and Canada to refer to language teaching in general, but are sometimes also used to contrast with EFL in the same way as ESOL is used in the UK. ELT is a more general term used to refer to the industry or teaching practices in general, covering all the above contexts.

A day in the life of an English language teacher

Graduates of the Trinity CertTESOL find themselves working in a variety of teaching contexts around the world, teaching adults, teenagers or children. Here is a fairly typical lifestyle snapshot provided by a recent graduate of the CertTESOL working in Italy:

> **" If you had told me before my CertTESOL that I'd be teaching kids in a year's time, I'd never have believed you! "**

*My name is Susie Bradshaw. I live in Siena, Italy, where I've been for the last nine months after completing my CertTESOL in the UK. I work as an English teacher to both adults and **younger learners** in a private language school. I do five and a half hours of teaching a day, from Monday to Friday, and occasional extra lessons (usually **one-to-one**) on Saturdays. My working day starts at 2 o'clock in the afternoon, which is really handy because I'm not a morning person! I usually get to work for about 12 o'clock to prepare my lessons. My first class is an enthusiastic group of Italian primary school teachers. We have a lot of fun together, although they are actually on a serious government funded course to improve their English. After a short break, at about 4:30, we have our younger learner classes. I have a small group of 7 to 10-year-olds that can be quite demanding, but as my **classroom management** skills improve, it's getting gradually easier. If you had told me before my CertTESOL that I'd be teaching kids in a year's time, I'd never have believed you! It's definitely harder work than teaching adults, but it can also be rewarding when the kids bring me pictures they've drawn at school or spontaneously start singing songs I've taught them! Then I have a longer break and a bite to eat before my final class. From 7 until 9 I teach a group of adult intermediate learners – my favourite group. They are on a **general English** course, but many of them also want a little bit of business English, making for an interesting mix. Some of them can be a little tired after a full day's work, so we have to blend study with communicative activities to make sure that they all remain involved and enjoy the lessons. I finish at 9 o'clock and sometimes go for a drink or a meal with either my colleagues or my students, some of whom have become good friends and helped me to settle into my new home. In my free time I'm learning Italian and authentic Italian cooking. I'm also taking an online course on teaching younger learners, which is really useful, and part funded by my employer. In terms of salary I'd say I'm comfortable, but I don't seem to be saving anything! Although I don't have much free time and I'm pretty tired by the end of the day, it's really cool to live in such an interesting city and I'm surprised how much I'm enjoying the job.*

Take a moment to imagine your own future career path:

- *Where do you see yourself in a year's time?*
- *Who will your students be?*
- *How will your life be different?*

You may already have a good idea of your future plans, or even have a job waiting for you when you have completed your initial training. Alternatively, you may be happy to wait and see what comes along. However, it stands to reason that the more carefully you visualise your potential goal at this stage and begin your research, the better your preparation is likely to be. You can start learning a language, find out more about a specific career direction or specialisation within English language teaching. Bear in mind that, unlike many other careers, becoming an English language teacher is likely to change your whole life, so it pays to prepare carefully.

B.1 Choosing your CertTESOL course

Spend some time thinking about the teachers who made an impact on you and make some notes about the behaviours, skills and characteristics that were important for you as a student. This can help you discover the kind of teacher you want to be.

Sinèad, CertTESOL trainer

Whether you are planning a long-term career in TEFL, looking for an opportunity to travel and work at the same time, or simply want to gain a useful qualification, it is important to choose your course carefully. Bear in mind that you may be heading overseas to a different country, where you will be doing a new job with new colleagues for a new employer, so your qualification needs to prepare you for this. While many employers in the industry are reputable, and require standard qualifications such as the CertTESOL from all applicants, there are others who offer the promise of a job either without prior qualification or with only a university degree and no specialist training. Beware especially of adverts that prioritise native speaker status over teaching qualifications.

Those who choose to start teaching without qualifications often find themselves working long hours for disreputable employers in schools where working conditions are poor, wages are low and learners dissatisfied. Stories of exploitation, fraud and even passport confiscation are not uncommon in such circumstances. Given the comparatively short length of initial training courses like the CertTESOL, it makes a lot of sense to train for the job properly. This will open up a much wider choice of responsible employers around the world and increase your chances of enjoying the job, simply because you will know more about what you are doing and how to do it.

A quick search for 'TEFL courses' online will return a wide variety of course providers offering certification in return for a modest fee, a few hours of online study and no classroom **teaching practice**. But beware; any course that does not provide classroom experience can hardly prepare you well for teaching in a classroom and the resulting certificate is likely to be worth no more than the paper it is printed on. The Trinity CertTESOL is one of only two initial ELT qualifications (the other is the Cambridge CELTA) that are internationally recognised by all reputable employers and accredited by OFQUAL (Office of Qualifications and Examinations Regulation) at level 5 on the UK Regulated Qualifications framework (RQF). Whichever course you choose, make sure that it is OFQUAL accredited and currently validated by the relevant organisation. The best way to check this for a CertTESOL course is to visit the Trinity College London website (http://www.trinitycollege.co.uk) where you'll find a list of validated **course providers** and advice on how to choose the best one for your needs. Before you do, let's look at some of the most important choices you will need to make.

Different study options

CertTESOL courses can be taken on a part-time or full-time basis, or integrated into a degree at some universities. Part-time courses tend to require attendance two or three evenings a week and sometimes Saturdays. They run for anything from twelve weeks to over a year. Full-time courses usually require eight hours of attendance per day, five days a week over a period of four or five (occasionally six) weeks. The obvious advantage to part-time courses is that, if you are working or in full-time education, you can study in your 'free' time. Other advantages are that they are less intensive, usually less stressful and allow more time for experimentation and learning to sink in. Unfortunately, such courses are only convenient if there is one nearby and if you're not in a rush to get qualified. Courses integrated into degrees are likely to be less intensive and to offer useful linkage to other aspects of the degree qualification itself.

Many people opt for the full-time CertTESOL, which is also called the 'intensive' CertTESOL for good reason. Especially if the course you choose is four weeks long, you will have little, if any, free time, even in the evenings or at weekends for the duration of the course. So, if you have a choice, think carefully before taking the decision to do an intensive course, and if you don't have a choice, make sure you are well prepared for the workload (see *Preparing for the Workload* below).

> *...teachers who know their learners' language and understand their culture have the ability to teach them better than those who don't.*

There is an important difference between CertTESOL courses run in the UK or other countries where English is spoken as a native language, and courses run 'overseas', where English is not spoken as a native language. In the former context, classes of learners will usually be **multilingual** (i.e. a range of different languages), whereas in the latter context, classes will usually be **monolingual** (i.e. sharing a **mother tongue** or first language (**L1**) while also learning English). These two contexts provide different advantages and challenges for the teacher. For example, learners in monolingual classes can share translations of vocabulary or concepts. They can also switch to their shared language whenever they have difficulty using English. Multilingual classes, on the other hand, provide opportunities for interesting discussions about cultural and linguistic differences and students are obliged to communicate in English. Despite these differences, the same basic methodology tends to be taught in both contexts. If you have a good idea of where you would like to work after your course, check to see if there are any course providers located in that country, as there are a number of potential advantages to training to teach with learners who have the same language and cultural background as your future learners. It also provides you with an opportunity to get to know the country, the language and to build up links with other teachers and language schools. While English-only approaches are encouraged in many classrooms around the world, the fact is that teachers who know their learners' language and understand their culture have the ability to teach them better than those who don't.

Key factors to consider

Once you have chosen roughly where you are going to do your CertTESOL, it is likely that you will still have a choice between a number of different course providers. The following list of factors will help you to make an informed decision and get the most out of your course:

- **Location:** The more convenient the training centre is to your home/accommodation, the less time you will spend commuting; this time is valuable if you are planning to take an intensive course.

- **Price:** In education, the old adage 'you get what you pay for' tends to be true, but there are exceptions. Things like: quality of trainers, course content and organisation of timetable can all influence the quality of the course without necessarily affecting the price. Be aware that some course providers do not include Trinity **moderation** fees in their quoted course price.

- **Reputation:** Word-of-mouth and online recommendations are important influences on our choice of course, so most course providers include trainee testimonials on their websites. If you know someone who has done a CertTESOL, find out if they would recommend the course provider or not. You might also want to Google the name of a potential course provider and find out if there are any independent reviews of their CertTESOL courses, or discussions in chat rooms. When you go for your interview (see below), it may be possible to meet some of the trainees on a current course and ask them how they are finding it.

- **Length of course:** A five-week intensive course is less intense than a four-week one, so if you don't work well under pressure, try to seek out such a course. The same goes for part-time courses, with courses of 20 weeks or longer allowing more time for reading, lesson preparation and learning than the shorter 12-14 week courses.

- **Timetable:** Some full-time courses start at 8 or 9am and finish at around 5pm each day. Others start a little later, around midday, and finish at 8 or 9pm. Many part-time courses include Saturdays; if so, these are not optional. Check your calendar carefully before signing up.

- **Help finding work:** Some course providers boast links to specific employers around the world. In some cases, these are tangible opportunities. In other cases, these may simply be links to recruitment agencies. Find out more and be sceptical of offers of guaranteed employment – you can often do much better yourself!

> *Some course providers boast links to specific employers around the world. In some cases, these are tangible opportunities. In other cases, these may simply be links to recruitment agencies.*

- **Resources and facilities:** All course providers will have certain basic resources such as photocopying facilities, computer access and a basic library. In addition to this, larger course providers will usually have cafes, computer labs, longer opening hours and more extensive libraries on site that trainees can benefit from. However, the flipside is that large organisations may have more bureaucracy, and less opportunity to be flexible on some issues.

- **Special offers and add-ons:** Some courses include free offers in their prices, such as photocopying allowance or required reading books. Find out about these when making your initial enquiries. Last-minute discounts may be available at quieter times of the year (usually winter).

Other factors that may influence your choice include: convenience of start dates, trainer qualifications and methodology, all of which should be provided on the course provider's website. There are two less obvious factors that you may also want to enquire about:

- **The pre-course preparation task:** How many hours does it take to complete? What does it involve? Longer tasks may seem less attractive beforehand, but they are likely to provide more thorough preparation, thereby easing the workload on the course itself (see below).

- **The learners in the teaching practice lessons:** Do they pay for the lessons? Do the learners in each group remain the same for the duration of the course? Learners who pay tend to be less forgiving of trainees' mistakes (although they are more likely to attend regularly), and stable groups allow for greater continuity and more positive **rapport** within the classroom.

B.2 Applying for a course

The Trinity CertTESOL is open to both native speakers and non-native speakers of English of any nationality. No previous teaching experience or foreign language knowledge is required, although some applicants have these. On many courses there is a combination of both native speakers and non-native speakers, experienced teachers and novices, recent university graduates and retirees, which usually makes for an interesting mixture of skills, expertise and knowledge, to the benefit of all involved.

Different course providers have slightly different requirements for applicants, although all of these must meet Trinity's minimum requirements, which are:

- **Minimum age:** 18 at the start of the course.

- **Level of English:** Non-native speakers of English need either to prove or demonstrate a level equivalent to C1 (advanced) on the Common European Framework of Reference for Languages (CEFR). Approximate indicators of this level include a Trinity ISE III or GESE 10, a score of 7.0 in IELTS in all 4 skills, a pass in the Cambridge Advanced Exam or a TOEFL iBT score of about 110. There is no requirement for trainees to speak with a British or other native speaker accent. Trinity encourages diversity in varieties of English.

- **Qualifications:** There are two options here, with the basic requirement being that applicants should have the necessary qualifications to enter higher education, either in the UK or in the applicant's home country. For an applicant from the UK this includes A-levels, national diplomas and other qualifications on Level 3 of the UK National Qualifications Framework. The second option allows course providers to accept applicants without such qualifications if the applicant can demonstrate the required academic study potential needed to complete the course. Some course providers may have an additional or more extensive interview and test that they use for such applicants. They make a value judgement of the applicant's academic study potential based on these.

Course providers retain the right to add additional requirements or higher standards if they wish, and may reserve the right to refuse an applicant who does not meet such requirements.

The interview

It is the responsibility of each course provider to verify that each trainee on a CertTESOL course meets the above requirements, has the aptitude to become a successful teacher and is also likely to complete the course successfully. For these reasons, all applicants for the Trinity CertTESOL must undergo an interview, usually face-to-face, although the use of Skype and telephone interviews is permitted. A typical interview will include a language awareness task, an on-the-spot, handwritten test of English and a face-to-face interview with a course trainer, lasting anything from 45 minutes to two hours in total. Bear in mind that the purpose of this interview is to assess your suitability for the course, so specific preparation is not normally expected or recommended. Try to relax, be honest and share any initial concerns you have with the trainer. This will help them to make an informed decision on your behalf. If you have any special needs (e.g. a disability) or a learning difficulty (e.g. dyslexia), discuss these with your interviewer and find out if they have the resources to provide any additional support that you may need. You will be required to show originals of any important qualifications or exam results at interview. Photocopies or scans will not be accepted.

The task usually happens before, or as part of the interview, and feedback on your performance is usually given during the interview itself. You can expect questions on **language awareness** (e.g. correcting spelling or grammar mistakes, explaining the difference in meaning between similar sentences or identifying similar vowel sounds), and sometimes also on teaching (e.g. questions on what you would do in a specific classroom situation or how you would explain the meaning of a word to learners with a low level of English). If they do ask you questions on teaching, don't worry if you don't have previous experience. At this point they are evaluating your reasoning skills and creativity. In written parts of the test, make sure your handwriting is clear and your spelling and use of English are 'standard' throughout.

Pause for thought

Ten example questions that are often asked at interview are listed below. You may find it useful to consider how you would answer them before your interview. Use common sense, honesty and experience to guide you:

1   *Why do you want to take the course?*
2   *What qualities do you have that you think will make you a good teacher?*
3   *What previous experience, if any, do you have of teaching, including informal opportunities with family, friends and colleagues?*
4   *What is your personal experience of learning foreign languages?*
5   *Which aspects of English do you think cause greatest difficulty for learners and why?*
6   *What are the characteristics of a good language teacher?*
7   *What skills does a language teacher need?*
8   *What would you say are your strengths and weaknesses with using English, both when speaking and writing?*
9   *What would you say are the advantages and disadvantages of working as an English language teacher?*
10 *How good are you at organising your time, working to deadlines and coping under pressure?*

The interview is, of course, a two-way process, so it's a good idea to prepare some questions to ask in advance. Depending on how informative the organisation's website or brochure is, you may have quite a few! Double-check what the fees do and don't include, and also course start and finish dates. See *Choosing your CertTESOL course* above for ideas for other questions.

You are likely to be informed of the outcome of the interview either immediately or soon after. Many course providers require a deposit to secure a place on a specific course. If you do not pass the interview, request clarification on the reasons. The trainer may have specific recommendations for how you can improve any weaknesses or develop required skills before applying for future interviews. You are entitled to apply for interviews with as many course providers as you like.

B.3   What happens on a CertTESOL course?

The 130 hours on a typical CertTESOL timetable are usually divided between five key elements:

- **Input sessions** that cover teaching theory, learning theory, language awareness and other aspects relevant to language teaching. These will normally be delivered to trainees in a language classroom and involve workshop-like activities and communication tasks similar to those used in a typical EFL classroom to provide you with ideas for your own teaching practice.

- Teaching practice (minimum six hours), when you, as a trainee, teach learners of English. The learners are always informed that their teachers are trainees and they may receive the lessons for free, or for a reduced fee. Lessons are observed by an experienced trainer, and feedback is provided afterwards. Trainees are also required to **self-evaluate** their own lessons, to observe each other's lessons and provide **peer feedback** on occasions.

- Working on assignments (details are provided in the relevant chapters of this book). This will include keeping a journal while you learn an unknown foreign language, interviewing and preparing a one-to-one lesson for one of your learners, creating your own teaching materials and learning about the grammar, **lexis** and **phonology** of English.

- Guided observation of experienced teachers. This provides you with an opportunity to see qualified teachers in action in their own classroom. Trainees keep a journal of their observation experiences.

- Preparation for teaching. A timetabled opportunity for trainees to prepare for lessons, often with opportunities to consult course trainers.

The way these elements are covered will vary from course to course, but they must meet the requirements of the Trinity CertTESOL syllabus, which can be found on the Trinity website: http://www.trinitycollege.co.uk. Course providers may provide example timetables on their website, or at interview.

B.4   Preparing for the workload

Before the start of the course, try to complete some of the recommended readings and watch some example classes on YouTube to get an idea of what'll be expected of you.
Ross, CertTESOL trainer

Intensive TESOL/TEFL courses are well known for having challenging workloads. Expressions such as 'in at the deep end', 'steep learning curve', 'rollercoaster' and even 'baptism of fire' are often used by teachers when recalling their training. This is unfortunate because any course that aims to train teachers in best methodology should itself be a positive experience that exemplifies best practice in teaching.

However, due to the evolution of these courses within the private sector and market-driven demands for cost-effectiveness, it tends to happen that the 'learning' is crammed into the smallest possible timeframe. The positive side of this is that you should get value for money. The negative side is the intensity. Because they allow more time for the learning to sink in, part-time courses feel less intense for some, although this will depend on your other obligations during the course.

As well as the timetabled hours on your course, you will need to spend considerable time working on assignments, background reading and lesson preparation, meaning that you will be busy every evening and most of the weekend during your course. Bear in mind that part of the challenge is the steep learning curve, so faster learners and trainees with previous teaching experience tend to suffer less from the intensity of the course even though they do not necessarily perform better. The good news is that with preparation and organisation, the course can become a lot more manageable. Let's look at some suggestions:

1 Experience some lessons

Depending on how much time you have before your course, you may be able to observe or even participate in language lessons yourself. Try doing a short classroom course in a foreign language at any level. If you've never done this before it will be an enlightening experience, allowing you insights into the mind of the learner and the practices of the teacher (thereby preparing you well for the Unit 5 assignment on the CertTESOL; see Unit 5). Keep a diary while you do this. Reflect on both your learning experiences and the teacher's behaviour. If this is not practical, search out opportunities to observe English language classes. You may know somebody who teaches English or you may be able to observe a lesson at your course providing organisation before the course starts. Failing all the above, or if you have little time, try searching online (e.g. using YouTube) for '*TEFL lesson*', '*ESOL lesson*', '*English language lesson*', etc. Make notes on any lessons or lesson extracts you find, and try to make sense of what you see, both from the point of view of the teacher (e.g. **objectives**, methodology and techniques) and the learner (e.g. needs, challenges and successes).

2 Study extensively and actively

Do as much background reading as possible, and begin as early as possible. This book will make a good start, but you should also read topic-specific titles (on pedagogy, grammar, pronunciation, etc.). All course providers will have both required reading and an optional list of other titles to read for the course. You will also find a similar list of recommended reading at the back of this book and in the Trinity CertTESOL syllabus, available from the Trinity website. When you read, try to do so actively. For example, if a book includes tasks, do these as you read, or if you prefer, take notes while you are reading. At the end of each unit or chapter, compile a list of bullet points, or a mind map to illustrate what you have learnt. Online resources are a useful alternative to reading, with publishers and methodologists offering webinars and YouTube clips on various aspects of teaching.

" Don't rush it, and take notes on anything that you find difficult to understand. "

3 Take time to complete the pre-course preparation carefully

According to Trinity CertTESOL specifications, course providers must provide pre-course preparation for enrolled trainees. This is usually in the form of a pre-course preparation task and may include required reading, short assignments, grammar exercises and opportunities to reflect on your beliefs about teaching and learning. Don't rush it, and take notes on anything that you find difficult to understand. Do extra research on these difficulties online, or consult the course provider if possible.

4 Learn your grammar and pronunciation basics

A significant amount of an experienced English teacher's 'content knowledge' relates to understanding how, why and when we use specific grammatical forms in English (e.g. specific verb **tenses**, sentence constructions, modal verbs, determiners, etc.). Especially if you are a native speaker of English, you are unlikely to be aware of the names of these forms and the rules that govern their usage. While you will need a significant amount of time to accrue this knowledge, you can prepare yourself for the course well by learning a little bit about the different parts of speech (e.g. nouns, verbs, adjectives, etc.), the names of different tenses (e.g. present perfect, past simple, future continuous, etc.), and other structures commonly taught in ELT. Much of this basic information can be found in pedagogic reference grammars such as *Practical English Usage* (Swan, 2005a), *An A-Z of English Grammar and Usage* (Leech et al., 2001) or *Grammar for English Language Teachers* (Parrott, 2010). Simpler grammar explanations and grammar practice material for learners can be found in *English Grammar in Use* (Murphy, 2012). Another area of knowledge that many trainees find challenging to absorb once the course has started relates to phonology: the sounds of English and how these differ from other languages, and from the spelling conventions of English. English phonemic script is a useful system of symbols for recording the pronunciation of words or utterances in written form (see Unit 2 p.86) not to be confused with the phonetic alphabet or phonics. By learning the symbols in the **phonemic chart** before your course starts, you will give yourself an insight into the complexity of sound-spelling relationships in English that will be very useful when you start teaching. A very readable title for exploring this in detail is Adrian Underhill's *Sound Foundations* (Underhill, 2005).

5 Learn to modify your language

One of the most fundamental skills shared by all language teachers is the ability to express themselves using simple, clear, easy-to-understand language. This doesn't sound like too much of a challenge, however it is something that many native speakers struggle with at the start of their CertTESOL course. For example, a surprisingly innocent question such as *'What've you been up to today?'*, especially if spoken at normal speed, will rarely be understood by learners at anything lower than an advanced level. It includes a contraction (*what've*), an idiomatic phrasal verb (*be up to*) and a verb tense that does not exist in many languages (present perfect simple). The word *'been'*, if pronounced quickly with a British English accent, sounds like the word *'bin'*. This combination of complexities once led a learner to respond to the above question by checking the rubbish bin and replying *'It's nearly full!'* …So how would one simplify the above question for lower-level learners? Ask: *'How are you today?'*

6 Get support from those around you

It may seem like an obvious point, but trainees who have both physical and moral support from their family and friends cope a lot better with the workload than those who don't. This doesn't mean getting them to help you with assignments or research; all that learning needs to happen in your head! It means letting them know that for the duration of your course you will have very little free time and may sometimes be under pressure and in need of reassurance. By preparing meals for you and taking weekend chores off your hands, they are winning you valuable time to spend either on the coursework itself or simply resting. By providing a sounding board for lesson ideas or a dummy student to explain grammar to they can help to **scaffold** your learning and even improve your performance in the classroom. Let them know well in advance about this and get them to promise to help you. And, if at all possible, cancel all non-essential appointments for the duration of the course.

B.5 The pre-course preparation task

As mentioned above, all course providers are required by Trinity to give future trainees pre-course preparation before they begin their face-to-face training, although Trinity does not specify the number of hours or the exact content of the preparation task. Thus, it varies considerably between course providers, with some offering this task online as a distance learning module and others requiring a handwritten 'assignment'. It can vary in length and complexity, and, especially in the case of longer pre-course tasks, may also allow for interaction with course tutors (e.g. through online chat, email or Skype). Universities may integrate this pre-course preparation into other modules on degree courses.

Here is a list of typical pre-course task activities selected from a variety of course providers:

- research specific areas of grammar, pronunciation and lexis in order to answer questions or explain learner errors
- identify verb tenses used in example sentences and research **meaning**, **form** and **usage** of these tenses
- read a specific book and complete tasks in relation to the content of this book
- watch a video of a lesson and answer focus questions
- reflect on different **learning styles**, learning preferences and learner motivation
- analyse or evaluate a lesson plan, or a page from an ELT coursebook
- read this book!

A recommended reading list is invariably provided with the pre-course preparation task, although usually only one or two titles are 'required reading'.

Answers for pre-course tasks are usually provided at the beginning of the face-to-face course, and sometimes individual feedback on pre-course task performance is given to trainees by tutors. On some courses there may even be an input session devoted to going through some or all of the task. Any marks or grades awarded for the pre-course task do not form part of a trainee's final assessment for the CertTESOL qualification itself.

Review of Before the course

Correct the mistakes

Each of the statements below is factually incorrect. Make all necessary corrections.

1 ESOL students do not live permanently in an English speaking country.

2 Susie Bradshaw teaches both EFL and ESOL learners.

3 The Trinity CertTESOL is accredited at level 3 on the RQF.

4 The term 'multilingual class' refers to a class that contains multilingual students.

5 Part-time CertTESOL courses involve more study than full-time courses.

6 You cannot take the CertTESOL unless you have A-levels or a degree.

7 Applicants with prior teaching experience do not have to attend an interview.

8 Get friends and family to help you with your assignments on the course.

9 Non-native speakers of English are likely to have greater difficulty with explaining grammar to learners.

10 This book is the only reading that you need to do for the CertTESOL.

If you need to, check your answers in the *Review Key* at the back of this book.

Now return to the learning opportunities provided at the start of the chapter. Tick the ones that you feel you have achieved and re-read the relevant sections for any you're not sure about.

unit 1 Understanding teaching practice

Learning opportunities

This unit will help you to...

- understand how teaching practice is organised on CertTESOL courses
- recognise key features of communicative language teaching
- describe lesson aims or outcomes and order activities in a lesson
- become familiar with typical language teaching lesson plans
- describe the basic steps for managing learning activities
- modify your spoken English to communicate with learners effectively
- deal with unanticipated occurrences during lessons
- understand why post-lesson reflection is important on the CertTESOL
- identify what you need to do to pass Unit 1 of the CertTESOL

Introduction

Unit 1 – Teaching Skills is the largest unit on the CertTESOL, constituting nearly 60% of the total hours on courses, as specified by Trinity. The reasons for this should be obvious. In the words of the syllabus itself:

> *As this qualification prepares the candidate specifically for the initial stages of the teaching profession, greater guided learning hours are attached to Unit 1 to ensure the vocational validity, relevance and professional integrity of the award…*

Trinity CertTESOL syllabus

In order to complete Unit 1 successfully, you will have to demonstrate the ability to plan lessons, teach effectively and evaluate your own teaching. All of these will be assessed by your course tutors, who will observe and provide feedback on your lessons, scrutinise your lesson plans and materials, and assess both written and oral **self-evaluation** of lessons. In addition to these three core aspects of **teaching practice**, you will also observe experienced teachers and keep a Guided Observation Journal to document your reflections on this. The final task of Unit 1, the Final Summary, is a short assignment in which you reflect on your development as a teacher through the course. All of these will contribute to your final grade for Unit 1, although greater weighting is given to the teaching practice element, as this is the core of the unit. The minimum number of guided learning hours for Unit 1 as specified by Trinity can be broken down as follows:

Hours	Component
6	Teaching practice: observed and assessed by course tutors
4	Guided observation of experienced teachers
64	Supervised input (e.g. **input sessions**, teaching practice feedback, supervised lesson planning)
74	Total

The 64 hours of supervised input will be integrated with other aspects of the course to ensure that your development as a teacher is holistic. For example, while some input sessions focus specifically on teaching practice, others integrate this with **language awareness** or materials analysis. In addition to these guided learning hours, you can expect to spend a significant amount of time preparing lessons and materials, reading up on what you need to teach and completing other written work (e.g. Guided Observation Journal, written self-evaluations and the Final Summary assignment). Thus, you can expect to spend over 100 hours on Unit 1, but the exact amount of time will depend on your aptitude and prior learning.

What actually happens in teaching practice?

Course providers differ in exactly how they organise teaching practice. The majority do so as follows:

- Trainees are put into small groups, called teaching practice (TP) groups and given guidance on what to teach for their initial lessons. Sometimes they are allocated lessons from a coursebook or in-house materials, and on other occasions they are given aims or objectives that they should try to achieve using their own choice of materials.

- Each TP group works with at least two groups of learners at two different levels (e.g. elementary and intermediate). They will usually have one group for the first half of the course and a different group for the second half. The course provider may organise special TP classes or arrange teaching slots for trainees with existing classes.

- The trainee teachers take turns to teach the learners (often consecutively), while the tutor and co-trainees observe each lesson. Lessons will often get longer as the course progresses.

- After teaching, tutors conduct feedback with the trainees. They **elicit** both self- and peer-evaluation of each trainee's performance and also provide their own feedback (both written and spoken) on the lessons taught. On some courses this happens immediately after the lesson, while on other courses there may be 'delayed feedback', usually on the following day.

As the course progresses, trainees will be expected to prepare for, teach and evaluate their own lessons with increasing autonomy, and the standard of teaching expected will also increase. Your tutors will encourage you to experiment during early lessons, thereby providing an opportunity to learn from your successes and mistakes. As a result of this, it is common for trainee performance over the course to vary within a curve of overall improvement, as shown in Figure 1, which also shows how the standard expected of trainees increases as the 'bar is raised' each lesson:

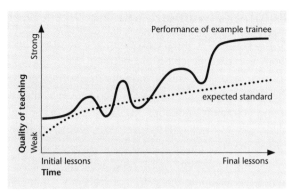

Figure 1.1:
A hypothetical trainee 'learning curve' in TP

1.1 Approaches to teaching

The way foreign languages have been taught in the last 100 years or so reflects not only our understanding and beliefs of how languages are learnt, but also changes in social development (e.g. increased investment in education), general trends in education (e.g. more participatory methods of learning), resources available (e.g. audio and video material) and even commercial aspects (e.g. the approach underlying a popular coursebook). The predominant approach in ELT today (promoted on many CertTESOL courses) is often referred to as the **Communicative Approach** or **communicative language teaching (CLT)**. It is an eclectic mix of dominant methodologies and beliefs of the last 40 or so years. However, like many of the approaches that preceded it, there may have been a tendency towards 'throwing out the baby with the bathwater'[1] when rejecting previous methods. Before describing CLT, let's take a brief look at what preceded it and why and how things changed. After all, every approach within the history of language teaching has something to offer a truly eclectic teacher.

[1] 'Throwing out the baby with the bathwater' is a common idiom used in British English to describe situations when something important or useful is lost when the beliefs with which it was associated are rejected.

Grammar-Translation

For the majority of the nineteenth century, language teaching theory was dominated by an approach now referred to as the Grammar-Translation method. It was used widely across Europe for the teaching of both classical and modern languages. Classes were dominated by written, often translation-based activities, with a strong focus on grammatical correctness and little interest in **communicative competence**. The most common aims of language learning courses at the time were to provide access to (written) classical literature and develop mental faculties rather than to facilitate communication with speakers of other languages. Although Grammar-Translation began to lose favour at the 'cutting edge' of language teaching around the turn of the 20th century, the method remained widespread, especially in school environments, for many decades. It even persists to this day in some parts of the world, due perhaps to a combination of cultural compatibility, ease of implementation and even inertia. In contexts where it was rejected, an important 'baby' was lost with the 'bathwater': the use of translation to facilitate language learning. Since 2000, a number of respected applied linguists and methodologists have argued for its reinclusion in modern teaching methodology (e.g. Butzkamm & Caldwell, 2009; Cook, 2010). Despite these appeals, translation still remains on the periphery of current language teaching methodology.

The Reform Movement and the Direct Method

Towards the end of the nineteenth century, a number of phoneticians and linguists rejected translation or explicit teaching of grammar rules and advocated greater emphasis on the use of spoken language. This change became known as the Reform Movement and quickly developed into a more dogmatic approach known as the Direct Method, which argued that the learning of foreign languages should try to replicate the acquisition of **first languages** in early childhood. As Cook (2010) points out, two key features of the Direct Method were the assumptions that the native speaker is the most appropriate **model** for language learning, and that classes should be English only, avoiding the learners' first language – assumptions that have been called into question more recently. The Berlitz chain, as the first large private language teaching institute, was one of the first exponents of the Direct Method, and signalled the beginning of significant commercial interest in language teaching.

For the first half of the twentieth century, teaching methods that had evolved out of the Direct Method became widespread in both private and government language learning institutions as English became the dominant language in international communication. This included Audiolingualism in the USA, and the Oral Approach and Situational Language Teaching in the UK. As well as the 'English only' emphasis and the focus on oral language skills, these methods recommended extensive use of spoken language **drills** and direct correction of mistakes. Creativity and meaningful language use on the part of the learner were not encouraged. A number of private language schools and online courses continue to use audiolingual approaches to this day, and they can also be found in watered-down versions in state school education around the world, where they have either replaced or been combined with aspects of the previously dominant Grammar–Translation methodology. Many communicative teachers also make use of a variety of drill techniques to hone learners' spoken skills, especially to improve their ability to transform specific structures quickly and accurately. Teachers may find that rhythmic or musical drills can be fun and engaging, especially for younger learners.

The Communicative Approach

By the late 1960s, following Noam Chomsky's criticism of the behaviourist theories underlying audiolingual language teaching approaches, a number of changes began to take place. The new scientific discipline of Second Language Acquisition (SLA) was establishing itself as distinct from (First/Childhood) Language Acquisition. A prominent researcher in this new field, Larry Selinker, coined the term 'interlanguage' (1972) to describe learner language development, after noticing that many adult learners seemed to learn foreign languages following a fixed, internal 'syllabus', that wasn't necessarily influenced by what their teacher taught them. Errors, which had been dealt with severely in Direct Method approaches, were recognised as a natural part of the learning process. In the abstract for an important paper of 1967, Pit Corder wrote:

By allowing the learner's innate strategies to dictate the language syllabus, rather than imposing upon him preconceived notions of what he ought to learn, a more effective means of language instruction may be achieved.

Influenced by these findings, a number of linguists and methodologists began to argue for a 'Communicative Approach' to language teaching in the 1970s (e.g. Widdowson, 1978; Wilkins, 1976). Communicative language teaching emphasised the importance of meaningful communication, recognised the importance of learner errors and argued that communicative competence (Hymes, 1972) should be the desired goal of language learning. Communicative language teaching also emphasised the importance of using **authentic texts** whenever possible for the practice of **receptive skills** (reading and listening), and authentic 'real world' tasks for the practice of **productive skills** (speaking and writing). As teachers absorbed these influences, they began to combine the more traditional grammar study and practice exercises with opportunities to communicate in order to practise language learnt in more meaningful activities. One of the most common models used today for structuring new language lessons, called PPP, originated at this time (Anderson, 2017). It stands for Presentation, Practice, Production, and can be used to introduce new grammar, **lexis** or **functional language**. First, new language is presented and analysed, then it is practised in controlled exercises and spoken drills and finally it is used in a freer production activity such as a role-play, discussion or creative writing activity.

Alongside the gradual evolution of mainstream communicative language teaching, a wide range of alternative approaches appeared in the 1960s-70s that should also be mentioned. With intriguing names such as The Silent Way, Total Physical Response, Community Language Learning and Suggestopedia, each has provided ideas, resources or techniques that are still alive, usually in significantly modified forms, in classrooms today. The need for brevity here prevents me from describing these methods, but for those who would like to read more about them, Richards and Rogers (2014) provide an interesting overview.

Instead we shall look briefly at three more recent approaches that have arguably had more impact on current classroom practice. The first of these, **Task-based Learning**, holds that communicative tasks should be central to the learning process, and that grammar and vocabulary are only important in that they facilitate performance in the task. Jane Willis's *Framework for Task-based Learning* (Willis, 1996) has provided an alternative paradigm for lesson planning to the more traditional models (such as PPP). The second of these, called the **Lexical Approach**, was developed by Michael Lewis (1993), who argued that traditional classroom practices place too much emphasis on grammar teaching when lexis (vocabulary) is actually far more central to effective language learning. Lewis underlined the importance of a number of features of lexis, including **collocations**, **fixed expressions** and, most importantly, learning language in **lexical chunks**. While the Lexical Approach has definitely had a significant impact on how we teach lexis in the classroom, especially English for academic purposes (EAP) or business English, its impact on published teaching materials has been somewhat limited, possibly because it has never prescribed a specific classroom 'method' (see Lewis, 1997, for some recommendations). The third approach, called Dogme or **Dogme ELT** (Thornbury, 2000), can be seen, in part, as a reaction to the overdependence on commercially available coursebooks in the adult EFL industry. Dogme holds that language learning can be more effective if it is based on learning content that's generated by the learners themselves, rather than a generic coursebook that may not suit their needs, interests or learning preferences. Task-based learning, the Lexical Approach and Dogme are all approaches within CLT that you may be interested in investigating, both on your initial training course and after.

CLIL and ELF

While it is always difficult to predict future trends in language teaching, two interesting concepts of note should be mentioned, as both are gaining momentum. The first of these is CLIL (Content and Language Integrated Learning), currently being used in secondary and tertiary learning environments in a number of countries. CLIL involves students learning 'content subjects' (e.g. social studies, sciences, humanities, etc.) in English using immersion techniques, and is argued by its exponents (e.g. Coyle, Hood & Marsh, 2010) to be no less effective at teaching the content subjects, and significantly more effective at facilitating the learning of English than traditional methods, although robust evidence to support these claims is lacking. A number of commentators on the future role of English in the world predict that CLIL is likely to become more widespread as part of a more general move in many countries to teach English at ever younger ages. The second concept, **ELF** (English as a Lingua Franca), has developed alongside the rise of English as the predominant language of international communication. Supporters of ELF (e.g. Seidlhofer, 2011) point out that the majority of communication in English around the world today takes place between non-native speakers of English, and that therefore the development of English cannot and should not be controlled by native speakers (e.g. British and American users of English). They argue that changes to the language itself may well (rightfully) occur, including possibly simplifications to grammatical structures and aspects of pronunciation alongside the development of **intercultural competence** necessary when non-native speakers interact in English. They also believe that learners of English should not be expected either to conform to **native speaker norms** or to take an interest in native speaker culture. ELF is already having an impact on what we teach, the role of culture in language learning and the role of native-speaker English in models and materials.

Hopefully, this brief excursion should have provided a little context for the methodology described in the rest of this chapter. In general, the underlying assumptions of the weak form of the communicative approach still hold true on most current teacher training courses, supplemented with an emphasis on contextualised grammar teaching, the analysis and learning of lexical chunks and collocations and a healthy dose of pronunciation drilling. Whether or not we find ourselves in the 'post–methods era', as some recent authors have suggested (e.g. Kumaravadivelu, 2003), I will leave you to decide at the end of the chapter!

Pause for thought

- *Which of the approaches described above remind you of your own experience of learning languages, either at school or after?*
- *If you have any self-study books for language learning, look at these again. Can you detect the influence of any of the methods in the way the content is presented?*

1.2 Lesson Planning

If we took a purely descriptive view of teaching, we could say that a lesson is basically a sequence of activities preceded by an introduction and concluded with a conclusion. Within this simple definition, 'lesson planning' means working out which activities to do, in what order and how.

So far, so good. However, our simple definition becomes somewhat more complex when we consider the question that must always begin any planning session: What do I want my learners to learn? In language teaching, the relationship between a teacher's perceived objectives and the actual learning that occurs in the mind of each learner in the class is surprisingly complex to understand and rather difficult to evaluate. This is because language learning is a multifaceted process involving various interconnected skills (e.g. sound pronunciation, word recognition) and types of knowledge (e.g. lexis, grammar). While all adult language learners will have honed these skills through first language use, the way that they develop in a new language is unpredictable and varies greatly between individuals of different age, language background and aptitude. The most important implication here, one supported by research into second language acquisition (Lightbown & Spada, 2013), is that, no matter how well we teach, learners don't necessarily learn language (especially grammar) in the order we expect, or want them to. An often quoted anecdote in ELT describes a rather confused-looking teacher who has just returned to the staffroom from a lesson. When asked by colleagues what she 'did' in her lesson, she replies *'Well, I did the present perfect tense, but I'm not sure what they did!'* Rather than being an admission of incompetence, this is a perceptive insight. Thus, any attempt to plan lessons must recognise the importance not only of what you would like them to learn, but also of the more natural language learning that you can't control but will happen anyway. In other words, as language teachers, we need to focus both on process and product; processes that facilitate natural language learning and products in terms of demonstrable **learning outcomes**.

Writing your lesson aims

For each of your assessed lessons on the CertTESOL, you will be expected to write a lesson plan, and nearly all lesson plans start by identifying the **learning aims** of the lesson. Some course providers prefer to use the term **objectives** and/or ask you to consider the learning outcomes of your lesson. As the focus of most TP lessons tends to involve the introduction of new language, the practice of skills or a combination of these, learning aims are usually of two basic types:

Systems-focused aims:
These include both learning of **explicit knowledge** about language (e.g. knowing how to use the past simple tense in English), and developing the **implicit knowledge**, or ability to use language appropriately (e.g. using the past simple to tell a story) in the three areas of grammar, lexis and pronunciation (or **phonology**).

Skills-focused aims:
These include improving ability in the four skills of reading, writing, speaking and listening and usually focus on developing specific **sub-skills**, functions or competencies (e.g. reading for gist, writing an email of complaint, introducing yourself or listening for specific information).

You may have noticed that none of these aims can be isolated from the others. For example, if you want your learners to be able to introduce themselves in English by the end of the lesson, which you might describe as a speaking skill, it is clear that the learners will also need lexis (the words they will use to introduce themselves), phonology (saying the words clearly and sounding friendly) and structure (getting the words in the right tense and the right order). In the same lesson, learners will also inevitably practise listening skills when they listen to each other or to you giving an example introduction. For this reason, when you are choosing learning outcomes for your class, it's a good idea to focus on one main outcome but also to think about other aspects of language use that will naturally develop during the lesson. Let's put the above example in more formal terms, as they might appear on a CertTESOL lesson plan:

Note that each course provider is likely to have their own specific requirements when it comes to writing lesson plans. Some will prefer to use the word 'aims', others will prefer 'objectives', and others like 'learning outcomes'. They will also differ in the way they want you to describe these aims.

[2] See page 120 for clarification of how learners can be categorised at different levels according to the Common European Framework Reference (CEFR)

Main aim

■ By the end of the lesson, the learners will have improved their ability to introduce themselves to new acquaintances in both formal and informal situations.

Secondary aims

■ Learners will become familiar with a range of fixed expressions used in introductions (e.g. *Pleased to meet you; How's it going?*; etc.)

We could easily add more, but these would probably be the main ones in the envisaged lesson. This lesson would probably be most useful at an elementary or pre-intermediate level (A1-A2[2]), especially for learners at the start of a course or for business professionals who need to make the right first impressions. These outcomes would probably be suitable for a lesson of 30-40 minutes.

Of course, we could state these outcomes with more ambition (e.g. the learners will be able to introduce themselves), or in much more specific terms (e.g. the learners will be able to use six fixed expressions in introductions), but in doing so, not only would we overlook the fact that there will be varying degrees of achievement of these aims within the class, but also that specifying a 'product' in too much detail may cause us to lose sight of other learning that is likely to happen during the lesson. In other words, keeping the aims a little flexible allows us to be realistic and honest about what the learners are likely to achieve, and flexibility during the lesson also allows us to take advantage of emerging learning opportunities.

Structuring a lesson

Now that we have described our hoped-for learning outcomes in a reasonable degree of detail, we begin to be able to imagine what might happen in the above lesson. This presents us with one of the biggest and most important challenges of lesson planning; working out which activities to do and in what order.

Pause for thought

Look at the following 10 activities, all of which might help in the achievement of the above-described lesson aims. Which of them would you include in a 40-minute lesson and which would you reject? Put them in the most logical order and remember to leave a few minutes for your lesson introduction and conclusion.

a   *Learners watch a few YouTube clips showing English speakers introducing themselves to one another in different situations. (5 minutes)*

b   *Learners **mingle** around the class, introducing themselves to each other, first informally, then formally. The teacher **monitors** and offers support when necessary. (10 minutes)*

c   *The teacher explains/elicits the meaning of six key expressions used in formal and informal introductions. (6 minutes)*

d   *The teacher demonstrates a formal introduction with one learner and an informal introduction with another. (3 minutes)*

e   *In pairs, learners practise reading out example introductory conversations while the teacher monitors and corrects pronunciation errors. (4 minutes)*

f   *The teacher drills the pronunciation of the most important expressions used in introductions; learners listen and repeat, first chorally (as a whole class) then individually. (3 minutes)* g   *The teacher gives groups of learners two introductory conversations cut up on strips of paper. Learners must sort the strips into the two separate conversations and put them in the correct order. (5 minutes)*

h   *In small groups, learners discuss cultural differences between how people introduce themselves to one another in different countries. (5 minutes)*

i   *Working in pairs, learners write down an example introductory dialogue (choosing formal or informal), while the teacher monitors and corrects any mistakes in their texts. (5 minutes)*

j   *Two confident pairs of learners demonstrate formal and informal introductions in front of the class. (3 minutes)*

Did you find that the activities you chose didn't fit in the allotted timeframe, or that you had to leave out some activities that would have been useful? Welcome to the biggest challenge of lesson planning! Choosing the right activities and getting them in the right order at this stage is essential for successful achievement of aims. Note that there are no 'bad' activities or red herrings given above; all would be useful, and all would contribute in some way towards achievement of the aims. Also note that there is no perfect solution, and that different experienced teachers would choose different activities from the list. What those experienced teachers would probably have in common, however, is the basic order in which they would do the activities, and this tends to follow common sense. Most of us would choose to begin with a clear, contextualised example of what we are trying to teach, which could be either the YouTube video clip (a) or the teacher demonstration (d). This would provide a context from which we could extract and analyse the **target language** (what we want them to learn). After analysing the meaning and practising the pronunciation of this target language, we would get the learners to use the target language themselves, at which stage it would be possible to evaluate how well the learners have achieved our aims. We could summarise these three lesson phases using a very simple mnemonic, which provides a useful starting point for planning:

C – context

A – analysis

P – practice

We will come back to this a little later in this unit, but for now, let's return to our lesson plan. I have to admit that my personal selection of the stages would probably depend in part on the learners in my class and resources available, but I'd probably choose the following stages in the order shown:

My choices	My reasoning
a Learners watch a few YouTube clips showing English speakers introducing themselves to one another in different situations. (5 minutes)	I chose this rather than the teacher/student demonstration (also a nice idea) because it would hopefully be quite realistic and would provide an opportunity for all learners to notice key features of introductions.
g The teacher gives groups of learners two introductory conversations cut up on strips of paper. Learners must sort the strips into the two separate conversations and put them in the correct order. (5 minutes)	Ideally, these would be the conversations from the YouTube clips, thereby enabling us to analyse the target language used in the context provided.
c The teacher explains/elicits the meaning of six key expressions used in formal and informal introductions. (6 minutes)	This is always the trickiest bit of a lesson, however the context provided should help. Whenever possible, it's good to elicit the meaning, which demonstrates that somebody understands it, but if nobody does, I would have to explain myself using context, gesture, simple definitions and synonyms.
f The teacher drills the pronunciation of the most important expressions used in introductions; learners listen and repeat, first chorally (as a whole class) then individually. (3 minutes)	This is the start of the 'practice' part of the lesson, which often moves from more **controlled practice** to **freer practice** in two or three stages.
e In pairs, learners practise reading out example introductory conversations while the teacher monitors and corrects pronunciation errors. (4 minutes)	This is a useful extra stage after the drilling which allows learners to focus on pronunciation at their own pace in the privacy of pairs. Correction is likely to be more useful and less intimidating if provided at this stage, rather than doing it in front of the whole class.
j Two confident pairs of learners demonstrate formal and informal introductions in front of the class. (3 minutes)	This could be done after the mingle as a consolidation activity, but it's a nice way to provide a challenge for these stronger learners. It also provides a useful opportunity to check that they have got the basics, that I haven't forgotten to clarify anything and that they have understood what to do in the next stage.
b Learners mingle around the class, introducing themselves to each other, first informally, then formally. The teacher monitors and offers support when necessary. (10 minutes)	This is the 'proof of the pudding'[3] stage. As well as providing vital practice, it also gives me an opportunity to assess how well the learners have achieved my aims.

Table 1.1:
Possible lesson activities

[3] A short form of the proverb 'The proof of the pudding is in the eating' meaning something can only be judged when it is tried out.

I also left out stage (h), the cultural differences discussion (while it would be interesting, it doesn't contribute directly to achievement of my aims and might be a bit challenging at lower levels) and stage (i), the dialogue writing stage (useful, but if the other stages have gone well, this would probably be overkill – the spoken practice is more important, given the time limitations). These choices would create a lesson of about 36 minutes, allowing several minutes for the introduction at the start of the lesson and the conclusion at the end.

Jim Scrivener once said that lesson planning *'is essentially a thinking skill ... imagining the lesson before it happens'* (2011 p.123). Hopefully we have done our thinking. Don't worry if you made different choices; remember that by trying out the lesson that you created and reflecting on how it went, you'll learn more than if you teach someone else's lesson.

Writing the lesson plan

We are now ready to move onto the next stage of lesson planning – the written plan. While experienced teachers don't always write detailed lesson plans (many just make a few notes), most would admit that their lessons generally go better when they do. On a CertTESOL training course, detailed lesson plans are essential and perform an important role in the learning process (and they are required as part of your assessed Unit 1 **Teaching Practice Portfolio**). Here are the key reasons why:

Before the lesson:

- they force you to think carefully about your aims and how to achieve them
- they help you to order the lesson activities and decide what to prioritise
- they help you to anticipate possible problems and think of solutions in advance
- they help you to notice what resources and materials you need

During the lesson:

- they give you confidence
- they help you to remember all the activities you have planned and get them in the right order
- they highlight issues of concern that you need to be aware of throughout the lesson (e.g. time management, potential challenges and possible occurrences)

After the lesson:

- they help you to learn from your successes and your mistakes
- when the lesson hasn't gone so well, a detailed plan can help both you and your tutor to see whether mistakes were made in the planning stage and/or during the teaching, and thereby pinpoint areas for improvement
- they provide a record of your training and development, useful for your tutors, the course **moderator** and most importantly, you

Different course providers have different templates or pro formas for their lesson plans. Here is a possible lesson plan pro forma, completed for the lesson above to a sufficient degree of detail for the CertTESOL:

Teacher	Name: Jason Anderson Lesson Number: 1 Date: 23/10/2017
Lesson	Length of students' lesson: 80 mins Length of trainee's lesson: 40 mins
Student Context	Number of Students: 12 Age Range from: 20 to: 45 Level of English: Pre-intermediate (A2) Educational / Professional Level: students and professionals First Languages: mainly Italian, Turkish, Chinese Reasons for Learning English: various, incl. immigrants looking for work and typical EFL students

All the information in this box is required by Trinity.

Aims of the lesson, expressed as learning outcomes:	How will you assess your learning outcomes?
Main aim • By the end of the lesson, the learners will have improved their ability to introduce themselves to new acquaintances in both formal and informal situations. **Secondary aims** • Learners will learn a range of fixed expressions used in introductions (e.g. *Pleased to meet you; How's it going?* etc.) • Learners will raise their awareness of the different intonation patterns used to show interest and friendliness in English.	**1** Observe learners' use of language during the final mingle activity – hopefully they will be introducing themselves appropriately in both formal and informal contexts. **2** Listen to learners' intonation patterns both during pronunciation pair work and the final mingle activity. It should be friendly and show interest.
Materials to be used:	**Personal action points for this lesson:**
1 Video from website: https://www.youtube.com showing three introductions. **2** Handout A – Two conversations cut up on strips of paper. **3** PowerPoint slides shown on interactive whiteboard: A – two conversations in correct order; B – six key expressions for introductions. **3** Handout B – The two complete conversations.	**1** I will try to speak slowly and clearly. **2** I need to watch time carefully; leaving plenty for final activity. **3** I aim to elicit as much as possible from students without lecturing them.

Lesson stage & aims	Time (mins)	Interaction	Procedure	Possible occurrences & reactions
1 Introduction To raise learners' awareness of anticipated learning outcomes.	2	T & Sts	**1** Greet learners. **2** Introduce lesson in simple language and board any key expressions (e.g. *introduction, formal, greeting*). **3** Check learners have understood aims by asking check questions (e.g. *How will this be useful?*).	–
2 YouTube video To provide examples of target language being used in context.	5	Sts watch video Pairs T & Sts	**1** Introduce task. Write observation question on board: *Which of the three introductions is a) most formal and b) least formal?* **2** Watch video. **3** Learners discuss observation question in pairs. **4** Get feedback.	Video may not work. Have backup saved on desktop.
3 Conversation ordering To provide further contextualisation in written form and facilitate noticing of target language.	4-6	Small groups T & Sts	**1** Introduce task, give clear instruction and check understanding by doing example. Give handout A to learners. **2** In three groups, learners separate and order two conversations. Monitor and help if needed. **3** Check answers by showing slide A. Praise learners. **4** If time, show 2 videos again.	Some pairs may find it more challenging. Provide extra help if necessary.
4 Check expressions To help learners to understand meaning and usage of target language.	5-7	T & Sts	**1** Show slide B with 6 key expressions underlined in conversations (*Alright?; How do you do?; Pleased to meet you; How's it going?; It was a pleasure meeting you.; See you later.*) **2** Get learners to find equivalents in the two conversations, eliciting meaning/usage of expressions, esp. which is formal/informal. Explain if necessary.	Bianca may ask lots of questions regarding grammar. Keep her on track and offer to answer individual questions in stage 6.
5 Drill pronunciation To provide both a model and practice of pronunciation of appropriate intonation patterns.	3	T & Sts	**1** Say each expression once, learners just listen. **2** Say expressions again, learners repeat chorally. **3** Check individual pronunciation, eliciting at random.	Some learners may not vary intonation (e.g. Han, Luis). Remind them of importance of sounding friendly.

Lesson stage & aims	Time (mins)	Interaction	Procedure	Possible occurrences & reactions
6 Pairwork controlled practice To provide controlled practice and correction of pronunciation in context.	3-4	Pairs	**1** Show handout B, provide instruction, give handout to students. **2** Students read both conversations. Monitor, correct, assist if necessary. **3** Praise learners' pronunciation.	Some pairs may want to do it twice, swapping roles. If there is time, allow for this.
7 Demonstrations To provide examples and check learners have understood lesson so far.	3	Pairs T & Sts	**1** Select two pairs of learners who have performed well in previous stage to come to front and to do example introductions for class. **2** Provide final advice/correction if necessary. **3** Get **peer feedback**/praise.	If one of demos is not very good, correct gently and encourage them to try again.
8 Mingle To provide freer practice of introductions in natural spoken context and to assess achievement of main learning outcome.	8-10	Whole class mingle	**1** Provide instruction. Check understanding. **2** Learners mingle, introduce themselves informally, chat briefly, then move on. Monitor, observe, make notes for correction. **3** Praise, provide correction of any common errors.	Some students may stick with their favourite partner (e.g. Bianca and Olga). If so, split them up.
9 Conclusion To conclude the lesson and raise learners' awareness of how well they achieved learning outcomes.	2	T & Sts	**1** Ask learners briefly how they found the activity and what difficulties remain. **2** Remind learners of lesson aims, invite evaluation of achievement. **3** Praise learners.	–

Notice how the individual lesson stage aims contribute to achievement of overall lesson aims.

Indicate here if your timings are flexible. (e.g. 2-4 mins)

'Possible Occurrences' includes things not under the teacher's initial control, such as student questions, problems, etc. From the teacher's perspective, they often seem like unwanted divergences from the lesson plan, but they also include fruitful learning opportunities (see below).

This lesson plan is intended as a simple example, not as a model. Bear in mind that a different choice of stages might achieve the aims just as well, if not better, and the effectiveness of the lesson itself will always depend on its compatibility with the students' level, preferences and previous learning.

Let us now return to the three phases in our C-A-P mnemonic and look at a few different lesson types from different levels that fit into this model:

Table 1.2:
CAP model
example lessons

C-A-P Phase	Example lesson 1 Intermediate level (B1) Making arrangements by email	Example lesson 2 Upper intermediate level (B2) Telling an anecdote	Example lesson 3 Advanced level (C1) Negotiating a business contract
C – context	Learners read and evaluate two different emails that make arrangements; one is clear and to the point and the other is not so good.	Learners listen to a recording of several friends telling amusing anecdotes from their childhood and match speakers to topics.	Learners watch a video of a business negotiation from a reality TV show and answer comprehension questions.
A – analysis	Learners study the structure of the better email and underline useful expressions and phrases (e.g. *How about if...?; Let me know...*)	Learners analyse which tenses the speakers used and why they used them (e.g. past simple, past continuous, etc.).	In pairs, learners watch the negotiation again on computers and make notes on effective negotiation techniques and language used.
P – practice	Learners write emails to each other to plan a weekend holiday and Cc in the teacher.	Learners spend five minutes making notes and then tell anecdotes to each other in small groups.	A role-play in which learners pretend to be buyers and sellers of a new range of computers.

You will see from these examples that all three lessons involve both receptive skills (either reading or listening) and productive skills (writing or speaking). On occasion we may focus on more extensive receptive skills work, or go into greater detail on an area of lexis, pronunciation or grammar. We will look at these possible lesson types in Unit 2, where we will also notice that, just as in the example lesson above, several practice stages are often necessary. This C-A-P mnemonic is a useful starting point for planning lessons, but you will soon find reason to start adding more complexity to the phases and to vary their order. Your course tutors will probably also encourage you to experiment with other models some of which are described in *The Knowledge* (at the back of this book).

Now that we have some initial ideas for structuring a lesson, let's look at the skills required to teach this lesson in class.

1.3 Teaching Skills and Strategies

To return to our purely descriptive definition of a lesson given above ('a sequence of activities preceded by an introduction and concluded with a conclusion'), the role of the teacher appears fairly straightforward; s/he is the 'manager' of these activities. For this reason, this aspect of the teacher's role is often referred to as **classroom management**.

But if we look at teaching from a more meaningful perspective, we might define a lesson as 'an opportunity for learning'. Within this definition, the role of the teacher changes subtly, but importantly. S/he becomes a facilitator of learning, not only 'executing' the lesson plan, but also noticing and capitalising on opportunities for learning that arise 'around' the intended lesson aims. The ability to find this balance between planning and improvisation, structure and freedom, or even order and chaos is at the heart of all good teaching. Getting the balance right on the CertTESOL is the difference between learning to teach and learning to teach well.

In our overview of planning above, we broke the lesson up into several specific phases (Context, Analysis and Practice), and within each of these phases we noticed that there may be several stages. We will now go into more detail regarding some of the key skills required during these stages, including:

- communicating with learners of English
- managing activities, including:
    - giving instructions
    - monitoring learning activities
    - conducting feedback
- responding to unanticipated occurrences
- managing the learning environment

We'll come back to the overall lesson structure, including introducing and concluding the lesson when we look at teaching different aspects of language in Unit 2.

Pause for thought

Look at the cartoon. What strategies does the man use to get his message across to the waiter? Which of these do you think would and wouldn't be useful for an English language teacher?

Communicating with learners of English

While some of the strategies used by the man in the cartoon are not recommended (e.g. adding Spanish grammar to English words!), the 'holiday instincts' that he displays demonstrate some of the key variables we need to consider when communicating with learners of English. These are shown in Table1.3, along with tips for how to control these variables at different levels:

Table 1.3:
Key variables for modifying speech with learners of English

Variable	At lower levels...	At higher levels...
1 speed of speech	speak more slowly	speak at a natural speed
2 clarity of voice	speak clearly and separate words or phrases from one another	relax your voice more
3 choice of lexis	simplify vocabulary	include more idiomatic language
4 complexity of grammar	keep it simple, but avoid pidgin English	keep it natural
5 use of body language	mime and gesture will help	only natural body language
	modify more	keep it natural

The basic rule here is the lower the level, the more we need to modify our speech, and the higher the level, the more natural we should keep it. However, at any level we should also modify our language depending on our purpose. If, for example, our main aim is to get a concept or instruction across to the learners, we need to modify our speech more than usual, speaking slowly and clearly, grading the vocabulary and keeping sentences short. But if our aim is to develop their listening skills, for example when telling a personal anecdote or doing a dictation activity, we want to challenge our learners a little, so our speed and complexity of speech should increase.

Trainee teachers often find it particularly challenging to modify their speech in initial lessons due to nerves, which often cause us to speak faster, mumble, **commentate** unnecessarily on what we are doing, use pidgin English and even try to fill silences with the sound of our voice, all of which can confuse learners or even cloud an important instruction. The good news is that with a little practice, the ability to modify your speech will become second nature. Listen out for modified speech carefully if you watch a low-level class during one of your guided observations. If you find it challenging in initial lessons, try **scripting** your explanations and instructions, and perhaps even have them on a clipboard as you teach. Also remember that learners will usually find a written instruction or explanation clearer than a spoken one, so providing both will help to ensure that everybody understands.

Pause for thought

The trainee in the following cartoon is suffering from first lesson nerves. How would you simplify his instruction to make it easier for learners to understand?

Check the Pause for thought Key [1] at the back of the book for one possible solution. There are many others!

Managing activities – The activity cycle

Most learning activities have three basic steps that will usually happen in a cyclical order. Let's call this the **activity cycle** (see Figure 1.2). With experience, the three steps will become second nature, but when you start teaching it's surprisingly easy to forget a step or muddle them up due to nerves, 'brain overload' or time pressure.

Figure 1.2:
The activity cycle

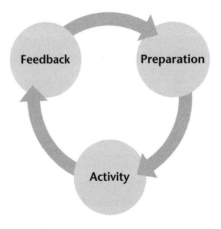

Pause for thought

Look again at the example lesson plan on page 30-32 and try to find two or three examples of activity cycles.

The preparation step – giving instructions

The most important part of the preparation step is giving the instruction, but there are several other preparatory steps that are nearly always necessary, and easy to forget. Poor preparation can lead to learners doing an activity incorrectly, which may have serious implications for the success of your lesson. This is a high pressure moment for any teacher being observed, so it's a good idea to rehearse the preparation steps for your lesson at home the evening before you teach it. Here is a simple checklist to help you:

	Action	Tips
1	Get the attention of all the learners	Make sure they are looking at you. If you have their eyes, you usually have their ears!
2	Introduce the activity	At lower levels keep this brief and simple. At higher levels you can link it to the previous activity or explain how it relates to your overall lesson aims.
3	Give the instruction	Pause for a moment to collect your thoughts. Make sure your delivery is slow, simple and clear. At lower levels, use imperatives (*'Tell your partner…' 'Write down three words…'*). If you want the learners to see the materials, hold them in front of your chest and point at them, but avoid giving them out at this stage whenever possible. Make sure you include the **timeframe** (e.g. five minutes) and the interaction (e.g. in pairs).
4	Check understanding	The simplest way to check understanding is to do an example (e.g. the first item in an exercise) or a demonstration (e.g. a role-play or game) with the learners. Alternatively, you could ask simple questions (called **Instruction Check Questions – ICQs**) to check key points (e.g. *'How much time do you have?' 'How many people should you interview?'* etc.) or get one learner to repeat the instruction back to you.
5	Give the materials to the learners	It may seem strange to do this at the end, but if you give the materials too soon, learners' eyes will focus on them and they may stop listening to the instruction. If you choose to check understanding by doing an example, it's okay to give the materials before step 4.

The activity step – monitoring the learning

When the learners are doing an activity, whether this is done in pairs, groups or individually, the teacher moves into a support role and monitors the learning. In this step, exactly what you do will depend on the activity type, but may include providing error correction, supplying useful vocabulary and offering a little tuition to individual learners during a writing activity or exercise. During a speaking activity you may want to take notes on both errors and successful language use for the feedback step to follow. At some point, notice how well they are doing the activity and progressing towards your learning outcomes; this observation (a type of formative assessment) will be useful during the post-lesson reflection after teaching practice (see *Post-lesson reflection* below).

When you do your guided observations or watch your peers teach on the CertTESOL, you will probably notice another reason for attentive monitoring: there are quite often one or two learners who haven't understood the instruction! Spotting this early and getting them on task is perhaps our first reason for monitoring. Another useful tip that you may pick up when watching more experienced teachers is that, during the activity step, there will often be time for you to consult your lesson plan, check your time management and even prepare any **boardwork** necessary for the next stage.

Towards the end of the monitoring step, start thinking about when and how to wind up the activity. On some occasions you may need to wait for everyone to finish before it is possible to begin feedback, but more often it won't matter if the slower learners haven't completed the final items, or answered the last question in the activity. In order to prevent faster learners from losing interest or even becoming disruptive after they finish an activity, you could think of a mini-extension task for them to work on while they are waiting. This is a type of **differentiation**, and might involve them writing down something they have told their partner, or heard from their partner, or even thinking of an example sentence or question using the target language of the activity. You can give the instruction for this task quietly to each learner or pair as they finish. Remember that it's okay to be flexible with your timeframe, as long as you are responding to the learners' needs, and to conclude an activity a little sooner than planned or allow it a little more time. If the learners are enjoying the activity a lot, or spending a long time on one of the stages, you may need to provide a time reminder (e.g. *'You have two minutes left.'*).

Whenever learners have done an activity individually, it's a good idea to get them to check answers or compare ideas in pairs before feedback. This serves several functions, including **peer correction** of most obvious errors, useful discussion of target language/topic and also promotes learner confidence if they share the same answers. After a listening activity, listen to your learners during this pair check to assess how well they did in the activity.

Here is a summary of the *'coulds'* and *'shoulds'* for the activity step. The *'shoulds'* can usually be performed in the order given and generally involve observing the learners. The *'coulds'* are divided into intervention tasks and preparation tasks and will always depend on the activity you are doing:

Observation tasks	Intervention tasks	Preparation tasks
You should...	You could...	You could...
1 check the learners are on task	1 provide direct correction of any errors that are impeding communication	1 prepare the board for the feedback step
2 take notes on errors and/or successful uses of language for feedback	2 supply any needed vocabulary or expressions	2 check you haven't forgotten to do anything on your lesson plan
3 assess how well the learners are moving towards your learning outcomes	3 provide brief tuition to individual learners	3 check your time management
4 decide when to conclude the activity	4 give a mini-extension task to learners who finish early	4 cue an audio or video recording
	5 get them to check/ compare answers in pairs (if they have done the activity individually)	5 decide which learners you will call on during feedback

*What would you do, if, two minutes into a five-minute **pairwork** discussion activity, one of the more demanding learners shouted out to you: 'We've finished!' All the other pairs are only halfway through the activity.*

Compare your ideas with the suggestion in the Pause for thought Key *[2].*

The feedback step - concluding the activity

After learners have completed an activity, it's important to get and give feedback appropriate to the activity they have just done. For example, if we give them an exercise with right or wrong answers (e.g. a reading comprehension task), it is essential to check these answers during feedback, which we can do by eliciting from individual learners, checking for agreement (if necessary) and then confirming ourselves. If, on the other hand, the activity does not have right or wrong answers, but many possible ways to complete it successfully (e.g. a pairwork discussion task in which learners describe their family), feedback may involve getting a few samples from the learners (e.g. *What did you find out about Mohammed's family, Ella?*).

Two other common features of giving feedback to learners are providing error correction and praising success. Be aware that, especially in classes where learners don't know the teacher or their classmates very well, they may be self-conscious about receiving individual correction in front of the whole class; so always be gentle, do it anonymously if you can (e.g. *'I heard this mistake during the activity. Who can correct it?'*), and trust your judgement of individual personalities. When providing praise, if possible, be specific about what impressed you; this is more effective than a generic *'Good!'* or *'Well done!'*. You may also want to respond meaningfully to the content of what you heard and conduct a brief plenary discussion (e.g. *'I didn't know that you went to the concert at the weekend, Keiko. Did anybody else go?'*). You may also see experienced teachers doing some **remedial grammar teaching** in the feedback step if they noticed any common errors in the learners' use of English. Don't forget to plan time for feedback, and note that this time will increase as you gain confidence and knowledge as a teacher. Some experienced teachers spend as long on feedback as they do on the activity itself.

Look at the following two activities, both designed for intermediate level classes. Make notes on how you would manage the preparation, activity and feedback steps. Then compare your ideas with those given below.

Activity A

Complete the sentences with these prepositions. There is one extra preposition you do not need. You can use some prepositions more than once.

> at   by   for   in   into   of   on   to

1 I'm afraid I haven't managed .... finish my project – could I have a few extra days, please?

2 Matt and his dad finally succeeded .... building a tree house in the garden. It was really cool!

3 Who's .... charge .... organising the trip on Saturday?

4 I know I can depend .... you .... tell me the truth.

5 In the school play, Jenny was transformed .... a wicked witch – she looked so funny with her black hat and a big nose!

6 I've seen Rich .... several occasions but I've never really spoken .... him.

7 The young children were staring .... the magician .... amazement – how did he do all those tricks?

8 Greece is famous .... its feta cheese.

9 I'm accustomed .... getting up early since I have to catch the school bus at 7.30a.m.

10 Our history teacher inspired us .... want to learn and to be interested .... the past.

Activity B

Student A

Your partner has a similar picture to yours, but there are 5 small differences. Describe your picture carefully to find these differences, but **DO NOT** show your picture to your partner.

E.g. *"On my picture, the bed cover is spotted. What about yours?"*

Student B

Your partner has a similar picture to yours, but there are 5 small differences. Describe your picture carefully to find these differences, but **DO NOT** show your picture to your partner.

E.g. *"On my picture, the bed cover is striped. What about yours?"*

Activity A is a fairly simple **gap-fill**, the kind of thing we do in the first stage of practice of new grammar or lexis. We can anticipate that most learners will be familiar with the procedure for such exercises. I would use it as follows:

1   Brief introduction: *'Now let's do an exercise to check our understanding of the prepositions we've been studying.'*

2   Instruction: *'Work individually...* (show the exercise by **chesting** the materials) *Do this exercise. Choose the best preposition for each sentence. Write your answers in the gap. You have five minutes. Let's do an example together.'*

3   Give out materials: *'OK. Number 1 ... Which option is best? ... Yes Felipe? Does everyone agree?'* etc.

4   Monitor discreetly, without interrupting. First check all learners are doing the right exercise in the right way. Then begin noticing how well they are doing. Make a note of which items have caused the most mistakes for the feedback step and which learners got the tricky answers right. Answer any individual questions quietly.

5   When most learners have finished, get them to check in pairs before feedback.

6   Feedback: nominate learners to read out their answers. Check others agree before confirming or correcting. Spend more time on any answers where several learners made mistakes, if possible eliciting the reason for the correct answer from a learner who got it right, providing specific praise here.

7   Praise the whole class and move onto next activity.

Activity B is a more complex **information gap** activity, in which students A and B have different pictures which they must describe to complete the activity. If any pairs misunderstand the instruction and show their picture to their partner, they spoil the activity. So a good instruction is essential for a successful activity. After getting their attention, I'd proceed as follows:

1   Introduction: *'Now we're going to do a speaking activity to practise using the language we've just studied.'*

2   Instruction: *'Work in pairs. Student A will get one picture and student B will get a different picture. Do not show your picture to your partner. You must describe your picture to your partner to find five differences. Do not write anything, just circle the differences in your picture...* (mime the act of circling) *You have eight minutes.'*

3   Check understanding using ICQs. These should be simple questions that avoid complex language: *'Can you show your picture to your partner?' 'Are they the same? What do you describe?' 'What do you have to find?'* etc.

4   Demonstration: *'OK, everyone watch Petros and Su-Jin. They're going to demonstrate the activity...'* (give the materials to these two students only, who do a quick demonstration) *'Okay, everyone now face your partner and begin.'*

5   Hand out materials and monitor like a hawk to make sure that they're all doing it correctly. Intervene now if any pairs have misunderstood. Monitor with notepad, taking notes on any common errors and any important vocabulary that the learners need. Correct any glaring errors that impede communication (esp. pronunciation) directly. If any pairs finish early, encourage them to write down some of their differences.

6   Feedback: nominate learners to describe specific differences and praise them for any correct use of the target language. Allow learners to show their picture to their partner,

and use this opportunity to write a few common errors and needed vocabulary on the board. Elicit the corrections for the errors and the meaning of the vocabulary before drilling it briefly and praising the whole group.

Responding to unanticipated occurrences

One of the most enjoyable aspects of working as a teacher is the eternal unpredictability of the classroom. Particularly in language teaching, when you combine the ever-present communication barrier with the multiple opportunities for misunderstanding and (in **multilingual** classes) a variety of nationalities together in one room, it may seem a marvel that we ever get through our lesson plans. And to be honest, on a day-to-day basis, we quite often don't! Interesting questions, stimulating discussions, language games and even lesson interruptions are all potential fodder for language learning opportunities. As long as there is a good **rapport** between the learners, and the flexibility to put off an activity or two for another day, these unplanned occurrences can liven up lessons greatly and provide the satisfaction that we are teaching the learners, not the lesson plan. Although this flexibility is rarely possible in initial teacher training, it is definitely something to look forward to once you qualify!

Day-to-day unanticipated occurrences include questions from the learners, misunderstood instructions and unpredicted responses to teacher questions. On occasions, learners may try to make jokes, express approval or disapproval, check the translation of a difficult word on their mobile phone, whisper something to their neighbour or start doing the next activity on their handout. The importance of dealing with unanticipated occurrences appropriately on the CertTESOL is evident from the lesson plan pro formas of course providers (often counterintuitively called 'anticipated problems/occurrences'), which usually provide space for trainees to attempt to predict these challenges in advance and consider how they would deal with them. If you find it difficult to predict these occurrences, ask your course tutors or classmates for advice, or try to make an educated guess based on your experience so far. But, by their very nature, some unanticipated occurrences will always remain unanticipatable! Knowing how to deal with them, like most things in teaching, takes experience and sound judgement. Trainees on a CertTESOL course usually lack the former and are often deserted by the latter when they need it most! So how can we prepare for the unanticipatable?

Let's return to the point made earlier in this chapter that good teaching is a balance between planning and improvisation, or structure and freedom. Making the right decisions at these 'occurrence moments' requires you to balance the learner's individual needs with your commitment to achieve your learning outcomes, especially on a CertTESOL course, where trainees nearly always find themselves pushed for time. Whenever you're in doubt, if your lesson is being assessed, remember that you can always deal with individual needs *after* the lesson, but that you should try to achieve your pre-planned aims *during* the lesson. We will look at this tricky balance between providing for individual needs and meeting aims designed for a whole group of learners more in Unit 3 – *Understanding Learners*.

The most likely type of occurrence in ELT lessons is the unexpected question, which could occur in one of two situations:

- when you are monitoring
- in front of the whole class

When you are monitoring, the spotlight is not upon you. One learner has asked you a question and the others are busy doing something else. In these situations, it's fairly easy to make the right decision. If you can answer the question and it won't take too long, do so. It will mean a lot to that learner. If you're not sure (e.g. regarding grammar), be honest. Tell them you will find out and get back to them next lesson. Far more challenging is the time when you get a question in front of the whole class. At these moments, your judgement as to what to do can be clouded by nerves or haste. So take a moment to RATE the question:

> **R** – Is it RELEVANT?
>
> **A** – Do you know the ANSWER?
>
> **T** – Do you have TIME?
>
> **E** – Will they understand the EXPLANATION?

If your answer to these questions is *'Yes'*, answer it! Otherwise, inform the learner that you will check and let them know next lesson. Often these questions reveal gaps in learners' knowledge that may be better dealt with by planning a future lesson or a quick activity on the topic in question, as long as you feel it isn't just one learner who has this gap.

The second most common type of unanticipated occurrence, quite common in initial training, is the (apparently) incomprehensible **utterance**. Especially if you are teaching a low-level class and are not used to the pronunciation features of your learners' first language(s), you will often find it challenging to understand their speech, and this can be frustrating. Tip number one: don't pretend you have understood if you haven't. I am reminded of one Monday lesson when a trainee was asking students what they had done at the weekend. After each answer, the trainee's stock response had been *'Good!'*. It was only during TP feedback, when we informed her that Pavel had tried to tell her he had spent Sunday at a funeral, that she realised her mistake! If you find yourself unable to understand a learner contribution, as well as the obvious advice, which is to try to negotiate meaning with the learner, or to modify the question, you could also ask the learner to say it another way (called **paraphrasing**; a useful skill), write it down or spell out the word that's causing difficulty. If all else fails, throw a quick glance at the other learners (especially any who speak the same language). If they have understood, they may be able to paraphrase. Most importantly of all, whenever this happens, find an opportunity (e.g. at the end of the lesson) to help that learner get that message across better next time. They will really appreciate it.

Most other unexpected occurrences fall under the category of unanticipated behaviour, and are less often directed at you. This includes the learner who checks a translation on her mobile phone dictionary, the learner who whispers something to his neighbour and the learner who wants to race ahead by doing the next exercise on the handout. Especially in adult classes, the basic rule of thumb is that if it isn't disruptive for any other learners or your lesson and if it doesn't break any school rules, let them do it. This allows you to stay focused on your lesson plan and more relevant behaviour in the classroom. Thus, I'd definitely let the learner check the translation; it's relevant and useful, I'd probably turn a blind eye to the whisperer (as long as it's a one-off and doesn't appear to upset the neighbour), but I'd stop the learner from racing ahead on the handout, which could lead to misunderstandings for him, or problems for his partner if I want them to do the activity in pairs. Other behaviour that can be mildly disruptive includes late arrivals (don't let them distract you from an important instruction or presentation), learners who don't like their partner (think of a pretext to swap partners) and learners who answer text messages or phone calls (remind them of the school rules at the end of the lesson). A good rule of thumb to remember here is: don't let disruptive behaviour disrupt your lesson. Stay focused and keep moving forward. We'll look at behaviour management in more detail in Unit 3.

One final tip: if you find you are often making the wrong choices when responding to unexpected occurrences, ask one of your co-trainees in your TP group to keep a note of these occurrences and how you respond when they observe your lesson. Not only will this help you to learn from your mistakes, but it will also reveal all the occasions when you reacted appropriately, and hopefully boost your confidence as a result. It has been estimated that teachers need to make over 1000 decisions during a 45-minute lesson, just in case you were wondering why you felt so tired after teaching!

Managing the learning environment

> *The CertTESOL course doesn't so much as give you the skills to teach as raise your awareness of the extent to which you already have those skills.*
>
> Will, CertTESOL trainer

The **learning environment** refers to the classroom and everything in it. This includes both the more obvious teaching resources such as the board, the CD player, TV and computer – if you have them, and the less obvious resources such as the walls, desks and floor and the view from the window. It also includes any real objects either in the class itself or brought in by you and your learners for the lesson (smartphones, clothes, bag, bag contents, newspapers, etc.), sometimes called **realia**. Beyond the physical objects themselves, there are other aspects to the learning environment whose management and organisation needs to be considered by the teacher. This includes arrangement of desks and seating, management of climate, sound and light and organisation of the learners.

Learner interactions

A number of **interactions** are possible during learning activities in a communicative ELT classroom, with some of the most common ones provided in the lesson plan earlier in this chapter (e.g. teacher and students – also called 'whole class', pairwork, **groupwork** and mingle). As well as these, learners should be given opportunities to work individually, most obviously during reading, writing or extensive listening activities. Your choice of interaction will depend on the aim of the activity, with individual work being best for personal reflection or individual assessment, pairwork being the simplest way to maximise speaking opportunities, and groupwork often most appropriate for certain games, discussions or project work activities. If your learners often seem tired or sluggish, mingle activities (where learners move around the classroom, interacting with each other on a one-to-one basis, like at a party) and **gallery activities** (where learners move around the class, usually in pairs or groups, looking at images, texts or posters on the walls of the class) can be effective ways to get them out of their chairs and interacting with their peers.

Pause for thought

Look at the images below showing two typical ELT classrooms. Within these classrooms, how easy would it be to organise the following?

1 individual work

2 pairwork

3 groupwork (with groups of four to five learners)

4 a mingle activity

5 a gallery activity

6 a 'board-centred' team game, with two large teams in the class

Which of the two classrooms would you prefer to teach in?

Classroom A

Classroom B

In both classes, individual work should be unproblematic, although the small tables on the **tablet chairs** in classroom A may make it difficult for learners to use large coursebooks. Many learners dislike this type of classroom precisely because they have no room to spread out their books and stationery. In both classes, pairwork will be easy, as learners simply turn to face the person next to them. Groupwork will be easy to organise in classroom A, as learners can easily move their chairs to face each other. In classroom B, groupwork becomes more difficult, and several learners may have to be re-seated (bring them round to the other side of the desks) to ensure that the they are close enough together to interact effectively. Mingle activities are easy to do in classroom A, but more difficult in classroom B. In such a classroom it's a good idea to get all the learners to come to the centre space of the classroom before beginning. Make sure that bags and other potential trip hazards are put on chairs or desks before you begin. A gallery activity will need a little preparation in both classes, but should work okay if chairs are moved away from the walls in classroom A, and pushed carefully under desks in classroom B.

The board

Probably the single most important resource in the classroom is the board, whether it is a traditional chalkboard, a standard whiteboard or an **IWB (interactive whiteboard)**, which is becoming more common. The board is the focus for key lesson stages. It provides a space to write down words, example sentences or answers to exercises and a sketch pad on which to draw diagrams or quick doodles. It can also be used for displaying images, **flashcards**, pre-prepared posters or lesson aims, and we can add variety by sometimes getting the learners to use the board. IWBs add a significant number of additional options to this, including Internet access, use of audio/visual resources, PowerPoint presentations and annotation of documents or texts.

Anybody who can write or draw a picture can use a board, but the skill of learning to use a board effectively, often referred to simply as 'boardwork' in teaching, requires both preparation and technique. During your initial training it's a good idea to plan your board for each lesson. Think about whether there is any information that needs to be on the board for the duration of the lesson (e.g. the lesson title, aims, key vocabulary, an important grammar rule, etc.); if so, where should it go? Will you need to keep part of the board free to display images, to note down answers to an exercise, or for students to provide feedback? The simplest way to plan it is to use a piece of A4 paper as your imagined board and a set of felt tip pens as your board pens. You can also plan to use different colours for different purposes (e.g. use green to mark pronunciation stress on words, blue to record new vocabulary, etc.). Once planned, your 'A4 board' can be stuck on the wall next to your real board during your lesson to guide you as you teach. Technique is also an important part of boardwork; effective teachers are able to write quickly and clearly and at just the right size, which may not sound too challenging, but to ensure that spellings are clear and punctuation indicated where necessary, you should normally write using lower case (i.e. not in CAPS LOCK) and avoid joining up your letters. If your handwriting is untidy, you will need to improve it, so get practising! There's no point in using a board if the learners can't read what you have written.

Using technology
The incredible changes that have happened in information and communication technology since the turn of the century are already having a significant impact on how we teach and how learners organise their learning. Every year new devices, programs, apps and websites for learning and teaching appear, many of them promising to make our job easier or to accelerate learning. For teachers who are confident with using new technology, this constant stream of innovation provides new opportunities and greater convenience, but for the self-confessed technophobes among us, it can be confusing at best and a serious impediment to doing our job effectively at worst. We have briefly mentioned IWBs above, which, for teachers who understand how to maximise their potential, can become extremely useful learning resources. For those who don't, they can quickly become a worst enemy… in the middle of the classroom! If possible, before your course begins, find out if your course provider uses IWBs on the course, and if so, what type (e.g. Smartboard™), and do a little background research. Often you can download the required software on a trial basis to familiarise yourself with it, even if you just have a PC or laptop. Even if you are not required to use one in your assessed lessons, ask for an opportunity to try out an IWB at the school to ensure you get familiar with it during the course.

Smartphones should no longer be seen as something that the learners have to turn off at the start of the lesson and hide in their bags. Most learners will bring smartphones to class equipped with dictionaries, cameras, music, Internet access and email. Add to this the wide range of apps available, some of these specifically for language learning (e.g. Sounds: the Pronunciation App by Macmillan – good for learning the symbols of the **phonemic chart**) and you have a very powerful learning resource. Despite these advantages, smartphones can also be distractions, ringing, pinging, updating and, on bad days, seemingly doing everything they can to disrupt your lesson! So it's a good idea to set a few ground rules regarding usage of smart phones in the classroom, making sure this includes positive uses (e.g. Googling images, checking unfamiliar vocabulary, taking photos of useful boardwork, etc.) as well as the potentially disruptive, including text messaging and compulsive checking of Facebook!

While your initial training will happen in a standard ELT classroom, we are currently entering an era when technology-based learning (generically called **e-learning**) is becoming more and more common in language education, with education management systems (e.g. Moodle, Blackboard), virtual learning environments (e.g. Adobe Connect) and video software (e.g. Skype, Google Hangout, etc.) taking the place of the classroom itself and the resources therein. This is likely to have a significant impact not only on classroom management, but also on methodology itself. The term **blended learning** is often used to refer to a combination of e-learning and face-to-face (i.e. real classroom) learning. For these reasons, during your initial training, you should take time to learn about the technology-based resources available on your course as well as the most popular websites and software used by teachers of English that can help you with background knowledge, lesson preparation and ideas for resources. If you can demonstrate to a future employer that you made use of the latest technology on your CertTESOL course, it may put you ahead of other applicants for a position.

Pause for thought

Imagine you have an intermediate level learner on the other side of the planet, and that both of you have computers and good quality Internet access. The learner wants general English one-to-one lessons twice a week.

- *What resources could you use to teach the four skills (speaking, listening, reading and writing) and the three systems (grammar, vocabulary and pronunciation)?*
- *What could you use instead of a whiteboard?*
- *What are the potential advantages and disadvantages of such an online learning environment?*

Check the Pause for thought Key *[3] for my ideas. Yours may be much better!*

1.4 Post-lesson reflection

Feedback is incredibly useful. Take notes and try to work on one or two key suggestions in your next lesson, as well as honing your strengths.
Samantha, CertTESOL trainer

You may be forgiven for thinking that we have covered the two most important stages in teaching practice: planning a lesson and teaching it. However, a third stage on the CertTESOL, referred to as **Post-lesson reflection** by Trinity and more often called **TP feedback** on courses, is arguably more important than the first two stages when it comes to learning how to teach better. After you complete your CertTESOL, with just a few hours of experience under your belt, you will begin your teaching career, and except for the occasional observations by your line manager, there will be no one sitting at the back of the classroom to help you. Thus, it is vital that as well as developing the planning and teaching skills needed to teach well, you also develop the reflective skills that will be of paramount importance if you are to continue improving as a teacher after the course. For this reason, post-lesson reflection is an assessed part of the CertTESOL, and you will be required to self-evaluate your own lessons both orally and in writing. and also provide constructive feedback to your co-trainees on their teaching on several occasions. It is notable that the trainees who are most perceptive during TP feedback are often also the ones who make the most progress on the course.

With some course providers, TP feedback happens on the same day as the lesson, often with just a short break between the teaching and the analysis. Other course providers choose to delay it, usually until the following day. As well as the trainees who have taught, other 'non-teaching' trainees from your TP group (up to 6 people) will be present and may also be expected to contribute to the feedback discussion. It usually involves several steps, typically in the following order:

Stage 1   Written self-evaluation

Trainees who have taught are expected to complete a written self-evaluation pro forma on which they reflect on how well they feel they achieved their aims for the lesson, any general strengths and weaknesses and suggestions for personal development. As well as providing a private opportunity to think about the lesson before the feedback session, the written self-evaluation forms part of the assessed portfolio, so it's important to complete it clearly and carefully. Your tutor should request a copy of this before the feedback discussion begins. After the feedback discussion, you will be asked to record further written reflections or add comments to your original reflections to demonstrate your understanding of the tutor's feedback.

Tips: When completing the pro forma, be as honest and objective as you can, providing evidence for achievement of aims (e.g. *'most of the students were using the target language well in their discussion'*), and reasons for non-achievement when this happens. Focus on strengths and weaknesses that have the biggest impact on achievement of aims, and also the degree to which you improved on any personal action points specified on your lesson plan. You can be fairly general in your initial self-evaluations, especially if the lessons are quite short, but note that as the course progresses: *'the degree of insight shown in self-evaluations should become more sophisticated…'* (Trinity CertTESOL Syllabus).

Stage 2   Oral self-evaluation

The teaching practice group normally gets together to discuss the lessons and the trainee who has taught self-evaluates their lesson, considering achievement of aims, strengths and weaknesses and development on personal action points (also called 'personal teaching aims'; see first page of example lesson plan above). The tutor may also ask questions at this stage, but will usually hold back on any evaluative comments until later.

Tips: While what you say should mirror what you wrote on your written self-evaluation, you have an opportunity here to go into more detail and your ability to do so will be assessed, so once again, be as honest and objective as you can. If your lesson has gone well, it is important that you are aware of this, so there is no need for false modesty. If your lesson hasn't gone so well, it's important that you pinpoint exactly what mistakes were made and when. Was it in the planning stage (e.g. you estimated timings poorly), or in the lesson itself (e.g. you forgot to keep an eye on the clock)? Achievement of aims is often partial, and will vary between learners, so it's good to be specific about who achieved which aims and how you know this (e.g. observation during monitoring).

Stage 3   Peer-evaluation

Co-trainees who observed the lesson may be asked to provide peer feedback. Course providers provide **peer observation tasks** for them to complete during the lesson (e.g. analysing instructions, focusing on one learner, etc.), and they will often be asked to provide feedback relating to these tasks.

Tips: As in the previous stage, it is important to be objective when giving peer feedback, however, this must always be tempered by sensitivity towards your co-trainees' needs and mood. In the **Professional Awareness and Development** course assessment criteria, trainees need to show *'...awareness of the value of mutual support in the teaching-learning-training environment.'* (Trinity CertTESOL Syllabus). You should show greater tact if a lesson hasn't gone so well, or if the trainee in question is especially sensitive to criticism. If you are receiving peer feedback, it's important to show receptiveness and interest in these comments (you may want to take notes). While your tutor will pinpoint priorities for improvement, peer feedback can often be useful precisely because it is provided by somebody who is undergoing exactly the same challenges as you – and also trying to find the solutions.

Stage 4   Tutor feedback

Your TP tutor provides feedback on your lesson. This usually comes after self- and peer-evaluation, because one of the main aims of feedback is for the tutor to assess the degree to which you are able to reflect effectively on the strengths and weaknesses of specific lessons, both your own and other people's. Some tutors like to take a 'feedback sandwich' approach (covering strengths first, then weaknesses, then recapping on strengths again), and others prefer to talk through the lesson, describing strengths and weaknesses as they do. A third strategy is to focus on the aims themselves and look at how what happened (or didn't happen) in the lesson contributed to achievement or non-achievement of aims. Your TP tutor will also provide written feedback on your lesson that will indicate whether your lesson was up to the required standard for this stage in the course or not. This is included to ensure clarity, and when required, the need for improvement. Trainees often become fixated on 'passing' lessons, however the relationship between your performance in each lesson and your final grade is more complex than this. Although all trainees must demonstrate that they have met the required assessment criteria by the end of the course, there is room for trainees to learn from their mistakes, especially in early lessons. The most important lessons to perform well in are the ones towards the end of your course.

Tips: If your lesson has gone well, it's easy to relax and take in the advice from your tutor, but if a lesson hasn't gone so well, this 'dissection' can be painful. After all the time and effort you put into preparing and teaching the lesson, your tutor still finds fault and expects more of you. It is quite common for trainees to be defensive, and tutors will be prepared to deal with this. However, a defensive approach is usually less effective than an analytical one. Make sure you understand exactly what the criticism is, what you could have done instead, and what recommendations your tutor is providing to ensure that you improve on this point for the future, so ask questions if you need to. Even if you feel your tutor is being too harsh or contradicting previous advice, take it all on board and sleep on it. If you want to query their criticism, do so the following day from a point of view of trying to understand how to improve, rather than taking it personally. In the Professional Awareness and Development course assessment criteria, it states that trainees are expected to show: *'… awareness of the need for development throughout the course, based on a constructive response to training input and feedback from tutors, peers and learners'* (Trinity CertTESOL Syllabus), so whatever personal action points you are given, you should act on these in your next lesson, and refer back to them during the feedback.

While your performance in teaching practice will constitute *'the greater part of the assessment'* for Unit 1, there are two other assessed elements to complete. These are the Guided Observation Journal and the Final Summary.

1.5 Guided Observation Journal

As a trainee teacher, you can obviously learn a lot by observing experienced teachers and reflecting on your observations. The Guided Observation Journal provides a structured opportunity to do just that. Trainees must observe at least four hours of teaching at a variety of levels, with at least one observation occurring before they begin teaching.

Your course provider will have a pro forma that you complete for each lesson observation. In this you document key details of the lesson (e.g. level, type of class, number of learners, etc.), along with the teacher's aims and a specific observation focus that will differ for each lesson. These observation foci may be similar to the peer observation tasks for teaching practice, and typically involve noticing both teacher and learner behaviour or lesson structure. Examples of teacher behaviour include classroom management (e.g. instructions, feedback, responses to unanticipated occurrences, etc.), modification of language at lower levels, use of resources and error correction strategies. Examples of learner behaviour include interaction with peers and/ or teacher, analysis of language produced and assessment of perceived learning preferences or **learning styles**. Examples of lesson structure tasks include analysing stages and inferring aims from lesson content. Figure 1.3 shows an extract from a typical Guided Observation pro forma in which trainees are asked to analyse a lesson from the point of view of Jeremy Harmer's ESA model (Harmer, 1998).

As an assessed component of the CertTESOL, the Guided Observation Journal must be completed correctly and in full. This part of Unit 1 should be a useful, enjoyable and unproblematic component of the course, as long as you follow the guidelines and devote sufficient attention to it.

Figure 1.3:
Extract from a trainee's
Guided Observation
pro forma

Guided Observation Pro Forma Lesson 2 Page 1

See Introduction to Guided Observation for instructions, guidelines and observation etiquette

Name of Trainee:	████████

Details of the Lesson and Class:	Date of Observation: _17 Nov 2011___ Video Observation or Live Lesson?: _Live_____ Length of Observation (in minutes): _90___ Trainee's Observation Number (1, 2, 3 or 4): _2____ Name of teacher: ███████████ Level of Class (elementary / pre-int / intermediate / upper-intermediate / advanced): _Upper-int_____ Type of Class (general English / business English / examination, etc.): _General_____ Number of students: __10_____ Approx. age range of students (e.g. 18-40): _20-40_____

Guided Observation Focus Task 2: Lesson structure and ESA (live observation)

During this observation, pay particular attention to the structure of the lesson you are watching. Make notes in response to the following 4 questions:
* **What is the ESA structure of the lesson?**
Make notes on how the stages fit together: Does the lesson start with Engage? Does Activation always follow Study stages?
* **How does the teacher Engage the students?**
Make notes on how the teacher does this and how effective you think it is.
* **What do they Study, and how?**
Make notes on what they study (grammar, vocabulary, skills) and how they do this.
* **What opportunities for Activation of language do the learners have?**
Make notes on how effective these opportunities are and whether they encourage learners to practise something they have already studied.

Notes on Guided Observation Focus Task:

ESA Structure of the Lesson:

I would describe the ESA structure in this lesson as a version of a patchwork lesson sequence in that the

opening Engage was followed by a short Activation stage and then a Study, returning to an Engage to

introduce the main concept of the lesson (To wish). The lesson moved in both directions between the

stages at fairly regular intervals, which kept the feel of the lesson fresh and quite energised. From the

---

1.6 Final Summary

Towards the end of your course you will be required to write a Final Summary (sometimes called 'Reflections on Teaching Practice'): a short assignment in which you document your development as a teacher over the course, typically commenting on lessons learnt, strengths and weaknesses and any areas that have been pinpointed for future development. Here is a brief extract from one trainee's Final Summary:

> *...Before I begin applying for teaching jobs I'm definitely going to do more research on grammar. I was really surprised in my early lessons by how much more the students knew about grammar than I did, which, as a native speaker, made me feel ashamed and also affected how useful my lessons were for them! While I made up for this by doing lots of preparation, especially reading about the grammar, I still feel like I'm bluffing it whenever I'm teaching grammar, and I constantly dreaded random grammar questions from the students. Doing this research will make me feel more confident, and help me to find the right information whenever I need it in the future. So the first thing I'm going to do is work my way through a self-study grammar book, which I've already ordered on Amazon...*

Trainees occasionally have to **resubmit** the Final Summary, especially if they haven't addressed any of the questions or criteria in the assignment rubric, but most trainees find this opportunity to reflect on their learning both useful and rewarding.

1.7 The Teaching Practice Portfolio

Your Teaching Practice Portfolio provides a record of your development as a teacher over the course. It is a required component which your TP tutors will use to evaluate your lesson planning and self-evaluation when considering your final grade at the end of your course. It will also be used by the external moderator, who will visit at the end of the course and 'sample' a range of trainees' coursework. While the external moderator does not observe any lessons or influence trainees' individual grades on Unit 1, the portfolios provide a 'window' into TP which the moderator can use to ensure that the course provider is meeting Trinity requirements.

Your portfolio will contain the following:

- all your lesson plans for assessed lessons
- all your materials for these lessons
- all your completed self-evaluation pro formas for these lessons
- all your written feedback from tutors on your lessons
- your Final Summary

On some courses the portfolio may also include other aspects of the trainees' assessed coursework, such as the Guided Observation Journal. Course providers usually have very specific requirements regarding the physical portfolio itself, and may provide you with a pre-prepared folder or request you keep an online portfolio.

It is extremely important that all the required elements for the portfolio are kept safe and sound for the duration of the course. Especially documents that are not stored on computer cannot be recreated retrospectively if lost (e.g. a handwritten lesson plan or self-evaluation). For this reason, all of these documents should be stored separately from more general paperwork, such as handouts from inputs, guidance documents, rough drafts and personal notes, and should never be left lying around. All of this sounds like obvious advice, but at the end of a long day on the course, it is surprisingly easy to misplace any one of the many documents that must be kept for the portfolio. A useful tip is to create a checklist of required portfolio paperwork, and on days when you are teaching, before going home, make sure you've checked off all the necessary documents and are aware of anything outstanding that needs to be added the next day.

One potential grey area regarding the documents in your portfolio is how to include 'soft copy materials', i.e. those that are not printed out for the lesson, but still form part of the resources used in the lesson itself. This may include the following:

- slides from a pre-prepared PowerPoint presentation or IWB file shown to the learners
- websites accessed during the lesson as part of planned learning activities (e.g. YouTube video)
- images accessed to help clarify meaning of vocabulary or grammar (e.g. Google image search)
- apps used on learner access tablets or Smart phones (e.g. a vocabulary game or pronunciation resource)

The first of these, as something you have created specifically for the lesson, should definitely be included in the portfolio, so print it off and add it. The remaining three should all be referenced in the appropriate place on your lesson plan, but, as accessed, rather than created resources, they are not essential for inclusion in the portfolio. Nonetheless, it is useful documentation of your resourcefulness if you can include something (e.g. a print off of the website, image search page or app screenshot) that will jog tutors' memories when they come to assessing your performance in Unit 1.

Review of Unit 1
Understanding teaching practice

True or false?

Read the statements below. For each one, decide whether it is true or false, based on what you have read in this chapter. Then put the statements in the order in which the answers are found in the chapter.

1   Post-lesson reflection will not be necessary once your course has finished.

2   The communicative approach still influences the practices of many teachers today.

3   Detailed lesson plans are necessary on the CertTESOL mainly because your lesson is being assessed.

4   You should begin lesson planning by choosing your activities carefully.

5   The expected standard required of trainees in teaching practice remains consistent throughout the course.

6   One of the reasons for monitoring learning activities is to carry out assessment.

7   The C-A-P mnemonic is appropriate for planning all lesson types.

8   Unexpected questions from the learners can help you to plan for future lessons.

9   The input for Unit 1 is provided separately from other aspects of the course.

10 'Commentating' is a useful skill for trainees to employ when communicating with learners of English.

11 Guided observation and peer observation are basically the same thing.

12 Pairwork is the best learner interaction if you want to maximise speaking opportunities for all learners.

13 Lesson aims in language teaching should always be specific and measurable.

14 You should never give out materials until the final stage of your instruction.

15 During TP feedback you should always defend the choices you made when planning and during your lesson.

If you need to, check your answers in the *Review Key* at the back of the book.

Now return to the learning opportunities provided at the start of the chapter. Check off the ones that you feel you have achieved and reread the relevant sections for any you're not sure about.

unit 2 Understanding and teaching language and skills

When teaching new language, remember that context is king! Making sure your target language is embedded in a meaningful context will help your students (and you!) to clarify meaning and usage.

Sinèad, CertTESOL trainer

Learning opportunities

This unit will help you to...

- describe the subject matter of language teaching as described in the CertTESOL syllabus
- become familiar with key areas of grammar, vocabulary and pronunciation that are typically taught in English lessons
- plan for and teach lessons with a grammatical or lexical focus
- understand how to integrate pronunciation teaching into different lesson types
- recognise the importance of receptive and productive skills practice in language learning, as described in the CertTESOL syllabus
- understand the role of functional language in productive skills lessons
- plan for and teach lessons on the four skills (speaking, listening, reading and writing)
- integrate combinations of these four skills appropriately in different lesson types
- identify what you need to do to pass Unit 2 of the CertTESOL

Introduction

Unit 2 of the Trinity CertTESOL is called *Language Awareness & Skills*. Let's find out exactly what this means. According to the Trinity CertTESOL syllabus...

> *Language Awareness (LA) is used as a generic term covering the areas of grammar, lexis and phonology... Language Skills (LS) is used as a generic term covering the receptive skills of listening & reading and the productive skills of speaking & writing.*

> Trinity CertTESOL syllabus

In other words, Unit 2 is about your subject knowledge of what you're teaching. Just as history teachers need to know what happened in the past and how to teach it, to be a successful English language teacher you need to know what the English language consists of and how to teach it. In the Trinity syllabus, **Language Awareness** covers the 'systems' of English, and Language Skills covers how we use spoken or written language to communicate, as shown in Figure 2.1.

The systems	grammar		
	lexis (or vocabulary)		
	phonology (or pronunciation)		
		Spoken language	**Written language**
The skills	**Productive**	speaking	writing
	Receptive	listening	reading

Figure 2.1:
The systems and skills of
English language learning

Notice that there are four skills in English, and three basic systems. Some writers argue that there are other skills (e.g. thinking, translating, conversing), and on a more technical level we can identify other systems such as **discourse**. Notice that the skills can be categorised either as **productive** (when we are producing language) or **receptive** (when we are receiving information via language), or according to the medium of spoken or written language.

This distinction between separate areas of language is useful for us to understand the scope of the subject knowledge of a language teacher, and the Trinity syllabus. However, the reality of much language use is that we blend these much more fluidly than this categorisation implies. It is impossible to say anything without words, and although you may not realise it you are always making use of complex rules of grammar and pronunciation when you speak. Although at first glance, it may seem that the skills are used more discretely, this is probably also a misnomer. Think about a conversation between two friends, which involves them both speaking and listening interchangeably. Now imagine they're talking about a text message from a third friend and discussing and drafting what to write in reply. All three systems and four skills are integrated simultaneously in their interaction. For more on this, see *Integrating Skills* at the end of this unit.

Why do I need to know about language?

Research on expertise among language teachers tells us that subject knowledge and knowledge of how to teach it (called **pedagogical** content knowledge) are essential to effective teaching (e.g. Tsui, 2009). If you are a native speaker (NS) of English you may think you know the system, and in a way, you do. However, there is a sense in which non-native speakers (NNSs) who have learnt English as a foreign language know the system better.

As non-native speakers of English have usually had to learn the language by studying it formally, their knowledge of it, including strengths and weaknesses, is different to the knowledge of native speakers. How would you describe these differences? And how might these differences influence how NSs and NNSs teach English?

Our knowledge of any language that we have learnt from a young age is instinctual. This native-speaker knowledge is sometimes called **implicit knowledge**. We have it and we can use it, but we can't always explain how or why we use it, and we can't always name the parts of the system involved (e.g. adjective, verb, etc.). This isn't a problem for everyday use, but it obviously causes problems when we need to teach it to somebody who doesn't have our implicit knowledge of the system. In contrast to this, the knowledge of a language that we build up by studying it formally (in classrooms or from self-study books) is often called **explicit knowledge**. As a result of undergoing this formal learning process, we usually know the names of all the parts of the language, the rules for **usage**, and we can sympathise with a learner who is undergoing the same learning process. This is where non-native speakers of English are often more knowledgeable than native speakers. However, they have to work hard to gain the native speaker's instinctual ability to use English without making mistakes. Thus, in order to be good language teachers, we need both types of knowledge: implicit and explicit, so that we can use language well and describe what we are doing when we use it. The characteristics of these two types of knowledge are summarised in Table 2.1.

Table 2.1 Differences between Implicit and Explicit language knowledge

Implicit language knowledge	Explicit language knowledge
instinctual, procedural knowledge	formally learnt (even by native speakers), declarative knowledge
often we are not aware of it, or can't describe very well exactly what we know	we are conscious of it and can describe our explicit language knowledge (e.g. as rules of usage, or the **meaning** of an expression)
native speakers always have this	non-native speakers usually have this
difficult to teach, learners need to use the language to develop their implicit knowledge	easier to teach, but learning it doesn't mean we can always use it when necessary

Assessment of Unit 2

As you might expect, the Trinity CertTESOL sees both implicit and explicit language knowledge as essential to being a good teacher. Your ability to use English competently and to provide an appropriate **model** for the learners is assessed before you start the course – applicants with a low level of English are not accepted by course providers. However, it is also assessed in your use of English in class and in assignments on the course. The majority of the syllabus described in Unit 2 relates to your understanding of the systems, how they are used and how you can help learners to use them through the four skills. This means you need to be able to do the following:

- describe the important components of each system (e.g. nouns, the passive voice, vowel sounds)
- help learners to understand how, when and why we use these components in a particular way (e.g. how we form the past continuous tense, and when and why we sometimes prefer it to the past simple tense)
- provide appropriate examples and model the language appropriately (e.g. when drilling the pronunciation of new vocabulary)
- plan and teach lessons in which learners learn about new parts of the system and practise them (e.g. a lesson where the learners learn new adjectives to describe personality and practise describing the personalities of people they know)
- show awareness of different types of English (e.g. British vs. American)

Assessment of these areas is distributed throughout the course elements. Many are assessed in your **teaching practice** and your assignments. However, your knowledge of the first two of these bullet points is also assessed through a Language Awareness test or assignment, which is likely to test mainly your explicit knowledge of English. See the *Outcomes* and *Assessment* sections of the Trinity CertTESOL syllabus for a more technical description of these areas of learning.

How important are the different components of the language system?

A famous linguist once said: '*When students travel. they don't carry grammar books, they carry dictionaries.*' (Krashen, 1987, cited in Lewis, 1993). Nowadays, they probably carry both on their smartphone, but that's beside the point. Languages contain far more words than they do grammar rules. Indeed, another linguist once noted that '*Vocabulary is the Everest of language*'. (Crystal, 2009, p.7), and from personal experience I would say that the majority of language learning involves memorising and remembering how to use words and expressions.

So does that mean that vocabulary is more important than grammar in classroom language teaching? Not necessarily. Despite repeated attempts to focus syllabi away from grammar and onto **lexis** by a number of applied linguists and methodologists over the last 30 years (e.g. Lewis, 1993), grammar still usually structures language learning syllabi. This is probably because for most of us, understanding the grammar is more challenging than learning the individual words. As such, we tend to need more practice with the grammar, and most importantly, it is with grammar learning that many of us feel we need the help of a teacher. However, let us note that these two parts of the system are very much intertwined; all vocabulary has grammar to it (even nouns and adjectives, see below), and all grammar needs vocabulary to mean anything. To quote a third and final (I promise) linguist, '… *while without grammar very little can be conveyed, without vocabulary, nothing can be conveyed.*' (Wilkins, 1972, pp. 111-112).

Most importantly from our perspective, it is with teaching grammar that trainee teachers tend to encounter some of their biggest challenges, so that's where we shall start. We will then look at lexis and then dive into the interesting area of pronunciation that many trainee teachers also find challenging. The four skills will follow after this.

*A useful tip – The next sections of this unit contain quite a lot of technical information, but you don't need to memorise all of this yet. Most language teachers only become knowledgeable about grammar, **phonology** and lexis by teaching them week in, week out, month after month and year after year. At this stage our focus is on getting an overview of the overall system, and noticing some of the most important features within it.*

2.1 Grammar

This section will cover the basics of English grammar, prioritising those areas that are often taught in English lessons and found in ELT coursebooks. See the Grammar reference section in *The Knowledge* to learn more about other important grammar areas, and make sure you have a good grammar reference book (e.g., Parrott, 2010; Swan, 2005a) to help you when preparing for lessons where grammar is likely to be a key focus. We will begin by looking at the labels we give to individual words (parts of speech), then we will look at verb grammar (e.g. different tenses), noun grammar, adjective and adverb grammar. After that, we will look at how we put bits of language together to make words and sentences (**morphology** and **syntax**) and finally we will look at some important differences between written and spoken grammar. Then we will focus on how to teach it to learners.

Parts of speech

The **parts of speech** of a language are the different categories or labels that we give to words. Words in the same category (**word class**) perform a similar function in a sentence. For example, you probably learnt some basic rules at school like 'verbs are the action words in sentences', and 'adjectives describe nouns'. Notice how in Table 2.2, we can select one word from each class to make a large number of grammatical, but not necessarily meaningful, sentences:

Table 2.2: Example word classes in English

Determiner	Adjective	Noun	Verb	Adverb
The	happy	doctor	worked	slowly.
That	front	door	squeaks	noisily.
His	incurable	condition	is deteriorating	every day.

Within each category, you often find subcategories. For example, determiners are often broken into four different category types, each with a slightly different function, but all usually coming at the start of a **noun phrase**:

1 articles (e.g. a, *the*)

2 possessive determiners (e.g. *my, your, whose*)[4]

3 demonstratives (e.g. *this, these*)

4 quantifiers (e.g. *some, many, every*)

[4] also called possessive pronouns or possessive adjectives

Pause for thought

Look at the following short extract from a story and see if you can work out what part of speech the underlined words/expressions are. Choose from the word types in the box.

Use the Grammar reference section *in* The Knowledge *to help you, and only then check your answers in the* Pause for thought Key *[4] at the back of the book.*

adjective (2) adverb (1) auxiliary verb (1) conjunction (2) gerund (1) modal auxiliary verb (1) pronoun (1) proper noun (1) phrasal verb (1) preposition (2) determiner (1)

As soon as we <u>got out</u>, they handcuffed us <u>and</u> told us <u>we</u> were <u>under</u> arrest.

'But what for?' said Colin <u>angrily</u>.

'For <u>stealing</u> a <u>silver</u> <u>Peugeot 206</u>,' said the <u>other</u> officer. 'We<u>'ve</u> got you on video, <u>so</u> I recommend you keep <u>quiet</u>. Anything you say <u>may</u> be used <u>as</u> evidence.

At this stage you will probably note some complexities creeping in. For example, a gerund is a type of noun derived from a verb, or for another example, a phrasal verb includes a verb and (usually) an adverb. You may have also noticed that the determiner 'other' follows another determiner, and that there are specific rules for how these can and cannot combine. Don't worry too much about all these rules yet; just be aware that there are different levels of analysis, and different ways to describe the elements of a sentence. Linguists refer to this process of sentence analysis as **parsing**.

Verb grammar

As teachers we tend to use the word '**tense**' to refer to different verb forms that imply different concepts of time, some in the past, some in the present and others in the future. Linguists often tell us that there are only two tenses in English; the present tense (*he lives*) and the past tense (*he lived*). They categorise other verb forms as **aspects**, such as the present perfect aspect (*he has lived*) and the present continuous aspect (*he is living*). For now, let's use the word 'tense' to talk about all of these, as teachers tend to do, unless we need to distinguish this from aspect. We will return to this distinction between tense and aspect in a moment.

While they are not necessarily the most important area of grammar, tenses are certainly the most well-known, and because of the complexities of formation and usage they are often the part of language that learners find most difficult to understand. What makes this even more challenging is the fact that different languages often have very different tense systems. Some (e.g. Malay) have no tenses at all, and others (e.g. Italian) have more than English. This means that different learners are likely to have different problems with different tenses in English.

Pause for thought

The table below shows the 12 main verb aspects in English. See if you can complete the missing ones.

↑ Tense & Aspect →	... simple	... continuous	... perfect (simple)	... perfect continuous
Past...	1	I was speaking English.	I had spoken English ...	2
Present...	I speak English.	I'm speaking English.	3	I have been speaking English ...
Future...	I will speak English.	4	I will have spoken English ...	I will have been speaking English ...

Check your answers in the **Pause for thought Key** *[5].*

Some interesting things can be noted by comparing the forms in this table. First notice that in the two 'true' tenses, the verb constitutes just one word (*speak* and *spoke*). The so-called 'future tense' in fact uses a modal verb that we often use to make predictions (*will*), to imply the future. Alternatively, we could use a different future form to do this (e.g. *I'm going to speak English*). Also note that we tend to use the same additions for each of the aspects. So to make a continuous form, we use a form of the verb *be* (*was, am, will be*) before the verb, and attach the affix *-ing* to the end of the main verb. Also notice that there are four different forms to the main verb in this example:

Base form/ infinitive	Past simple form	Continuous/active participle	Past participle
speak	spoke	speaking	spoken

Pause for thought

Speak is an irregular verb. Try changing the verb forms in the above table to 'play tennis' (play is a regular verb), then answer the following:

1 What do you notice about the past simple and the past participle forms?

2 How do we form past simple and past participle forms with regular verbs?

3 Think of two or three more examples of regular and irregular verbs.

4 Which would you teach learners first? regular or irregular verbs? Why?

Check your answers in the **Pause for thought Key** *[6].*

Another important area of verb grammar that learners need to practise is the formation of negatives and questions. Try turning the sentences in the verb table above into negatives (e.g. *I didn't speak English.*) and questions (e.g. *Am I speaking English?*). Notice that the question forms require a change in word order, and that some simple tenses require the addition of an extra **auxiliary** verb (*do/don't*) to form negatives and questions, but the continuous and perfect aspects make use of the auxiliary verbs already present to do this (e.g. *I <u>wasn't</u> speaking English.*; *<u>Have</u> I been speaking English?*). English has a complex system for the formation of negatives and questions, and it is quite natural for learners to confuse auxiliaries, or get the word order wrong at early stages in language learning. Here are two typical mistakes with this area that you may have heard before:

[5] An asterisk is used to show non-standard or grammatically incorrect sentences or utterances

*I no speak English. * [5]*

*Where you are going? **

Because of the challenges presented by verb grammar, it's often overlooked that other parts of speech also have important grammar. Let's look at three of them here, all common in English language textbooks: noun grammar, adjective grammar and adverb grammar.

Noun grammar

The most obvious area of noun grammar is how to make plurals. Most nouns in English do this by adding -*s*, but there are some irregular ones, such as *man – men*. Can you think of any others?

A much less obvious area of noun grammar that learners need to know about, especially if it doesn't exist in their **L1**, is the idea of **countability**. Have a look at the following errors. You will be able to correct them, but can you work out why they are wrong?

- *I only have a few money. **
- *I need an information. **
- *My father hasn't got any hairs. **

Of course, all of these errors are to do with countability. Some nouns are countable (also called 'count nouns'). This means that we can pluralise them and count them. It also means that we can only use them with certain quantifiers. The opposite is uncountable nouns (also called 'non-count nouns'), which can never be plural (e.g. *information*) and also have specific quantifiers (see Table 2.3).

Table 2.3:
Countable and
uncountable nouns

	Countable	Uncountable
Example noun	(a) problem / problems	(some) information
Example quantifiers	a **few** problems how **many** problems...?	a **little** information how **much** information...?

Adjective grammar

The most common area of adjective grammar covered in ELT coursebooks is comparative and superlative forms. Comparatives and superlatives are one of the 'nice' areas of grammar to teach. The rules are fairly simple, they are not too difficult for learners to grasp, and there are lots of ways we can practise them in English lessons (for example comparing people: *Dan is older than Nick*, or talking about world records: *He's the fastest man on the planet*.). They are usually categorised in three basic groups in ELT coursebooks, with just a few irregulars (see Table 2.4).

Table 2.4: Comparative and superlative adjectives		Base adjective	Comparative adjective	Superlative adjective
One-syllable adjectives		slow	slower	slowest
Two-syllable adjectives ending in '-y'		happy	happier	happiest
All other adjectives		expensive	more expensive	most expensive
Irregulars		good	better	best
		bad	worse	worst
		far	further	furthest

Notice how the 'y' changes to 'i' in the second row of the table. Somewhat trickier is the *as … as* structure that we often used to make comparatives negative, e.g. *He isn't <u>as sensible as</u> his sister.*

Adverb grammar

Adverbs have some surprisingly tricky grammar. One basic rule of thumb if you are parsing a sentence: if you don't know what it is, it's probably an adverb! The underlined words in each of the following sentences are adverbs:

- *I'm <u>off</u> to New York <u>tomorrow</u>.*
- *I <u>really</u> can't sleep <u>well</u> at the moment.*
- *<u>Unfortunately</u>, he <u>still</u> hasn't apologised for acting <u>so</u> <u>rudely</u>.*

There are also some expressions that function as adverbs. These are called 'adverbials'. The three words *'at the moment'* in the second sentence constitute an adverbial, which basically means 'now', which is also an adverb!

One area of adverb grammar which is quite often taught in English lessons relates to where we can and cannot add adverbs in sentences. The truth of the matter is, there is a lot of flexibility to where they can go, but the only place we really don't like them in English is between a verb and its object:

- *He closed quickly the door. ***

And if you're not exactly sure what an 'object' is, read on! It's coming up in the next section.

Morphology and syntax

Grammarians often separate grammar into two basic areas: morphology and syntax. Morphology refers to how the form of words changes depending on grammar. Here are some examples from above, with the **morpheme** underlined:

live – live<u>d</u>   *slow – slow<u>er</u>*   *problem – problem<u>s</u>*   *speak – <u>spoke</u>*

Compared to some languages (e.g. Spanish or Russian), English doesn't have many morphemes, and the only significant challenge regarding morphology for learners of English is learning the past tense and past participle forms of irregular verbs (*write – wrote – written, ring – rang – rung*, etc.).

Syntax refers to the order of, and relationship between, words in a sentence. The basic syntax of English declarative sentences tends to follow a subject-verb-object/complement (SVO/C) word order. Here are some examples of that:

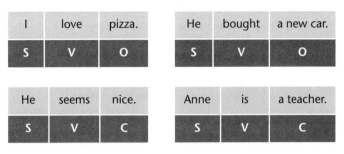

Verbs like '*love*' or '*buy*' require a direct object (a noun) to complete the sentence. However, verbs like '*be*' or '*seem*' require complements (additional information about the subject). Some verbs don't need anything to complete them. They are called **intransitive verbs**:

So far, so good, but unfortunately things start to get complicated when we look at the logic of more complex sentences, such as sentences with more than one clause, which can be parsed at various levels:

Table 2.5:
Parsing of a
complex sentence

declarative sentence								
noun phrase (subject)	verb phrase (predicate)							
	verb (past)	noun phrase (direct object)	subordinate clause					
			noun phrase (subject)	verb phrase (predicate)				
				verb (past)	prepositional phrase (adverbial)			
						noun phrase		
pronoun	transitive verb	noun	conjunction	pronoun	intransitive verb	preposition	determiner (article)	noun
I	met	him	when	he	came	to	the	party.

This is just a taste of the delights of syntax, which is rarely analysed to this degree of detail in English language lessons (phew!). If you want more, see *The Knowledge*, where three grammatical features with complex syntax are described: conditional structures, the passive voice and relative clauses – all are commonly covered in ELT coursebooks.

Spoken versus written grammar

The vast majority of grammar introduced in ELT coursebooks tends to describe rules we are very likely to follow when writing, but not necessarily when speaking. Given the emphasis on spoken English that has dominated English language teaching, at least in theory, for at least the last 40 years, this may come as a surprise. However, as most grammar tends to be presented and studied in written form (e.g. in reading texts or grammar practice exercises), perhaps this shouldn't be so surprising. Indeed, until scientists started recording and analysing spoken data quite recently, few linguists were really aware of the extent to which spoken grammar differs from written grammar. More recent grammars of English have begun to look into this (e.g. Biber et al., 1999; Carter & McCarthy, 2006) and have surprised many of us with their revelations, including the following:

- Sentences, as used in writing, are difficult to identify in spoken language.
- Vocal cues such as **intonation** and pauses are essential for clarifying meaning.
- Speakers regularly interrupt each other, finish each other's sentences or talk at the same time.
- Sentences are often left unfinished (**false starts**), and words which are understood are often omitted completely (ellipsis).

The following extract, involving native speakers of British English, demonstrates many of these features very well (from Carter & McCarthy, 2006, p.165):

A: *I'll just take that off. Take that off.*

B: *All looks great.*

C: *[laughs]*

B: *Mm.*

C: *Mm.*

B: *I think your dad was amazed, wasn't he, at the damage?*

A: *Mm.*

B: *It's not so much the parts. It's the labour charges for…*

D: *Oh that. For a car.*

B: *Have you got hold of it?*

A: *Yeah.*

B: *It was a bit erm…*

A: *Mm.*

C: *Mm.*

B: *A bit.* (continues)

Despite the interesting features of spoken grammar, surprisingly little has changed regarding how we teach structure. However, a few bits of spoken grammar have made their way into (some) standard textbook grammars over the years. These include the following:

- Question tags: *He's late again, isn't he? You did it on purpose, didn't you?*
- **Vague language**: *It's like a sort of adventure game where you collect, like, prizes, and stuff.*

Pause for thought

One of the key skills that experienced language teachers have is the ability to identify areas of grammar, whether this is in a reading text, or something a learner has said. Let's try honing this skill now. The following sentences all include examples of grammar that we have looked at so far. See if you can complete the tasks in the right-hand column.

Example sentences	Task
1 They've been playing football all afternoon.	Identify the tense.
2 Then I got so angry when the car broke down.	Find the adverbs in this sentence.
3 We will be taking a break for lunch at 1 o'clock.	Turn this sentence into a negative and a question.
4 I was only joking, wasn't I?	Identify the feature of spoken grammar.
5 Can I have two breads, please? *	Identify the cause of the error.
6 I thought the sequel was more interesting.	Identify the tense and the adjective grammar.

Check your answers in the **Pause for thought Key** *[7].*

2.2 Teaching grammar

Over the last 50 years, the field of Second Language Acquisition (SLA) has attempted to describe how we learn new languages. While many of its most important discoveries largely confirm what common sense tells us about learning foreign languages, one of its most interesting findings is that we don't necessarily learn the grammar of a foreign language in the order that it is taught, and that there is probably a 'natural order' of acquisition influencing the learning process (Ellis, 2008). Interestingly, this depends mainly on the language being learnt (e.g. English), and less on the learner's **first language** (L1).

Pause for thought

■ *What are the implications of this research finding for grammar teaching?*

Compare your opinion with the ideas provided in the **Pause for thought Key** *[8].*

Preparing to teach grammar

Obviously the first question we must consider when preparing to teach grammar is: *What grammar should I teach?* While a few lucky teachers can choose the grammar they teach, most of us are required or expected to follow a syllabus (this includes the 'implied syllabus' of an ELT coursebook) which specifies the areas of grammar to cover and probably even suggests an order. However, the research findings described above indicate that we are likely to get better results if we choose our grammar based on our learners' current needs. Thus, even if we have a prespecified syllabus, wherever possible we should try to prioritise or rearrange elements to meet these needs. The following questions may help you to predict what grammar your learners are ready to learn:

1   What areas of grammar are they starting to use, but still having difficulty with?
2   What ideas did they have difficulty expressing yesterday?
3   What common mistakes are many of them making?
4   What bits of grammar are they noticing in the world around them?

Let's say, for example, that your pre-intermediate learners (A2 level) are starting to use comparative forms in their natural spoken English, but they're still making mistakes with them and have been asking questions about them. Here are some of the mistakes you've noticed recently:

■ failure to use the grammar: *His phone is very expensive than mine.* *
■ overuse/misuse of the grammar: *It's more funnier, I think.* *

So you decide to teach a grammar lesson on comparatives. Before you can go into class, there are several things you need to do:

■ research your grammar
■ plan your lesson
■ prepare your materials

The Trinity syllabus recognises the importance of researching new grammar, lexis and phonology as one of the two main learning outcomes for Unit 2 (the other is applying knowledge gained from such research). When researching grammar, it's probably not a good idea to Google it, at least initially. There are several different types of grammar description, some of which aren't for language learners or language teachers. If you look at a grammar for linguists (e.g. on Wikipedia), it may provide very technical terminology not appropriate for learners, and give you much more information than you need. There are also quite a few websites designed for learners (or by learners) that are not very accurate in their description. Two useful sources for grammar research are 'pedagogical grammars' (grammar books designed for teachers and learners of English) and the coursebooks that teachers use in class. Whereas pedagogical grammars tell you everything you are likely to need to know about the grammar (e.g. Swan, 2005a) and about the challenges that learners have with it (e.g. Parrott, 2010), coursebooks usually provide a fast, simple overview (in the grammar reference at the back), and possibly some practice exercises to help you to consolidate your understanding. Coursebooks also have the advantage that they provide ideas for contextualising, analysing and practising the grammar. Thus, I usually recommend trainees research their grammar in both pedagogical grammars *and* coursebooks.

The process of planning a lesson is covered in detail in Unit 1, where an example lesson plan is also provided. Although the lesson provided there isn't a grammar lesson, the suggested structure is appropriate for any lesson where you are introducing new language. Let's revise this now with a suggested skeleton structure including C-A-P (Context, Analysis and Practice). Bear in mind what you have already established about the learners' needs, that at least some of them have some knowledge about the grammar, but they are still making mistakes or missing opportunities to use it.

Context	A short text comparing two cities, London and Paris, that will include several examples of comparatives.
Analysis	Learners underline comparatives in the text and match them to rules regarding comparative adjective formation. You then plan to ask questions to check their understanding (e.g. *How do we make comparatives from one-syllable adjectives? Which adjectives are irregular?*).
Practice	Learners complete a **gap-fill** grammar exercise which requires them to use comparative forms. They then prepare written notes for a speaking activity in which they compare two cities in their country.

Preparation of materials may involve creating or adapting texts or exercises on a computer, photocopying pre-existing materials (don't forget to source materials for copyright reasons), and collecting any objects or images you may need. If you have an **interactive whiteboard**, you may also be able to prepare some useful materials for the analysis stage, such as example sentences, useful images, etc. If you want to save time during the lesson, you could also create a poster with the important grammar rules that you can display or hide when needed, and use it to **elicit** key concepts or check understanding. And of course, if you are preparing an assessed lesson for the CertTESOL, you will need at least two copies of your lesson plan; one for your tutor and one for you.

Teaching a grammar lesson

In Unit 1, we looked at how to manage learning in any type of lesson, focusing our attention on **classroom management**, **activity cycles** and dealing with the unexpected. In this unit we look at how different lesson types may influence this structure, starting with perhaps the most challenging lesson type for trainee teachers – grammar lessons. While all lessons do, of course, include grammar, by 'grammar lesson' we mean a lesson in which our main intention is to help learners to improve their ability to understand and use a specific grammar feature (or features) appropriately.

Introducing grammar lessons

There is strong evidence from educational research that learners are more likely to learn what we are teaching if we make our intentions clear at the start of the lesson (Hattie, 2009), something that, in English teaching, can be applied in grammar lessons where complex concepts and explicit knowledge are involved. At higher levels, we could explain these intentions verbally, but it can be a good idea to indicate these in written form as well (especially at lower levels). This could be in the form of a lesson menu on the board, a set of aims simplified from those written on your lesson plan, a set of questions that you hope to answer, or a set of outcome statements. Let's choose the last of these for the lesson provided above, and imagine that they are written at the top of the learners' handout for the lesson, as shown below:

Using comparative adjectives

- ◼ I can identify comparative adjectives in a text.
- ◼ I understand how to form sentences with comparative adjectives.
- ◼ I know when to use comparative adjectives.
- ◼ I can talk about places I know using comparative adjectives.

If we expect that learners have prior knowledge of this topic, we could begin the lesson by getting them to self-evaluate their current ability. We could get them to put a number next to each of the statements, where 0 means 'not at all', 1 means 'a little', 2 means 'fairly well' and 3 means 'definitely'.

Providing context for grammar

The Context phase for this lesson involves the learners reading a short text that compares the cities of London and Paris. We can use the *activity cycle* (see Unit 1) for this reading task, but given that it's the first activity of the lesson, it's a good idea to precede this with a warm up that orients the learners onto the topic of the text. We could do this by getting them to find the cities on a map, asking them what they know about them and whether they have visited them. If they have mobile phones, they could use them to find some photos of the cities. This all serves to stimulate prior knowledge, which aids comprehension when reading. We can then use the text to link this prior knowledge to the new language through an appropriate reading task. Such a task will help us to check how much they understood and what they noticed during feedback.

Look at the three following reading tasks. Which would you give, and why?

1   Read the text and underline any comparative adjectives you find.

2   Read the text and find five differences between London and Paris.

3   Read the text and decide which of the two cities you would like to live in and why.

Later in this unit we will look in more detail at comprehension questions for longer reading activities (see *Receptive Skills*). The main purpose of this text is to contextualise the new grammar, so it may seem logical to go for Task 1. However, there are a couple of problems with it as a contextualisation task. It's quite boring, and doesn't really encourage the learners to engage with the content of the text or to find personal meaning in it. Also, if learners know what comparative adjectives look like, they may be able to complete the task without understanding the text. The second task is much better for understanding, especially because we can elicit possible answers during feedback. However, many of us would probably most enjoy doing Task 3, which would also allow us to assess understanding effectively. During feedback, it would become evident fairly quickly whether the learners have understood key information in the text. Also, importantly, when they try to answer the question 'why', they will probably find a need to use comparative adjectives (…*because it's beautiful of London… how can I say?**), and by creating this need, we are hopefully stimulating the part of their brain that helps them to learn new grammar.

Other suggestions for providing context

■   Instead of using written text, use an audio recording or a short video extract to contextualise the new language. This is very useful if the new language typically occurs during dialogue (e.g. question forms). If you want learners to see the new language written down, you can provide a printed tapescript of the conversation.

■   Try using the classroom as a context. You can contextualise prepositions of locations just by describing the location of objects (*behind, under, next to,* etc.). Similarly, for possessive pronouns, you could collect a random assortment of the learners' possessions and ask questions to elicit them (e.g. *'Is this bag yours?' 'No, it's hers.'*).

- Tell the learners a story, and weave your grammar into the story (e.g. past continuous tense: 'She _was walking_ along the road...'). You could leave the story unfinished, and get the learners to finish it during the practice phase of the lesson.

- Use images, including printed photos, images from magazines, or even images displayed on the board, or students' smartphones. Describing images often involves using specific grammar structures such as present continuous (e.g. 'A man _is walking_ by the river...'). Using two related images is good for comparatives or the present perfect (e.g. '_In this picture, the house _has been painted_.').

Analysing grammar

Let's return to our comparative lesson where our learners were providing feedback on why they would prefer to live in one of the two cities. An experienced teacher can probably use this opportunity to move seamlessly into the analysis phase by picking up on some of the sentences that the learners produce when comparing the two cities, writing these on the board, and analysing, or correcting their use of comparatives. This is quite a difficult skill, so if you prefer, you can give them a specific activity to start this phase. For example, as they have already focused on the meaning in the text, it would now be okay to give them Task 1 above (underline the comparative adjectives) to help them to notice the grammar. You can get them to do it in pairs, which would enable them to help each other and also provide useful feedback to you as you **monitor** their **pairwork** conversations. You can make a note of what problems they have and how much they already know about the grammar (see Figure 2.2).

Figure 2.2

Check the answers during the feedback stage and clarify any problems, but avoid touching on what you are about to explain next.

Now comes the crucial 'teacher-led' part of the analysis. The learners have noticed our **target language** (comparative adjectives) and now need to understand how to form sentences with comparatives, and when to use them (see the **learning outcomes** above). It may seem logical to provide a short 'lecture' here, explaining the grammar rules for forming comparative adjectives, and mentioning that they are often used with a preposition (... _bigger_ _than_...). However, lectures are not a good idea during the Analysis lesson phase. This is because a lecture can be difficult for language learners to understand and doesn't allow the teacher to check understanding. It's a better idea to ask questions and elicit the key information from the learners. This helps us to assess how many learners understand the grammar and also provides a useful opportunity to **scaffold** the learning by leading them through the stage step-by-step.

Table 2.6 below compares what a lecturer might say about the grammar, and what a good English teacher might elicit to make the same point clear. Read the two completed rows, and then try to work out what the English teacher should say for the other two rows. Let's assume that learners have been taught some important words for describing language, such as syllable, preposition, etc.

**Table 2.6:
Effective eliciting**

The lecturer says...	The English teacher elicits...
With one-syllable adjectives, such as *slow*, add the suffix *-er* to the end of the adjective to make the comparative: *slower*.	T: Look at this adjective. [points at 'slow'] How many syllables does it have? Ss: One. T: One, yes. Good. What do we add to it to make the comparative form? Ss: '-er' T: Exactly. Well done!
With longer adjectives of two syllables or more, we form the comparative by adding the word *more* before the adjective.	T: Look…
After a comparative adjective, we use the preposition *than* to link it to the object of comparison.	T: Okay. Look at this comparative sentence. [shows a comparative sentence from the text] What word comes after the comparative adjective? Ss: 'than' T: Correct. What type of word is 'than'? Ss: It's a preposition. T: Well done!
Comparative adjectives are used to highlight a difference between two things, such as places, people or objects.	T:

Check your answers in the **Pause for thought Key** *[9]*

In the above exercise, it seems very easy to get the learners to say what you want, but of course, in reality it's a bit more challenging! Don't forget that if your attempts to elicit something fail, it's okay to tell them, but speak slowly and clearly and show an example. Then check they've understood by asking simple questions. Such questions that check understanding of the meaning of important lexis or structures are called **concept check questions**, or **CCQs** for short.

So far, so good. We've checked the meaning and the form of the language. With areas of grammar which involve difficult or unpredictable pronunciation, we should also check pronunciation. The easiest way to do this is to drill it, perhaps using example sentences on the board. Drilling usually involves several stages and is discussed in more detail below (see *Teaching Pronunciation*). Here's a common two stage drill appropriate for our comparative lesson:

1   Model the pronunciation and get all the learners to repeat in chorus (**choral drill**).

2   Choose a few individual learners to say the sentence while the rest listen (**individual drill**).

Let's remind ourselves of the intended learning outcomes for this lesson. Hopefully the learners will have made reasonable progress towards the first three:

> - I can identify comparative adjectives in a text.
> - I understand how to form sentences with comparative adjectives.
> - I know when to use comparative adjectives.
> - I can talk about places I know using comparative adjectives.

In order to progress towards the fourth learning outcome, they will need to practise using the language themselves. As you might expect, this happens in the Practice lesson phase below, but before we do this, let's quickly look at a range of other techniques that we can use to help learners to analyse language. Exactly how you put these techniques together will depend on what you're teaching, the level of the learners, the type of class and the sociocultural context.

Other suggestions for analysing grammar:

- **Discovery learning worksheet:** Rather than asking elicitation questions, especially if you think this is quite challenging, you could create a worksheet with the questions on it and hand it out for the learners to do in pairs or small groups.
- **Word order flashcards:** A fun way to check the learners understand the form of a structure where word order is important is to give out example sentences that have been cut up for learners to rearrange. This is effective with complex syntax like conditional structures or passive voice.
- **L1 use:** If you share the L1 of your learners, there are several ways it can be used during language analysis (Cook, 2010). For example, you could elicit a translation for a target language sentence or provide a short explanation of the meaning of the grammar in the learners' language. However, bear in mind that the CertTESOL expects you also to show the skills required of a teacher working with **multilingual** classes (learners who have different L1s) so it's important not to rely on translation all the time during the course. Show that you can also clarify meaning in other ways.
- **Matching activities:** These can be quite useful for eliciting or checking understanding. For example, if you are teaching several different meanings of the present perfect tense, learners can match example sentences to the meanings.

Practising grammar

Practice is necessary in almost all types of learning. If you are learning to use a new computer program or a new card game, a little practice should be enough. If you are learning to play a musical instrument, touch type on a computer or use new grammar in a foreign language, much more practice is required. It is this practice that helps us to 'proceduralise' our explicit knowledge of the grammar so that we can use it instinctively as implicit knowledge. Thus, in order for a grammar lesson to be useful, extensive practice is essential, unless you're only teaching the grammar for passive recognition. With regard to our Comparatives lesson, we want the learners to be able to use the grammar by the end of it, so it would probably be a good idea to devote a substantial portion of the lesson to practice. Skill learning theory indicates that two stages to practice are necessary (Fitts, 1966; Anderson, 1983). In language teaching these stages are often referred to as **controlled practice** and **freer practice** (or production), as shown in the example lesson plan in Unit 1.

- **The controlled practice stage** is an opportunity for learners to check and consolidate their understanding of what has been taught. It may involve either spoken activities such as drills, or written activities such as gap-fills or sentence completion exercises. It's also an important opportunity for the teacher to check understanding and to correct any 'conceptual mistakes' before moving on.

- **The freer practice stage** is an opportunity for learners to use the new language in a situation similar to how they would use it outside the classroom. This could also include written or spoken language, such as writing an email to a friend, or performing a role-play in pairs.

Trainee teachers on the CertTESOL sometimes find it difficult to work out whether an activity is controlled or freer practice. A very simple rule of thumb is that if the activity has right and wrong answers (such as a grammar exercise), it's controlled practice, and if it doesn't (such as a role-play or discussion), it's probably freer practice.

Controlled practice of grammar

Let's return to our comparatives lesson. Given that much of the Analysis lesson phase involved studying the formation of comparative adjectives, it makes sense to provide learners with some controlled practice of this, for example using a gap-fill activity:

1 The film was _____ than I expected. (interesting)

2 Hamid is three years _____ than his sister. (young)

3 I am much _____ in my new job. (happy)

You can do this as an activity cycle, but remember that the learners will probably want an opportunity to check their own understanding of the new grammar, so rather than starting them off in pairs, they can try to do it individually and then check in pairs. This allows for a period of silent concentration during the individual work, when you can monitor and provide individual help to anyone who is struggling, and also allows for some useful peer-teaching during the pairwork. During feedback you can ask individual learners to read out different sentences, thereby further checking pronunciation. By the end of feedback, you should have a good understanding of whether they have understood the grammar in question, and they should be ready for some freer practice.

Other suggestions for controlled practice of grammar

- **Error correction activities:** For example, showing the learners written sentences that each include a common grammar mistake that they must find and correct.

- **Sentence transformation activities:** For example, when learners transform a positive to negative statement or an active to passive sentence.

- **Spoken transformation drills:** You provide a prompt and learners respond using the target language, either chorally or individually.

- **Controlled writing activities:** For example, when learners write short answers to questions that prompt them to use the grammar, or when they complete unfinished sentences.

- **Matching activities:** For example, where learners select phrases from different columns in a table to make a number of logical sentences.

- **Sentence jumbles:** Learners must put words in the right order to make logical sentences.

Look at the controlled practice activities below. Match each activity to one of the suggestions above.

Activity 1
Put the words in the correct order to make a true comparative sentence:
than bicycle better a for Riding the is car environment a driving

Activity 2
Rewrite the following sentences using 'not as (adjective) as':
Example: Gold is more expensive than silver. *Silver isn't as expensive as gold...*
1 Cairo is hotter than London.
2 Football is more popular than cricket.
3 Organic food is better for you than fast food.
etc.

Activity 3
Correct the mistake in each of the following sentences:
1 That exam was much difficulter than I expected!
2 He is taller of his brother.
3 Malaria is a more big killer than AIDS.
etc.

Activity 4
Draw lines to link phrases in the three columns to make logical sentences.
One example has been provided:

1	2	3
My father is	faster	than summer.
Winter is	older	than the main road.
The motorway is	colder	than my mother.
etc.		

Activity 5
Complete the following sentences about public transport:
1 Travelling by train is slower...
2 Cycling is better...
3 Taxis are more...
4 Riding a motorbike isn't as safe...
etc.

Activity 6
Note: Students have a handout with
1 Paris – London.
2 London – Tokyo.
etc.

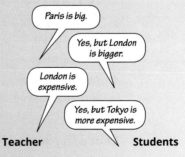

Teacher   **Students**

Check your answers in the **Pause for thought Key** *[10]*

Freer practice of grammar

Whenever possible, freer practice activities should aim to get the learners using the new language as 'naturally' as possible. By this, I mean that you should try to create a situation inside the classroom that replicates how they would use the language outside the classroom. One of the simplest yet most effective ways to do this is to refer back to the Context phase of the lesson, and to get the learners using the language in a similar context. This has the added advantage that they will already be familiar with some of the necessary vocabulary and **schemata**, and will be able to focus their attention on expressing their own ideas and using the new language. For our comparatives lesson, this would involve the learners comparing two cities that they are familiar with. If you are teaching a class of learners from different countries, they will find it interesting to learn about each other's countries. If you're teaching a class of learners from the same country, you could adapt the activity slightly and get them to compare the city where they are now with another city they know well.

This activity should take the form of a more extensive activity cycle. At pre-intermediate level they will find it useful and achieve more success if they have time to prepare by taking notes. Once more, you can monitor at this stage and provide individual help. Then, when they are ready, put them into pairs or small groups to tell each other about the two cities they have chosen to compare. Don't expect them to use the grammar perfectly at this stage. They will make mistakes, even if you've taught it faultlessly. Indeed, these mistakes are both evidence of learning and opportunities for you to demonstrate your ability to '*deal with errors in an appropriate manner*' as specified in Unit 1 of the CertTESOL Syllabus. This might include correcting their mistakes directly as they speak, providing appropriate recasts of what they wanted to say, or taking notes on the errors and providing feedback afterwards. **Peer-correction** (where learners correct each other) is also possible at this stage, and can be encouraged if culturally appropriate. Specific strategies for error correction are covered later in this chapter under *Productive skills (Speaking).*

Other suggestions for freer practice of grammar

- **Role-plays:** Learners role-play a specific situation that requires them to use the grammar. For example, an interview between a journalist and politician before an election, in which the politician makes promises to practise future verb forms.

- **Information gap activities:** Learners work in pairs to exchange information, usually to complete a specific task. For example, the *spot the difference* activity on page 40 in Unit 1.

- **Discussions and debates:** Learners discuss questions or a topic that provides a natural context for using the grammar. For example, a debate on the possible impact of climate change is a good way for learners to practise using future conditional forms.

- **Creative writing:** Learners are encouraged to write stories (in the past), newspaper articles (in the present) and imaginary worlds (in the future) encouraging them to use the grammar.

- **Mingle questions:** Each learner in the class gets a different question that is likely to elicit the target grammar. They stand, mingle and ask each other their questions. Tell them to listen out for the most interesting or the most unusual answer.

Concluding grammar lessons

Just as it is important to make intentions clear at, or near the beginning of lessons involving the teaching of explicit knowledge, it's equally important to return to these intentions at the end of the lesson. This could involve recapping on what has been learnt, eliciting this from the learners, checking what they've learnt using CCQs, or getting learners to self-evaluate progress. This last option would be appropriate for our example comparatives lesson. They can return to the outcome statements which they evaluated at the beginning of the lesson and add a second mark to assess personal progress:

Before	After	
2	3	I can identify comparative adjectives in a text.
1	2	I understand how to form sentences with comparative adjectives.
1	3	I know when to use comparative adjectives.
0	2	I can talk about places I know using comparative adjectives.

This concludes our discussion of grammar. We've looked at the grammar itself, and identified some common areas that are taught in English language lessons. We've also looked at how we can teach grammar, focusing on contextualising it, analysing it and practising it. There are, of course, many more ideas for teaching grammar, which you can find in resource books, coursebooks or online. Alternatively, if you want to challenge yourself, start from your aims and see if you can build the lesson structure, develop the activities and create your own materials from scratch.

2.3   Lexis

The relationship between grammar and lexis is often perceived as one in which grammar provides the underlying structure upon which items of lexis (vocabulary) are 'hung', rather like clothes being hung on a washing line. However, as we have seen above, all aspects of lexis have grammar, including nouns, adjectives and obviously verbs, indicating that they are important to structure as well as meaning in language use. This led an influential writer on lexis in language teaching, Michael Lewis, to note that: '*language consists of grammaticalized lexis, not lexicalized grammar*' (1993, p. 34). Thus, while it is grammar that tends to dominate SLA research, language learning coursebooks and many English lessons, it may be that lexis has a more fundamental role in language itself. We might think of language more as chunks of lexis of varying size, length and shape that hold together by virtue of their internal grammar, a bit like jigsaw pieces in a puzzle. Some of these chunks are obvious single-word pieces, such as *dog*, *run* and *heavy*, and others seem to be longer pieces that involve more than one word, such as *run out of*, *heavy defeat*, *in the doghouse* and even whole sentences. Try finishing this one:

You can't make an omelette without...

In this section we will look at some of these important features of lexis, especially those most often taught in English lessons and assessed in the Language Awareness test/assignment on the CertTESOL, then we will look at how lexis is often taught in ELT. As with grammar, this initial introduction to lexis is not intended to be comprehensive, and should be supplemented with more specialist reference books whenever you are teaching a specific area of lexis. The series *A Way with Words* (Redman & Ellis, 1990-2014) has some good practical ideas for teaching and recycling lexis.

Lexical words and grammatical words

An important initial distinction that we can make is to note that some words carry the majority of the meaning in a text, including nouns, verbs, adjectives and adverbs. These words are sometimes called lexical words (or content words) Others seem to perform a more grammatical role, often called grammatical words (or function words), and include all other word classes, such as determiner, conjunction, preposition, etc. Try taking all the grammatical words out of a text and you can still identify the topic, and possibly even the points being made. Take all the lexical words out of the text, and you won't have a clue what it's about. The number of grammatical words in English is fairly limited at around 300 or so, although they include some of the most commonly used words. The remaining 600,000+ word forms in the Oxford English Dictionary are lexical words – the 'Everest of language' that we read about earlier. Interestingly, while all proficient speakers of English know almost all the grammatical words, many know less than 10% of the lexical words in the OED. The implication of this is that we need to be very careful about deciding which items of vocabulary are useful for our learners to learn now, and which are not.

Word formation

Words are made up of smaller bits. We can call the smaller bits morphemes, and met these briefly in *Morphology and syntax* above when we looked at grammatical morphemes. A morpheme is simply the smallest bit of a language that has meaning. Here are examples of two common words, each with three morphemes:

> *refundable   unhappiness*

Pause for thought

- *Can you work out what the three separate morphemes are?*
- *Identify the meaning or function of each morpheme.*
- *Which of the morphemes are complete words on their own, and which depend on other morphemes to exist and make sense?*

Check your answers below.

refundable		
re	fund	able
prefix	*root / stem*	*suffix*

unhappiness		
un	happɏi	ness
prefix	*root / stem*	*suffix*

Notice that the root of both words can exist on its own – these are called **free morphemes**. *Fund* is a verb or noun, and *happy* is an adjective. The **prefixes** and **suffixes** cannot exist on their own, so they are called **bound morphemes** (although -*able* is also an adjective). Now notice that the function of the prefixes and the suffixes in the above examples is slightly different. While prefixes most often change the meaning (e.g. *un-* always makes a word negative), suffixes more commonly change the word class (e.g. adding -*ness* to an adjective always turns it into a noun). These rules are useful for learners to know, so that they can guess the meaning and word class of unfamiliar new words. Let's now look at how words often come together to make larger 'chunks' of language.

Collocations

Words seem to have preferences regarding the company they keep. For example, the word *unrequited* very often precedes the word *love*. We can call these two words together a strong **collocation**. Here is another example. Which is the strongest collocation, and which would be unusual in English?

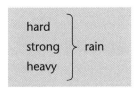

While the expression *strong rain* is easy to understand (and is used in other languages, such as Russian), it's not common in English. We tend to prefer *heavy rain* (a strong collocation), or possibly *hard rain* (a weak collocation) and we would never say *thick rain*, unless we were aiming for a specific poetic effect. *Unrequited love* and *heavy rain* are examples of adjective + noun collocations. There are other types of collocation too:

verb + noun collocations	adverb + adjective collocations	verb + adverb collocations
make a mistake tell the time	highly successful fully furnished	wait patiently speak (a language) fluently

Research has indicated that learners who pick up and use common collocations develop greater fluency in all four skills (Yazdandoost et al., 2014), so it's a good idea to teach them.

Idioms

Idioms are unusual or colourful expressions whose meaning is different to the meaning of the individual words combined and cannot be taken literally. For example, if I tell you that my friend 'blew his top', you probably understand that I mean he got very angry, and I don't mean that his head exploded. Learners may have difficulty guessing the meaning of idioms, which are used mainly by native speakers. Here are some other examples of both common and uncommon idioms. Which do you think would be most useful for learners? And which would be most difficult to guess the meaning of?

> *at the end of the day   not my cup of tea   the last straw   kick the bucket*

Idioms are quite difficult for learners to learn, as most are fixed expressions, the parts of which often cannot be altered. For example, you can say '*It's not my teacup.*' or '*My grandfather kicked a bucket last week*', but these tiny changes stop them from being idioms, and we understand the literal meaning of the sentence.

Multi-word verbs

As its name suggests, a **multi-word verb** is a verb that consists of two or more words, such as

- **two-word verbs:** verb + adverb (*go away*) or verb + preposition (*look after*)
- **three-word verbs:** verb + adverb + preposition (*get on with*; *run out of*)

Many people also call them 'phrasal verbs', although properly speaking, the term 'phrasal verb' should only be applied to multi-word verbs that have idiomatic meanings (i.e. like idioms). Let's look at an example multi-word verb that has a number of meanings, some of which are literal and others are more idiomatic:

1 *Should I <u>take off</u> my shoes?* (literal)

2 *The plane <u>took off</u> about half an hour ago.* (partly idiomatic)

3 *Our business really <u>took off</u> when we moved to the new premises.* (idiomatic)

The last example of *take off* is a typical phrasal verb, and students would have difficulty guessing the meaning unless they had a clear context. English has a large number of multi-word verbs, many of which are very common and idiomatic in their meaning, making them quite a challenge for learners.

Pause for thought

Find examples of collocations (both strong and weak), idioms, multi-word verbs and words with several morphemes in the following short text.

> **If I had to provide a description of my uncle Arthur, I'd say he's quite a card, and anybody who meets him generally warms to him very quickly. He has an unforgettable laugh and a great sense of humour. I have heard rumours that once he was pulled over by a policeman for speeding, and he managed to talk his way out of it using his unbelievable charm.**

Check your answers in the **Pause for thought** *Key [11].*

2.4 Teaching lexis

Earlier in this chapter we learnt that language learners probably acquire features of grammar in a specific order, meaning that we need to be sensitive to our learners' needs and current state of development if we are to teach grammar successfully (Ellis, 2008). The good news is that lexis is not subject to the same constraints, and there is evidence that if you teach it well and it is useful to their needs, learners are likely to learn lexis largely as it is taught (Ellis & Shintani, 2014).

Learners learn lexis all the time. Irrespective of whether you're trying to teach grammar or trying to develop their skills, lexis is always involved. Learners are internalising collocations, noticing unfamiliar words, checking them in dictionaries, jotting them down and consolidating what they have learnt. As a catalyst to this natural learning process, there are a number of occasions when communicative teachers intentionally 'teach' lexis in language lessons:

1 A vocabulary lesson, in which the teacher introduces and the learners practise a number of related lexical items.

2 Integrating the teaching of lexis into a receptive skills lesson (reading or listening) or productive skills lesson (writing or speaking). This may include pre-teaching lexis (often part of receptive skills lessons) or providing useful phrases and expressions before learners embark on a specific speaking or writing task (in productive skills lessons).

3 Unplanned vocabulary teaching, for example when learners ask the teacher about the meaning of a word they have seen or heard, or when the teacher is discussing something with the learners and interesting or important vocabulary 'crops up'.

We will look at the second of these later in this chapter when we look at language skills. But firstly, we will look at the structure of a typical vocabulary lesson and then cover unplanned vocabulary teaching afterwards.

Teaching a vocabulary lesson

Vocabulary lessons often involve thematically related lexis (e.g. food and drink, daily routines, money and finances, etc.), which allows us to introduce and practise the lexis within the context of the chosen theme. For example, a lesson on food and drink may include a recipe reading activity, a role-play in a café and a restaurant review for a writing activity. But let's imagine for our example vocabulary lesson that you have a class of upper intermediate (B2) learners who often like to chat about the films they have seen. However, you've noticed quite a few mistakes in the vocabulary they use, so you decide to do a lesson on vocabulary to describe films and film plots. Here's your 'skeleton' plan with three basic stages:

Context	A short film review text, which you adapt to include a wider range of vocabulary appropriate to your learners' needs.
Analysis	Learners match vocabulary items from the text to prepreared definitions, then notice a number of important features of meaning, form and usage.
Practice	Learners complete a written exercise by correcting common learner mistakes when talking or writing about films, and then they write their own reviews on films they have seen recently.

Introducing lessons on lexis

As with grammar lessons, it's a good idea to make your intentions clear to the learners at the start of lessons on lexis. Given that this is a higher level class, it would be appropriate to introduce these orally as follows:

'I've noticed you often like to chat about films together, so in today's lesson we are going to learn about 10-15 new words and expressions for talking about movies. We'll check the meaning and pronunciation, then practise them. This will lead into a film review writing activity which we'll start in class and finish for homework. You can then upload your reviews to the class blog for each other to read. How does that sound?'

Providing context for lexis

Just as with the example grammar lesson described above, written texts are a useful way to contextualise new vocabulary, and a film review is a natural context for film-related lexis, one that's likely to be familiar to the learners. You could provide an effective lead-in to such a reading text by showing the learners the title of the text, getting them to guess what film it is, and finding out who has seen it and what they thought of it. This could then lead into a contextualisation task in which the learners read the text to identify the reviewer's opinion, including what she liked and disliked.

Other suggestions for providing context

- **Use realia:** The term **realia** is used to refer to real objects used for language learning in class. If you're teaching 'concrete' vocabulary (i.e. real things such as clothes or kitchen implements), you could make use of what is already present in the class or bring in the items yourself. This obviously makes the meaning clear, and context can be provided by getting learners to describe each other's appearance (clothes) or by pretending to cook a dish (kitchen implements).

- **Use images:** Photos or illustrations can be very useful for providing context for new lexis. Images of rooms from a home furnishing catalogue can be used to teach furniture, a map of the world can be used to teach nationalities, and an online grocery website to teach fruit and veg.

- **Context from listening:** Listening activities are less often used for contextualising new lexis, as it's often difficult to notice new words in a stream of spoken language. Nonetheless, audio texts can be used to help consolidate new language, or, after listening to a recording, learners can be given a written transcript and their attention can be directed towards the target lexis, much like with a written text.

Analysing lexis

The most obvious way to help learners to understand the meaning of new lexis is to provide definitions. Sometimes it's useful to get the learners to use dictionaries for this purpose, as the practice develops their study skills. Spoken definitions are also possible (either provided by the teacher or elicited from members of the class). In our film lesson, let's imagine you preprepare 12 definitions of lexical items from the text that you think the learners will find useful. These could be presented on a handout without the items themselves, so that learners have to find them in the text. This search and find task, an example of 'noticing', is likely to help them to remember the target lexis once found.

Hopefully, this task will help to make the meaning clear, although it's a good idea to check this using either CCQs (if learners don't share their L1) or by eliciting an appropriate translation (if they do).

Pause for thought

Which of the following CCQs do you think would help you to check learners' understanding of the word 'director' as used in filmmaking? Which would not be useful?

1 Is the director present during filming?

2 Does the director appear in the film?

3 Does the director provide the money?

4 What does the director often say?

5 Who can give me examples of famous directors?

6 Would anybody here like to be a director?

Check your answers in the **Pause for thought Key** *[12].*

As well as checking the meaning of newly introduced vocabulary, it is useful to check aspects of the form (including written form, collocations and pronunciation) and the usage. Table 2.7 shows some examples of this from our film lesson, which the teacher could either explain or elicit by asking questions:

Item	Notable aspects of form and usage	Useful elicitation questions or CCQs
scene	Form: Pronunciation often causes problems. A homophone of *seen*. Model and drill (see Teaching Pronunciation below). Usage: In many languages the word is used to describe location, but in filmmaking it is more commonly used to refer to part of the film (e.g. *in this scene they decide to…*).	How do we pronounce it? Is the writer using it to describe a place or a part of the film?
wooden (performance)	Usage: Somewhat idiomatic, and clearly critical. Often collocates with *performance*.	Do you think it's positive or negative? What word follows it?
movie vs film	Form: Pronunciation of the dark 'l' in *film* can cause problems. Model and drill a few times. Usage: *movie* is more common in American English, and *film* in British English, although *movie* is increasing in the UK to refer to Hollywood-type films.	How do we pronounce this word? Is the 'L' silent? Which is British and which is American?
act vs play (the role of)	Usage: Often confused by learners. *Act* is rarely used except to describe the performance of the actors (*he acts well*), but *play* is more common to link an actor to a role (*She plays the mother*).	What's the difference in meaning? Can you give an example from a famous film?

During this Analysis phase, keep an organised board where all important items are listed clearly (e.g. on one side) and retained through the latter stages of the lesson if appropriate. Record part of speech next to each item (e.g. write (n.) in brackets for noun, (v.) for verb, etc.) and phonemic script for any items which are likely to cause problems with pronunciation.

Other suggestions for analysing lexis

■ **Translation:** A fast way to provide or elicit the meaning of new lexis. In bilingual classes, this is an effective technique (but beware of **false friends** or differences in usage). In multilingual classes, many learners naturally want to check translation to their L1 using smartphone dictionaries. This can also be useful, but it can lead to errors, so if you use this strategy, back it up, for example by asking CCQs.

■ **Focus on collocations:** Ask learners to underline or highlight important collocations in a text, for example, words that collocate with 'movie'. You could also get learners to Google a word to see what it collocates with.

- **Brainstorming:** Brainstorming tasks can be quite effective in covering core items in a lexical set, especially at higher levels. Learners can brainstorm in groups (e.g. words to describe personality), followed by elicitation to the board when meaning and pronunciation can be checked. New items can be added as appropriate. As brainstorming is a fast activity, there are a number of possible team games that can be played (e.g. a 'board relay race' with two or three teams racing to add words to separate columns on the board).

- **Use context:** Encourage learners to guess the meaning of a new item from context. Note that the success of this task depends on the clarity of the context, the ease of the text (learners need to understand the surrounding words or 'co-text') and the idiomaticity of the word (more idiomatic words are generally less guessable).

- **Words inside words:** For words that have several morphemes (e.g. *unimaginable*) or for compound nouns (e.g. *tablecloth, raincoat*), get learners to guess the meaning from prior knowledge of the constituent parts.

Practising lexis

Just like grammar, lexis is often practised in two stages: controlled practice and freer practice. Activity types tend to be similar to those used in grammar lessons, so they are discussed briefly here.

In our example lesson, the controlled practice activity involves providing learners with a written exercise including a number of sentences using the target lexis. The learners must identify and correct any mistakes in the sentences. Such an activity can raise awareness of potential mistakes before they are made, and is likely to encourage **peer correction** of such mistakes if they happen:

1 Leonardo DiCaprio acts the leading role. *

2 The film sets in a fantasy world. *

Other suggestions for controlled practice of lexis

- **Matching activities:** These can include matching images to words, matching two parts of a collocation, or matching synonymous expressions.

- **Odd one out activities:** Get learners also to identify why the odd item is different. For example, *bus, car, road, bicycle* (*road* is the odd one out because it is not a form of transport).

- **Labelling activities:** Learners label a picture or pictures. For example, a cross-sectional illustration of a house in which learners have to label all the items of furniture they see.

- **Translation activities:** For example, translating a number of sentences from L1 to English that require the target lexis (only possible in bilingual classes).

- **Collocation brainstorming:** Learners think of all the words that can collocate with a key noun or verb (e.g. *work*).

- **Categorisation tasks:** Learners sort words into several categories of their own choosing (e.g. food items which learners sort into vegetables, meat, fruit and others).

Freer practice of lexis

As with the grammar lesson above, given that learners met the new lexis in a film review, it makes sense to get them either to write a film review or to tell their classmates about a film they have seen. Let's imagine you opt for the written film review, preceded by a brief pairwork speaking activity in which learners tell their partner about their chosen film. A possible structure or outline can be provided for such a text (see *Writing* in *Productive skills* below), and learners can begin in class, where the teacher can offer guidance and support, and possibly finish their reviews for homework. Classes with access to the Internet may enjoy publishing their film reviews on blogs for classmates to read and comment on.

Other suggestions for freer practice of lexis
These are largely similar to the suggestions provided above for free practice of grammar, including role-plays (e.g. in an airport to practise lexis associated with flying), information gap activities (e.g. a spot the difference activity focusing on clothing), discussions and debates (e.g. a debate on which is the greatest film of all time to finish the above lesson), creative writing (e.g. learners invent a newspaper article to make use of crime vocabulary), personalisation questions (e.g. learners talk about their favourite… anything!) and mingle questions, which can focus on different aspects of the topic area you have chosen.

Pair and **groupwork** projects can also be effective, particularly for lexical sets, with learners researching within an appropriate thematic field. For example, to practise lexis relating to environmental issues, groups could conduct case studies on environmental problems around the world and prepare posters, webpages or presentations.

Concluding lessons on lexis
At the end of a lesson on lexis, given the challenge that learners often face in retaining all the new words that have been introduced, the Conclusion is an invaluable opportunity to review the lexical items learnt. At this stage you can also check they have made a note of all the new lexis and provide a homework task to assist with memorisation. Here are some useful ideas:

- Use items listed on the board to prompt recall. You could provide definitions for which learners have to shout out the lexical item being defined, or challenge learners to provide these definitions. Alternatively, have them use items in personalised example sentences.
- Peer-testing tasks in which learners test their partner on new items learnt.
- Conduct a quick spelling or pronunciation test to revise the form of new items.
- Quick brainstorming tasks similar to those mentioned under *Analysing lexis* above.

Unplanned vocabulary teaching

Good planning can prepare you for much of what happens in an English lesson, but not everything. Some of the most useful teaching that we do happens on the spur of the moment, either in response to a learner question, a learner error or something that crops up organically during discussion. Such events should not be allowed to take over your lesson (at least not during teaching practice), but by showing your ability to respond to the **emergent language** and the needs of the learners, you are showing your ability to teach well. Just as with responsive pronunciation teaching discussed later in this chapter, you can capitalise on such opportunities using an appropriate combination of the following strategies.

When an unplanned item of vocabulary crops up in the lesson you can:

- write it on the board, indicating whether it's a noun (n.), verb (v.), adjective (adj.), etc.
- explain the meaning, remembering to keep your use of English slow, simple loud and clear as we learnt in Unit 1

- model and drill pronunciation (see below)
- provide a quick translation (if you share the learners' L1)
- provide a synonym if one exists
- provide a simple example sentence

Alternatively, rather than doing the hard work yourself, you can often elicit such information from your learners. As well as challenging and involving them, eliciting also gives you time to think if a word is difficult to spell, explain or exemplify. An elicited definition may sometimes be unclear, but you can always add to or modify it. Learners often come up with good example sentences in such instances, showing awareness of the most common contexts or collocations for lexical items.

2.5 Pronunciation

The Trinity CertTESOL syllabus identifies four areas of subject knowledge with regard to phonology (pronunciation). These are:

1 **Phonemes:** the individual sounds that make up words

2 **Words and phrases:** This includes **word stress**, contractions (e.g. *I am = I'm*) and features of connected speech (the changes that happen when we speak quickly).

3 **Sentences and discourse:** This looks at features of pronunciation in longer stretches of speech, including stress patterns in sentences, and intonation.

4 **General:** This focuses on how the features of phonology link to other areas of language and its relevance for your practice as a teacher, including how grammar and pronunciation are linked, understanding how learners' L1s influence their pronunciation in English (called **contrastive analysis**), understanding the challenges learners face when listening to English, and even your awareness of your own pronunciation challenges when you are learning languages.

Just as for grammar, your learning of these areas of subject knowledge is assessed throughout the course. Most obviously, you will be required to teach aspects of pronunciation during teaching practice. It will also be necessary to demonstrate your understanding of these areas through the Learner Profile (Unit 3) when you analyse the features of a specific learner's English and the challenges they face learning it. During the Unknown Language Assignment (Unit 5), there will be an opportunity to reflect on your own challenges with the phonology of a foreign language, and it is also likely to be assessed during your Language Awareness assignment or exam.

As with the *Grammar* and *Lexis* sections above, what follows is intended as an introduction to phonology for the CertTESOL. You will need to develop your knowledge and understanding of pronunciation and how we teach it throughout the course, and you may find it useful to also read an introduction to teaching pronunciation, such as Adrian Underhill's *Sound Foundations* (2005). Let's begin by looking at each of the four areas on the Trinity syllabus in more detail, and then we will look at teaching phonology.

English – an evolving language

As we discuss phonology, it's important to remember that English, as a 'world language' is evolving rapidly. The majority of English speakers are no longer native speakers, and given that they are often using the language to communicate with other non-native speakers, there is no need for them to sound like British, American or Australian speakers. As an influential linguist points out, this appropriation of English is an important part of its development (Widdowson, 1994), and especially with pronunciation, we should not presume that native speaker pronunciation is an appropriate model for all learners. Indeed, some of the easiest accents to understand in the world are non-native speaker accents, and possibly one of the most difficult to understand is the rapid speech of the educated middle class from the south-east of England, sometimes referred to as 'received pronunciation' (RP). The Trinity CertTESOL recognises the importance of diversity in pronunciation, and there is no requirement for course participants to sound like native speakers. Jenkins (2000) provides an alternative model in her Lingua franca pronunciation core for those who are interested to read more about this. The pronunciation model described below (including the **phonemic chart**) is based on a fairly standard southern British accent, which currently tends to be the default model on the majority of CertTESOL courses, but this does not mean that it has to be your accent. Whether you have a Yorkshire accent, a Nigerian accent, a Texan accent or an Indian accent, your variety of English is just as valid as any other.

Phonemes

Phonemes are the smallest units of the spoken language. Just like letters in the written language, we put them together to make words. In many languages, there is a fairly consistent one-to-one relationship between phonemes and letters (e.g. Italian, Swahili, Turkish), but unfortunately this is not true for English. This creates a number of challenges for learners. First and foremost, when they see a new word it is difficult for them to predict how to say it. And even more frustratingly, when they hear a new word, they may not know how to spell it, and so they have difficulty looking such words up in a dictionary.

Let's look at this tricky relationship between sounds and letters using two words that are identical in spelling, but slightly different in pronunciation in most accents. The written word *close* could represent an adjective or a verb. Look at the following two example sentences and decide which is which. Then do the *Pause for thought* task:

a   Could you <u>close</u> that door please?

b   It's <u>close</u> to the school.

Pause for thought

1   Say the two words. What difference in pronunciation do you notice?

2   Which of the letters is not pronounced at all?

3   Try separating out the individual sounds of the two words. How many sounds are there?

Check your answers by looking in a dictionary; most British English learner's dictionaries share the same phonemic script we are going to use (some American dictionaries use different systems). Did you notice that the 's' is pronounced /z/ in one word, and /s/ in the other? Note that the two symbols /əʊ/ make up just one 'double sound', or diphthong, in English. It's also the second sound in 'no'.

The phonemic chart is often found on the walls of English language classes. It shows all the sounds of a standard British accent separated into three groups: monophthongs, diphthongs (together these make up the vowels of English) and consonants. Your accent of English may not have all these sounds. For example, American English does not need the /eə/ and /ɑː/ sounds because 'r's are pronounced more often than in UK RP.

You will probably come across several different versions of this chart: it will normally contain the same sounds, but may vary in its layout. In this version, by Adrian Underhill, the sounds are grouped according to where they are made in the mouth, thus giving teachers and students a lot of information about how and where the sounds are made.

Vowels						
Monophthongs ('single vowels')				Diphthongs ('double vowels')		
iː see	ɪ it	ʊ good	uː you	ɪə near	eɪ name	
e ten	ə letter	ɜː girl	ɔː four	ʊə sure	ɔɪ boy	əʊ go
æ at	ʌ come	ɑː car	ɒ lot	eə where	aɪ five	aʊ how

Consonants							
p pen	b big	t teach	d do	tʃ children	dʒ June	k camera	g get
f find	v very	θ three	ð the	s say	z is	ʃ she	ʒ television
m me	n now	ŋ morning	h have	l look	r red	w why	j yes

Looking at our first example word above, the four sounds in the verb *close* include three consonants and one diphthong: /kləʊz/. As there is only one vowel sound in this word, it has one syllable. A word with two vowel sounds, usually separated by a consonant, will have two syllables. Simple! More about that later.

You may also note that the top two rows of consonants are in pairs of similar sounds (e.g. /p/ and /b/). The main difference between each pair is that the first is **voiceless** (/p/) and the second is **voiced** (/b/), pronounced with a vibration of the vocal chords in the glottis (your Adam's apple). Voiceless consonants are whispered when pronounced in isolation – as if you have lost your voice (e.g. /p/, /t/).

Pause for thought

Let's explore this phonemic chart a little more. Find the answers to the following questions

1 *How many monophthongs are there?*

2 *How many diphthongs?*

3 *How many consonants?*

4 *How many voiceless consonants are there?*

5 *Find five phonemes (other than diphthongs) that may represent more than one letter in English (e.g. ð = 'th').*

Check your answers in the Pause for thought Key *[13].*

We can write words in English using these phonemes. When we do, it is called writing in 'phonemic script', and we usually put forward slash symbols to mark the beginning and end of the transcription (e.g. /mæn/ – 'man'). Let's look at some examples from the chart, all transcribed as if spoken with a fairly standard British accent:

Written word	Phonemic script	Notes
come	/kʌm/	Notice how the first letter is pronounced /k/, and that there is no /c/ symbol on the chart.
girl	/gɜːl/	Notice how the letter 'r' is pronounced as part of the vowel in British English. The : symbol means the vowel is a long sound.
pen	/pen/	Notice how some words are pronounced just like the written word. These words can be called 'phonetic' or 'phonic' words.
television	/telɪˈvɪʒn/	Notice the differences between the written vowels and the vowels we pronounce. The second 'e' letter is actually pronounced /ɪ/ or /ə/ and the last vowel sound, is very weak, and pronounced as part of the final /n/.

Pause for thought

Let's try 'reading' and 'writing' in phonemic script. Using the phonemic chart to work out the pronunciation of each of the phonemes, write the words in the first column in normal handwriting. Then try writing the words in the second column in phonemic script. Two examples have been provided. Check your answers using a dictionary.

Reading practice

/liːv/   *leave* ....

/ˈdɒktə/ ....

/ˈmʌðə/ ....

/ˈheləʊ/ ....

/kraɪm/ ....

/bəˈnɑːnə/ ....

Writing practice

bad   .... */bæd/* ....

house ....

know ....

think ....

cheese ....

understand ....

On the CertTESOL your tutors will expect you to use phonemic script. This will include using it in assignments to describe features of a learner's English (Unit 3), or features of the unknown language (Unit 5). It is also useful for many learners if you use phonemic script when teaching. For example, if you are teaching a new word with tricky pronunciation, you can write the phonemic script next to the spelling on the board. If you're teaching a multilingual class, you'll often find that certain nationalities (e.g. Japanese, Korean, Thai) like to record words using the phonemic script.

Words and phrases

We've already begun exploring the pronunciation of words by reading and writing them in phonemic script. Let's now look at syllables and word stress. The last two words from the previous *Pause for thought* task both have more than one syllable. As mentioned above, this is because they have more than one vowel sound. You can find out how many they have, either by counting the number of vowels written in phonemic script or by saying the words slowly. Alternatively, try clapping the syllables or humming the word with your mouth closed:

/bəˈnɑːnə/   banana   /ʌndəˈstænd/   understand

You will have noticed that they have the same number of syllables: three, and that they both have an apostrophe. This symbol indicates that the subsequent syllable is stressed. But what exactly do we mean when we talk about 'stress'?

Stress means different things for different languages. Japanese has almost no word stress, and in Italian, intonation is the main indicator of word stress, which gives it its musical quality. In English, there are four important factors in word stress (Roach, 1991):

1 loudness – the stressed syllable may be louder

2 length – the stressed syllable may be longer

3 pitch – the stressed syllable may be either higher or lower

4 vowel quality – one sound never occurs in stressed syllables: /ə/

The balance of these factors may vary between individual speakers, which contributes to our distinctive tones of voice and accents.

The stress pattern of words features quite regularly in ELT coursebooks, where it's often represented using small and large circles over the syllables. The following *Pause for thought* task provides a typical example of this, a categorisation activity.

Pause for thought

Write the words in the correct column according to their stress pattern. Then check your answers in the **Pause for thought Key [14]**. *One example is provided:*

jeans   unique   monkey   trousers   photograph
calculate   ~~detective~~   abroad   computer

●	●•	•●	•●•	●••
....	....	....	*detective*	....
....	....	....	....	....
....	....	....	....	....

Let's now look at some other features categorised under '*Words and phrases*' in the CertTESOL syllabus:

Weak forms

In many accents of English, because certain syllables are stressed quite strongly, the vowels in other syllables often change their quality, especially those right next to the stressed syllable. They become 'weak' syllables, or **weak forms**. *Banana* is a good example of this. Despite the fact that the three vowel letters are the same, because the second syllable is stressed, the first and the last syllables become weak forms, involving the /ə/ sound, which is the most common sound in a standard British accent, and has its own name: schwa. How do you say *banana* in your accent?

We can see the changes that word stress exerts on other syllables by comparing the words in the following word family. The stressed syllable is in bold, but notice how the pronunciation of the underlined vowels changes when they are not stressed:

*ph**o**t<u>o</u>graph   ph<u>o</u>t**o**gr<u>a</u>ph<u>e</u>r   ph<u>o</u>t<u>o</u>**gra**phic*

Contractions

In many English accents (but not all) when we speak quickly, it influences the 'shape' of words. Some of these changes have become standardised. For example, a number of auxiliary verbs lose initial vowels or consonants, and these are represented in the contractions we use when writing informally, or reporting spoken English:

I'<u>ve</u> got a new job.   She'<u>s</u> really friendly.   We'<u>re</u> off tomorrow.   I'<u>d</u> love to.

Notice how other contractions are less standardised, but still used when attempting to represent spoken English:

I'd've called, but I couldn't 'cause I was out wi' my friends.

Cryin' and singin' the blues. (Song title)

Features of connected speech

There are a number of other changes that tend to occur especially when we speak quickly in many English accents. Let's look at a few of them now:

- **Assimilation:** When a sound (usually at the end) of one word influences the pronunciation of a sound (usually at the start) of another word. For example, we might say: '*in the*' like this: /ɪnnə/.

- **Elision:** When a sound disappears. For example, we might say '*waste of money*' like this: /ˈweɪstəˈmʌniː/

- **Linking and liaison:** When we add a sound, or pronounce a sound that's normally silent to make it easier to link words together. For example, we might say: '*who owns*' /huːwəʊnz/ (intrusive /w/), or we might say: '*here are*' /hɪərəː/ (linking /r/; note that the 'r' is not pronounced when an RP speaker says 'here' in isolation).

- **Catenation:** When two words are pronounced as one, usually because the consonant at the end of the first word is pronounced in the same syllable as a following vowel. A good example of this is '*an apple*'. The way it's pronounced occasionally causes young children to think that '*napple*' is the name of the fruit!

All of these features caused by the fast pronunciation of native speakers (sometimes called

'rapid colloquial speech') can create significant problems for learners. Interestingly, they also make a number of jokes possible in spoken English. One that you may find interesting (but probably not funny) combines a number of these features:

Why are there no aspirins in the jungle? Because the paracetamol.

If you don't get it the first time, say it more quickly!

Sentences and discourse

This includes two areas of pronunciation: **sentence stress** and intonation.

Sentence stress (also called 'prominence') refers to how speakers accentuate a specific word or words in a sentence to convey a particular meaning (Underhill, 2005). For example, the following sentence can be said in several different ways, depending on what the listener did wrong. The word in bold has extra prominence:

*No! **You** should've told Anna.*   (It was your responsibility to tell her, not mine!)

*No! You should've told **Anna.***   (But you told Gary!)

*No! You should've **told** Anna.*   (But you sent her an email instead!)

Intonation is the music of our voice. It's an important feature in our identity, as expressed through our accents, and it also conveys important information about what we're saying and how we feel about it. This information can be attitudinal (for example, when we use intonation to say something angrily or ironically), accentual (closely related to sentence stress) or grammatical. A simple example of the grammatical function of intonation is the fact that in many languages, including English, we can turn a statement into a question just by changing our intonation:

It's too expensive.   *It's too expensive?*

In English, it has been noted that different question types often have different intonation patterns. Imagine someone saying the following two similar questions; what difference in intonation can you hear?

1 *Did you tell her?*   **2** *When did you tell her?*

Exactly how intonation is used to convey meaning is the subject of much discussion among scientists, and plenty of disagreement. For example, older guides to English pronunciation suggest that the intonation on *tell* (the stressed syllable) is more likely to rise in question 1 above (a *yes/no* question) and fall in question 2 (a *Wh-* question), but more recent analyses of real data have not really supported this. It's an area of language study where, rather than attempting to explain to learners how we use it, it's probably more useful to teach it intuitively, providing appropriate models when we drill sentences, getting learners to notice and repeat intonation patterns, and using rhyme, rhythm and song to raise learners' awareness and develop a 'feel' for the intonation of English.

Pause for thought

You can explore the important features of sentence pronunciation and discourse by playing a game. Try saying the following sentence in different ways to convey the different meanings below. You can play in pairs and try to guess which meaning you are conveying:

It's 9 o'clock.

1   Time for bed!

2   Time flies!

3   I'm late for my meeting!

4   Think I'll go to bed.

5   There's a film I want to watch starting now.

6   It can't be that late!

'General' features of pronunciation

This area of the Trinity phonology syllabus focuses on how the specific features of the pronunciation system of English (individual sounds, word pronunciation and pronunciation of sentences) link to other aspects of the system (such as grammar or vocabulary), and also how your knowledge and understanding of the pronunciation system can usefully inform your practice as a teacher. Much of this is covered in the next section: *Teaching Pronunciation* and also in other units, but let's focus briefly on some important features of note.

Firstly, a number of areas of grammar often studied in English lessons have specific pronunciation features. The intonation of questions has already been mentioned above, but we can also note other links, such as the fact that negative words in sentences are nearly always stressed, or that there are three different ways to pronounce the regular past tense morpheme *-ed*, and the present simple morpheme *-s* (compare: *tried, kicked* and *visited*).

Equally, aspects of lexis also have specific pronunciation features. For example, many two-syllable verbs become nouns if we change the stress (compare: *I ob**ject** to that.* and *That defeats the **object**.*), and the fact that important content words in a sentence, such as verbs, nouns and adjectives are much more likely to be stressed than the grammar words linking them together. Indeed, this observation shows how all three areas of the system, grammar, vocabulary and pronunciation link closely together to create the system we teach as language teachers.

Also included in this part of the syllabus is your ability to understand the challenges caused by pronunciation that learners face when learning English, both when producing it and listening to it. I remember the case of one diligent student who, despite having studied English for several years, still was not able to make herself understood when trying to order a 'latte' in a coffee shop on the way to school every morning. In her language, as in many languages around the world, there is no difference between the /l/ and /r/ sounds, sometimes bringing her to tears in her frustration to produce it. We have probably all experienced similar difficulties when trying to communicate in a foreign language. We will look in much more detail at these other areas of the Trinity phonology syllabus in Units 3 and 4 when we focus on understanding learners and experiencing learning respectively.

2.6 Teaching pronunciation

In most classrooms around the world where English is taught as a foreign language, pronunciation lessons tend to be less common than grammar lessons or vocabulary lessons. While it is possible that teachers could devote a whole lesson solely to an important area of the pronunciation system (e.g. an introduction to the phonemic chart), pronunciation is more commonly integrated into other types of lessons focusing on systems or skills, particularly listening and speaking. Here are three examples of lessons that do this:

1	Listening and pronunciation	The pronunciation teaching is integrated into a lesson on listening skills. Learners listen to a monologue or a dialogue, and then focus on features of pronunciation of the speakers. Such a lesson is likely to develop pronunciation as a receptive skill: understanding speakers of English.
2	Grammar and pronunciation	The lesson focus is an area of grammar where pronunciation is important. For example, the modal verb *can*, which often causes learners significant difficulty when trying to differentiate the positive and negative forms. Such a lesson is likely to focus on both receptive pronunciation (understanding speakers) and productive pronunciation (making themselves understood).
3	Speaking and pronunciation	The lesson focus is to develop the learners' speaking skills and confidence. The lesson may focus on a specific function (e.g. agreeing and disagreeing), or on a discussion or role-play activity. Depending on the lesson type, the teacher may include extensive drilling of useful expressions before the speaking activity and/or correction of pronunciation errors during and after the activity.

Pronunciation can also find its way into lessons in smaller doses in any of the following situations:

1 The teacher drills the pronunciation of example sentences or expressions during Analysis lesson phases.

2 The coursebook the class is using includes a pronunciation activity, and the teacher decides either to do this in class or to set it for homework (more about pronunciation activities below).

3 The teacher notices a shared problem with pronunciation during a speaking activity (e.g. learners have difficulty differentiating *fourteen* from *forty*) and provides clarification afterwards.

4 A student has difficulty making him/herself understood. The teacher recognises a pronunciation error and provides clarification, or simply correction.

5 A student has difficulty understanding the teacher. Through negotiation, the teacher realises there is a receptive pronunciation problem and provides clarification.

6 A student sees a word somewhere (e.g. in a book), shows it to the teacher and asks how to pronounce it. The teacher provides clarification.

Pause for thought

How many of these 'small doses' of pronunciation could have been planned by the teacher? What implications does this have for trainee teachers on the CertTESOL?

Responsive pronunciation teaching – modelling and drilling

Much of the most useful pronunciation teaching tends to be reactive, rather than proactive. In other words, a pronunciation challenge crops up in the lesson, and we respond to it. This includes situations 3-6 above. Trainee teachers quite reasonably express concern at the idea that they cannot plan for such events. However, the good news is that it is not too difficult to provide this responsive pronunciation help. Let's imagine a learner, or several learners are having difficulty with one of these three pronunciation challenges, all of which are common among learners with different L1s:

A   pronouncing the two words *won't* and *want* identically

B   adding an extra syllable onto past simple verb forms, so that /lɪvd/ is pronounced /lɪvɪd/

C   pronouncing *photograph* with the stress on the last syllable

Here are five things you could do in such situations, although the order chosen may vary. Some teachers prefer to write it first and others to drill the pronunciation first, and write it later:

1	**Write it**	Write the word (or words) on the board, either in isolation or in an example sentence. Highlight the word or syllable that's causing problems by writing it in a different colour or underlining it.
2	**Elicit it**	Ask the class how to pronounce it. This helps them to notice the pronunciation problem. Try to elicit an intelligible model and provide praise.
3	**Model it**	Model the item yourself. In many cases it's a good idea to break the word down into bits. For example, with challenge B above, you could first say /vd/, because it is this cluster of consonants that often causes problems, then add the vowel /ɪvd/, then say the whole word. With challenge C, you could start with the stressed syllable 'pho', and build it up this way. Then say the word in the sentence context. Encourage learners just to listen at this stage, and remember to make sure everyone is looking at, and can easily see, your mouth.
4	**Drill it**	Now repeat 3 again and this time get the whole class to repeat after you (choral drilling). Keep your eyes on who is and isn't participating, and sensitively encourage all to try.
5	**Check it**	Select individual students to say the word (individual drilling). Begin either with confident students or those who were pronouncing it well during the choral response.

Of course, you probably don't need to do this every time you notice a pronunciation problem. Sometimes just modelling it and drilling it chorally two or three times will be fine, and can take as little as 10 seconds. Here are some other things you could do that are particularly useful for more challenging problems:

■   Write the phonemic transcription on the board.

■   Draw learners' attention to key features of the item such as a silent letter, an unusual spelling or a difficult consonant cluster.

- Think of other words which may share the same challenge (rhymes are easy to think of quickly), and model and drill these. For example, in A above, *don't* rhymes with *won't*, and *font* rhymes with *want*.

- Draw learners' attention to the shape of your lips, the position of your tongue and other physical aspects involved in pronouncing a sound, syllable or word.

- Compare the challenging item with the learners' language (only possible in classes that share L1), possibly showing the closest equivalent or explaining in the L1 how to pronounce it.

- Get them to practise the pronunciation in pairs for a minute or two. Monitor and provide assistance.

Practising pronunciation

Pronunciation practice activities may focus either on 'segmental' areas (dealing with the separate segments of pronunciation such as sounds, syllables or words), or 'suprasegmental' areas (phrases, sentences and texts). Here are some activities that are often found in English lessons and textbooks:

Sounds, syllables and words

Categorising words: Provide a list of words for learners to categorise according to some aspect of their pronunciation. The word stress activity above is an example of this. Other common examples include categorising words according to vowel sound or number of syllables.

Minimal pairs: A minimal pair is two words that only have a single difference in their pronunciation. For example, *light* and *write*. Only the first sound in these two words (/l/ and /r/) is different. Minimal pairs can be chosen in sets to focus on specific contrasts that cause problems for our learners. The following set would be useful for learners who have difficulty making the /l/-/r/ distinction:

light / right   law / raw   alive / arrive   fly / fry

Rhyming words: Learners think of words that rhyme with an example word, or categorise a set of given words into rhyming sets. Note that words which rhyme in English don't always look the same (e.g. *bird, word, heard, slurred*).

Odd one out: Learners identify one word in a row that is different in pronunciation to the others. For example, which of the following words starts with a different sound?

sugar   chef   sure   sheep   sun   chute

Phrases, sentences and texts

Dictation activities: Dictation doesn't sound like much fun, but it's very useful for practising receptive pronunciation. You can dictate individual words, short phrases or sentences. Learners listen, write down, compare in pairs and then feedback. Alternatively, you can play a short recording several times and get learners to build up the text gradually. You can also get learners to dictate sentences to each other. There is even

Figure 2.3:
Running dictation

a famous dictation game called 'running dictation' generally loved by teachers and learners alike: Learners work in pairs, with one member of the pair running to a short text posted on a distant wall, remembering a phrase, running back and dictating it to their partner who writes it down, then going back for another phrase. The team that finishes first wins the game (see Figure 2.3).

Reading aloud: While silent reading is the default way to help learners develop reading fluency and comprehension skills, when appropriate, reading aloud can be a useful pronunciation practice activity, helping them to focus on word and sentence stress without also having to think of meaning and grammar. Be aware, however, that some students may find it stressful to read aloud in front of classmates and will prefer to do it in groups. Learners can read out extracts from appropriate texts, such as plays, speeches or news stories (they can pretend to be newsreaders). Poems are enjoyable opportunities for learners to practise adding expression to text, and also include features of rhythm, rhyme and metre. Poems for children are often useful with lower level language learners, such as the following one. Notice how it focuses on one vowel sound. Which one?

> *There is no need to light a night-light*
> *On a light night like tonight;*
> *For a night-light's light's a slight light*
> *When the moonlight's white and bright*
>
> Anonymous

Rhymes, chants and songs: Rhymes and songs have several advantages for practising pronunciation. Their repetitive nature helps learners to practise structures without losing interest. They help learners with the rhythm of English (limericks are good for this), and can focus on specific challenges without making learners self-conscious (e.g. tongue twisters). Hopefully, if you choose enjoyable songs and fun rhymes, learners can have a great time both listening and chanting or singing along. 'Jazz chants', developed by Carolyn Graham specifically for language learners (see Graham, 2000), also provide similar practice of the rhythm of English. Here is a fun limerick that learners enjoy practising:

> *A wonderful bird is the pelican.*
> *His beak can hold more than his belly can.*
> *He can hold in his beak*
> *Enough food for a week!*
> *But I'm damned if I know how the hell he can!*

Role-play and drama presentations: Mentioned both above (see *Practising grammar*) and below (see *Speaking*), role-plays can also provide useful opportunities to practise pronunciation if learners are encouraged to prepare for and then perform role-plays for their classmates. They provide an opportunity for learners to focus on discourse elements of pronunciation, such as sentence stress and intonation. Some classes will even enjoy preparing mini-drama activities for other classes.

Pause for thought

Imagine you have noticed the following pronunciation challenges. What would you do, and when would you do it? Would you provide help immediately, a little later in the lesson, or prepare something for a future lesson?

1 *You have heard several of your intermediate (B1) learners recently saying* 'work' *so that it sounds identical to* 'walk'.

2 *Your advanced (C1) learners have complained that they often have difficulty understanding a specific accent in English.*

3 *Several of the students in your upper intermediate (B2) class speak fluently but with flat intonation, making them sound cold and disinterested.*

Compare your ideas with those in the Pause *for thought Key [15]*

Introduction to the four skills

In order to improve our proficiency in a foreign language, we need to practise using it, either through speaking, listening, reading or writing. Two of these skills are natural to all humans: speaking and listening. Every child learns them instinctually. The other two are artificial, part of a system created by our ancestors to represent the spoken language in permanent form: reading and writing. If we do not learn them formally, we do not acquire them. As such, it may seem logical for us to look at reading and

writing skills together, and indeed this is useful if we are teaching English to very young learners or students who have low levels of literacy in their L1 or the Latin alphabet. However, as nearly everybody in the world learns some English in primary or secondary school nowadays, the majority of English language learners that CertTESOL graduates teach are likely to already have a basic level of literacy in English as a foreign language. Given that on the CertTESOL we are focusing on how to *teach* these skills, we shall group the two receptive skills together for our analysis below, as lessons based on these two skills tend to have a similar structure. These are investigated first. We will then look at the two productive skills (speaking and writing), as there are also similarities in how they are typically taught. The Trinity syllabus requires trainees to demonstrate the following learning outcomes with regard to the four language skills:

1 an understanding of a variety of relevant **sub-skills** that make up each of the four skills

2 the ability to apply this understanding within a communicative teaching approach

3 the ability to reflect on and evaluate your successes

2.7 Receptive skills (reading and listening)

Regular practice of reading and listening skills is essential to foreign language learning for two main reasons. Firstly, it provides us with 'input': data from which we can learn new words, grammar and phrases in a foreign language. Secondly, such practice helps to improve our receptive fluency: our ability to understand different types and speeds of speech when listening, and our ability to decipher and interpret written texts appropriately when reading.

Thus, it stands to reason that if we want our learners to learn English effectively, we need to provide regular opportunities for them to receive such input, both inside and outside the classroom. While **extensive reading** (such as reading novels) and **extensive listening** (such as watching films) play an important role in this, given typical lesson lengths, reading and listening activities in class tend to be shorter and more focused, what we often call **intensive reading/listening**. We will look at intensive practice first and then look at ideas for extensive practice after this.

Intensive reading and listening

On CertTESOL courses trainee teachers often learn the framework shown in Table 2.8 for reading and listening lessons initially. It provides a useful starting point, and is also used by many practising teachers.

Table 2.8: A starting point for structuring receptive skills lessons

Main phase	Sub phase	What to do
Pre	Lead in	Share your intentions or aims for the lesson. Engage learners on the topic of the text.
	Pre-teach vocabulary	Introduce learners to any important vocabulary in the text that they will need to know before listening/reading.
During	Global comprehension task	Learners read or listen quickly to complete a task that focuses on the general topic or main ideas in the text.
	Detailed comprehension task	Learners read or listen more carefully to complete a more challenging task, typically involving a number of questions.
Post	Language analysis	Learners analyse the language used in the text (optional).
	Extension activity	The text provides stimulus for productive language use, with the learners possibly involved in a discussion relating to the topic of the text, or producing a similar text themselves.

The following should be noted:

- ■ 'Text' means either the written text for a reading activity or the audio recording for a listening activity (all coursebooks include a large number of audio listening activities).

- ■ This is a guideline framework only, and there are many reasons for departing from it. For example, we may prefer to focus learners' attention on the vocabulary after the global comprehension task, thereby providing more context for understanding the vocabulary. Alternatively, especially with listening tasks, learners may need a third, or even fourth opportunity to listen to the text. Also, after the comprehension tasks, there is significant variation as to what may follow; we may choose to do only language analysis, only an extension activity, or neither.

Here is a typical reading text designed for intermediate level students (B1). Imagine you have been asked to teach a 90-minute lesson using this text. Decide on the following, and then compare with the ideas provided below the text:

1 *an appropriate lead-in task*

2 *what vocabulary to pre-teach*

3 *appropriate global and detailed comprehension tasks*

4 *possible areas of language that the learners can analyse*

5 *an appropriate extension activity to finish the lesson*

Talking To The Animals

For hundreds of years, scientists have wondered if animals can talk. Parrots, apes, dogs and even dolphins have been used in experiments, but with little success. Many animals could understand and even produce single words, but no animal has been able to understand and respond to language in sentences, until now.

A chimpanzee called Kanzi has learnt to understand sign language without even being trained. Just like a child, he managed to pick up language while researchers tried unsuccessfully to teach his mother, who wasn't able to learn more than a few words. When they noticed Kanzi's ability, his trainers continued to teach him as a human mother teaches her children, and the results are remarkable.

At the age of 23, Kanzi has a vocabulary of about 500 words. While this alone isn't unusual (a gorilla called Koko understood about 2,000 words), what sets Kanzi apart from all other animals is that he can understand and respond to language in sentences. In many different experiments, Kanzi has responded to instructions, such as *Go outside and get the ball*, predictions, such as *Liz is going to tickle Kanzi*, and questions, such as *Where is Rose's shoe?* Kanzi can also use a large keypad with small pictures on it to communicate. He can compose sentences of three or four words himself.

Kanzi has been trained by Sue and Duane Rumbaugh at the University of Georgia in the USA. He also has two friends, Panzee and Panbanisha who have similar language ability. Their typical day includes playing children's games, doing tests and even watching films on TV. They tend to like films with apes in them! Kanzi has also succeeded in making stone-cutting tools, improving them over time.

Sue believes these discoveries are very important in our relationship to intelligent animals. If we take seriously the fact that the chimpanzee has an understanding of language and an ability to produce language, it raises all kinds of other questions. Are they conscious? How should we treat them? Perhaps one day, Kanzi himself will be able to answer even these questions.

Table 2.9:
Outline of example
reading lesson with
commentary

Stage	Possible activity	Notes
Lead in	Brief discussion on animal intelligence and/or animal communication. Show the learners the title of the article to see if they can guess what it's about.	This should provide useful context for the text, and some important vocabulary.
Pre-teach vocabulary	wonder (v) ape (n) pick up (v) remarkable (adj) set (smb) apart from (v) conscious (adj) treat (v)	There are quite a few difficult verbs in this text. Notice the phrasal verbs: *pick up* and *set apart from*. *Conscious* and *ape* will need drilling due to unpredictable pronunciation.
Global comprehension task	Learners read the text to find three ways in which Kanzi is unique.	This task isn't too challenging, and allows different learners to find different answers.
Detailed comprehension task	Learners read the text again to answer the following questions: 1 Which animals have scientists used in talking experiments in the past? 2 What couldn't these animals do that Kanzi can do? 3 How did Kanzi learn to understand language? 4 What kind of sentences can he understand? 5 How does he communicate with his trainers? 6 What is Kanzi's typical day like? 7 What are his other achievements? 8 Why does Sue think that Kanzi's language ability is important?	These questions focus on specific details in the text, some of which require learners to interpret the content of the text. They are fairly typical of detailed comprehension questions. Other possible tasks include true/false statements and multiple-choice questions. Usually we ask learners to try to find the answers working individually and then compare in pairs.
Language analysis	Learners look for structures in the text that describe ability (e.g. *'wasn't able to learn'; 'he managed to pick up'; 'no animal has been able to'*). A gap-fill activity from a grammar book could provide a useful consolidation exercise.	These expressions to describe ability are quite varied and some can be tricky for learners to understand and use.
Extension activity	Learners could discuss whether they agree with Sue or not. This could lead into a whole class debate based on the following motion, with one group arguing for it and the other arguing against it: *Apes should have the same rights as people.*	This would get the learners using most of the language from the text and the language analysis. It would also be lively, providing a nice contrast to the more silent study earlier in the lesson.

Let's now imagine that the above reading text is an audio recording, for example, an interview with Sue, Kanzi's trainer, in which the same information is provided. Notice that the same basic lesson stages could be used, and even the comprehension tasks could remain largely the same. For both tasks the teacher would typically play the whole recording without pausing. There is, however, an important additional mini-stage in the listening lesson not required in an equivalent reading lesson. Before they listen the second time, the teacher will typically give them time to read through and discuss the detailed comprehension questions in pairs. The questions themselves provide useful structure for the detailed listening task and clues about the content. The discussion also provides an opportunity to check what they have understood during the first listening, which may include some of the answers to the detailed comprehension questions. This helps them to pinpoint what they need to listen for during the second playback. The language analysis and extension activity after this would need little modification from the reading lesson, although learners may need a copy of the tapescript if language analysis requires them to identify specific structures in the text.

Important listening and reading sub-skills

The Trinity syllabus identifies a number of specific sub-skills, relating to reading and listening lessons. Table 2.10 shows some of the most important ones that are typically practised during intensive skills lessons, drawing examples from the reading and listening lessons described above. Obviously, it is not necessary to demonstrate all these sub-skills in every lesson:

Table 2.10: Example listening and reading sub-skills

Both listening and reading sub-skills in the CertTESOL syllabus	Predicting content, vocabulary and answers	The lead-in task provided above should do this fairly well by getting them to predict the content of the text from the title.
	Distinguishing main points from supporting information	The global comprehension task is likely to develop this sub-skill by focusing learners' attention on what makes Kanzi unique.
	Making inferences	Often practised as a higher level skill, the following question would provide practice of this sub-skill: *What are the implications of Kanzi's achievements for animal rights?*
Listening sub-skills in the CertTESOL syllabus	Listening for gist	This is listening to understand the main idea or gist of a text, often encouraged through global comprehension tasks.
	Listening for specific information	This would be achieved through some of the detailed comprehension questions (e.g. 5, 6) above.

	Recognising **genre** from format and layout	By looking at a written text, we can tell whether it's a newspaper article, a text message or an extract from a novel. All of these are examples of genre, often identified during lead-in tasks.
Reading sub-skills in the CertTESOL syllabus	Navigating titles, subtitles, index, etc.	Learners will benefit from analysing the grammar of newspaper article titles, academic text subtitles or finding a specific passage in a book by using the index.
	Skimming	Often used as a global comprehension task, skimming involves reading a text quickly to identify the salient content (similar to listening for gist).
	Scanning	This is a very common reading sub-skill which involves scanning quickly through a reading text to find something specific.

Important differences between listening and reading lessons

While there are clear and useful analogies between the structure of receptive skills lessons, there are, of course, a number of important differences between reading and listening lessons apart from the extra mini-stage to listening lessons mentioned above. The majority of these refer to the greater challenge of understanding listening texts for learners:

1 **Pace:** Students can go at their own pace during reading activities, but during listening activities the pace is dictated by the speaker, and to some extent the teacher, who is usually in control of the audio recording.

2 **Noticing lexis:** Students are more likely to notice difficult lexical items and want to check them in reading lessons (because they can see them) than in listening lessons, when they will often pass unnoticed. Be prepared for related questions in reading lessons.

3 **Equipment:** Reading lessons don't require use of audio or IT equipment, but listening lessons do (unless it's 'live listening' – see below), so make sure you know how to operate your equipment for a listening lesson.

4 **Receptive pronunciation challenges:** Often learners have difficulty answering comprehension questions to listening texts because of features in the pronunciation of the speaker(s). To help them to overcome these challenges, we may need to replay short segments of the listening and analyse the features of connected speech that are causing problems. This can influence **time management** and requires skilful use of equipment.

Creative listening and reading lessons

In order to keep learners interested and engaged in the learning process, it's a good idea to be creative with choice of texts and tasks for reading and listening practice activities. Here are some ideas, most of which are well-known to experienced teachers:

Jigsaw reading

Different students in the class read different texts. They then get into small groups and tell each other about what they read, ideally comparing and discussing the content of the different texts. There may be two, three or four different texts, and they will normally be thematically related (e.g. three texts describing different holidays - learners summarise the holidays, discuss the relative merits of each and then have to agree in their group to go on only one of the holidays). See *Teamwork* (Anderson, 2004) for examples of such jigsaw reading activities.

Using authentic texts

While most coursebooks include plenty of texts for you to use, learners will find it useful to read or listen to texts that have not been designed for the language classroom (e.g. newspaper articles, websites, podcasts, blogs, YouTube videos, etc.), especially at higher levels. **Authentic texts** can be challenging for lower level learners, so keep tasks simple and don't expect full comprehension.

Live listening

Instead of using an audio recording, the teacher produces the text 'live' in the class using his/her voice. If two speakers are required, the teacher may get a colleague or a strong student to help. Good ideas for live listening include telling a story, sharing a cultural insight and role-playing a dramatic scene. Try to avoid reading aloud from scripts – keep them organic and natural.

Using stories

Stories can be read or told by the teacher, or even by students. All of us enjoy a good story, and they can be made more interesting through dramatic presentation. Short stories are easy to find (try Googling *Aesop's Fables*), and they can be retold in jigsaw activities.

Tapescript gap-fills

For a detailed listening comprehension activity, try giving your learners a copy of the tapescript of the recording with gaps in it that they have to fill as they listen. Textbooks usually have such tapescripts in the back which you can photocopy and adapt to create the blanks (don't forget to source photocopied materials).

Using songs

Songs are a great way to learn new languages. Listening to them repeatedly helps us to acquire new grammar and lexis, and singing along helps us to improve pronunciation. They can be used effectively for integrated listening and reading skills. First, learners can listen only to try to understand what the song is about. Then you can provide a copy of the lyrics and a challenging task for the second listening (e.g. provide a gap-fill activity or jumble up the lines of the song and get learners to order them). Don't forget to finish with a singalong!

Using video

Video material can easily be found on the Internet, especially through YouTube. You may be able to play it on a TV, a computer screen or an interactive whiteboard if you have one. The key advantage of video is that it provides visual context and often shows the speaker's lips, both of which help learners to understand more. Subtitles improve understanding but tend to lead to learners reading rather than listening, so avoid using them, at least initially.

Extensive reading and listening

Extensive reading and listening are not as common in typical ELT classrooms as intensive reading and listening. Why? Mainly because learners expect more from the teacher. Many will argue that they can read a book or watch a film at home, but when they come to school they want the clarification, interaction and practice that lessons typically provide. Nonetheless, our learners will all improve faster if they engage in regular extensive reading and listening, and there are two obvious ways we can get them to do this:

Using novels, short stories and easy readers

Over the course of a term, you can encourage your learners to choose and read a novel or short story (depending on their level) in English, which can then provide input for language lessons. If they select different stories, you can get them to do brief presentations (e.g. one or two a week) or book reports, and if the class choose to read the same story, it can be discussed several times a term during lessons, and useful language can be pre-taught or analysed during class. This is easy to organise if your school has a library, where there are likely to be 'easy-reader' books for low level learners. It's more difficult if there is no library, but there are plenty of stories available for free online.

Using films

A well-prepared film lesson can be rewarding and enjoyable for learners. Choosing the right type of film, carefully selecting the vocabulary to pre-teach and knowing when to pause the film to check understanding are all part of the preparation. Remember also to keep an eye out for appropriate English-language films on television. In many countries, these are now common and usually subtitled. You can get learners to watch a film for homework and then discuss it, analyse content or re-enact scenes from it in the subsequent lesson.

2.8 Productive skills (speaking and writing)

While there are clear and obvious analogies between the structure of typical reading and listening lessons in ELT, similarities between how we usually practise the two productive skills are fewer. You will have probably noticed that speaking tends to be practised regularly in all lessons – in lead-in activities, during pair and groupwork, when responding to teacher questions and, of course, during the practice phases of grammar and lexis lessons. In contrast to this, the only writing activities we have come across in Units 1 and 2 are the notetaking and film review tasks in the grammar and lexis lessons above. This imbalance between the attention devoted to the two productive skills to some extent reflects the relative importance afforded to them in the **Communicative Approach** to language teaching. Indeed, the very idea of a 'communicative classroom' conjures up images of learners chatting, discussing and interacting with each other, and not of learners writing. However, it's important to note that the balance between the amount of classroom time devoted to the practice of productive skills may be very different in other contexts. For example, in large primary or secondary classrooms in low-income countries, writing provides a useful opportunity for each learner to practise using language without classes becoming too noisy, and in ESOL classes for refugees in high-income countries, improving basic writing skills may be a key priority of learners aiming to get jobs.

The first obvious similarity between the two productive skills is that both are appropriate for practising new language in the final phase of grammar and lexis lessons. Such practice, as well as providing an opportunity to use the new language, also helps to develop these two important skills. However, often in such lessons, the focus is on making use of the new language rather than developing more specific communication skills, such as agreeing and disagreeing, making formal requests, ordering in a restaurant or tweeting good news. The expressions that learners need to perform these communication skills are referred to as **functional language** in ELT. They often constitute the main input for speaking and writing lessons. As such, a focus on functional language is the second feature often common to productive skills lessons. So let's begin this section of the chapter by looking at functional language and then we will look at the two productive skills separately.

Functional language

All language use is functional, but when we talk about teaching functional language, rather than focusing on elements of the system (grammar, lexis and phonology), we are focusing on a specific reason for communicating (e.g. asking permission to do something). We often teach learners a range of expressions or **exponents** for doing this (e.g. *Would you mind if I …?, Is it okay if I …?*). As such, a lesson on functional language is likely to include a number of grammatical elements and possibly some new lexis, but these are not usually analysed in detail. As long as learners understand when to use them and what they mean, they can be taught as formulaic 'chunks' to be used in subsequent speaking and writing activities. This is recognised in the Trinity CertTESOL syllabus for both writing and speaking sub-skills: *Selecting appropriate vocabulary and lexical chunks to express desired language functions.*

The example lesson in Unit 1 on the topic of formal and informal introductions involves the teaching and practice of functional language. Table 2.11 shows a selection of other functions often studied in English lessons, along with example exponents:

Table 2.11: Functions and exponents

Function	Exponent
Beginning and ending telephone calls	Could I speak to …? May I ask who is calling?
Responding to a comment on a blog	Thanks for sharing, Salma. Check out my previous post on …
Agreeing and disagreeing	Oh, absolutely! I'm afraid I can't agree with you there.
Writing an email of complaint	The problem started when… What made it even worse was…

Have a look at the Contents pages of a typical ELT coursebook to try to find the functional language (Tip: previews are often available online). Spoken functional language may come under a section with a practical slant called 'Everyday English', 'Practical English' or 'Real life', but written functional language is nearly always taught under a section called, rather uninspiringly, 'Writing'!

Let's now look at each skill in more detail.

Speaking

The skill of speaking comes so effortlessly to us in our first language that it's easy to forget how many elements are involved. Before we even begin speaking, we need to make assumptions about who is listening and what they know. Then, as noted in the Trinity syllabus, we need to use appropriate grammatical structures with accuracy, apply syntactical rules correctly and form phonemes and stress patterns appropriately, all as we are thinking about the meaning of what we are saying. While some of the underlying skills are transferred naturally into foreign languages, the difficulty of rapidly coordinating features of grammar, phonology and items of lexis inevitably leads us to make more mistakes than we do when composing written text. With regard to this, we will look at the area of spoken error correction shortly.

As discussed earlier in this chapter, one of the ways that we succeed in communicating effectively when speaking is to build up a repertoire of fixed expressions and chunks of language that can be drawn upon to express common fixed meanings, as well as **fillers** (e.g. *you know, I mean*) to give us time to think. We also make use of **vague language** (e.g. *kind of, like*), and we are also willing to start sentences and then abandon them partway through if necessary (called **false starts**).

See how many typical features of spoken language you can identify in the following extract from a recording of a native speaker of English talking about finding work:

> …well, you know, I suppose one of the reasons is, it would just be easier to get a job. I mean, you can like go overseas or, or if you don't fancy that, you can try… I dunno, stay here and look for something…

Far from being 'sloppy language', as was often thought before scientists began analysing spoken grammar, all of these elements are important, necessary components of fluent speech, enabling us to think and produce language simultaneously (Carter & McCarthy, 2006). It stands to reason that if native speakers need them, language learners are also likely to find these features useful.

An example speaking lesson – giving advice

As mentioned above, speaking practice is a feature of almost any communicative lesson, however, we may also sometimes decide to build a whole lesson around a specific speaking sub-skill and/or function, including a little context, a little analysis and then lots of practice, probably with a planned intention to provide correction, as in the lesson skeleton in Table 2.12, appropriate for a pre-intermediate (A2) level class:

Table 2.12:
Lesson skeleton for
a speaking lesson

Context	Come into class and pretend to the learners that you have a small problem (e.g. 'I'm having difficulty sleeping at night.'). Elicit advice from the learners.
Analysis	Write some of the exponents that the learners use on the board (correcting mistakes if necessary), and add a few more: *You should / shouldn't* (+ verb) … *Why don't you try* (+ verb+ing) …? *It might help if you* (+ verb) … Elicit any differences in meaning between the different exponents and check learners can form sentences using them. Model and drill the example sentences.
Practice	Give individual synopsis cards to the learners, each describing a minor health complaint. Tell them to stand, mingle, describe their problems and offer advice as in the following example exchange: **Learner 1:** I have a terrible cold and a temperature. **Learner 2:** How long have you felt like this? **Learner 1:** Since yesterday morning. **Learner 2:** I see. Perhaps you should stay at home tomorrow and have some rest. It might help if you take lots of vitamin C as well.
Correction	Show learners a number of the errors heard during the mingle activity (e.g. on the board). Get them to discuss potential corrections in pairs and then elicit feedback.

Notice that there is no controlled practice stage in this lesson but there is a correction stage after the practice phase, when learners have an opportunity to notice and correct their own mistakes. This does not necessarily stop you from providing more immediate correction during the activity – both are useful, as is praise for effective language use.

Spoken error correction strategies

While many trainee teachers are often nervous about correcting students' English, learners are usually very appreciative of correction, as long as it's done sensitively. After all, that's why they're here! However, overcorrection can stifle the learners or cause them to lose face in front of their peers, so, if they are producing a lot of errors (e.g. at lower levels), it's often a good idea to focus your correction on the specific area of language that you are practising, which in this lesson would be exponents used to give advice. Here are some of the most common spoken correction strategies that can be used in any type of lesson, including grammar lessons, lexis lessons and skills lessons. Let's imagine the student who makes the mistake is chatting with another student during the practice stage of the above lesson and the teacher is monitoring.

A   Correction during an activity:

1   Direct correction – when you hear a mistake, pause the learner and provide the correct sentence:

Student: *…so you should to stay at home tomorrow and…*

Teacher: *Careful. Say 'you **should stay** at home', without 'to'.*

2 Prompting – when you hear a mistake, indicate this to the learner and get them to correct their own sentence:

> Student: *...so you should to stay at home tomorrow and...*
>
> Teacher: *Careful. Check the structure on the board.*
>
> Student: *Ah yes. **You should stay** at home tomorrow and take some rest.*

Sometimes classmates will also hear the mistake and prompt, and may offer the correction (peer-correction).

3 Recasts – when you hear a mistake, try responding to the meaning of what the learner has said naturally, so that you weave a correct reformulation of the mistake into your response:

> Student: *...so you should to stay at home tomorrow and...*
>
> Teacher: *Oh, that's a good idea. You should stay at home. I wish I could!*

4 Correction notes – when you hear a mistake, write it down on a slip of paper and pass it to the learner who made the mistake.

B After the activity:

5 Feedback on the board – Write a number of the sentences that included mistakes on the board, and elicit corrections from the class. You may also want to include one or two correct sentences in the list – examples of effective use of the target language – and learners can be further challenged to spot the correct sentences among those with errors.

6 Delayed feedback – Send emails to individual learners after the lesson with their personal mistakes for them to note, correct and email back to you for checking.

Note that activities 4, 5 and 6 require you to take notes during the activity.

Pause for thought

What factors do you think will influence a teacher's choice of error correction strategy? Make notes and then compare your ideas with those provided below.

Which error correction strategy to use?

Experienced teachers will often use of variety of strategies during an activity. They tend to have an instinctual knowledge of which error correction strategy to use at any given time, and many will have personal favourites. Here are some guidelines to help you as you begin:

■ Use direct correction, or prompting if a mistake is particularly important and you want to draw the learner's attention to it, for example, if the learner has made a mistake with a basic aspect of the grammar that you have been teaching today.

■ Prompting is only effective if a learner is likely to be able to self-correct after a second or two of thinking. Avoid using it if you're not sure that this is true.

■ Use recasts if you feel the meaning of what the learner is saying is more important, but you still want to offer correction.

■ Use correction notes or delayed feedback if you don't want to correct a learner in front of his/her classmates or partner, for example, if they are self-conscious.

■ Use feedback on the board if you notice an error several times and/or think it's an important area for all learners to notice.

■ For errors caused by carelessness (sometimes called 'slips'), you may want to agree on a specific strategy with a class and encourage learners to peer correct their partners using the strategy. For example, if a learner forgets the 's' on a 3rd person verb, you could agree to draw an 's' shape in the air with your finger.

Effective ideas for speaking practice

Role-plays

Role-plays are one of the simplest and easiest ways for learners to practise speaking skills. They provide opportunities for them to imagine they are someone else, somewhere else using English meaningfully. As such, they lend themselves particularly well to practising functional language. Let's take an example context, such as a hotel, familiar to almost all students. It would be easy to think of a wide range of role-plays in this one context practising functions such as making enquiries, making requests, making complaints, introducing yourself, ordering food, paying compliments, engaging in small talk, apologising, etc. A distinction is sometimes made between role-plays and simulations; while role-plays involve learners pretending to be someone else, simulations require them to be themselves, just in a different situation outside the classroom. See *Role Plays for Today* (Anderson, 2006) for a wide range of ideas, from structured functional role-plays to full dramas.

Personalisation questions

We all love talking about ourselves. We also know a lot about ourselves. This makes personalisation questions extremely useful, because the content of what we say is already very familiar, leaving more brain cells free to focus on the communication. Personalisation questions can be thought of for almost any topic (e.g. food, finances, music, film, love, holidays, etc.), and it only takes a few minutes to think of them. Most questions with the pronoun 'you' in them are personalisation questions. (e.g. *What do you usually eat for breakfast? What do you eat when you're on a diet?*)

Discussions and debates

Just as we all love talking about ourselves, we also love expressing our opinions. One of the advantages to this is that we don't have to know much about a topic in order to have an opinion on it. Expressing opinion constitutes a very large part of interactive language use – just try visiting a local pub to test out this theory! Discussions are also useful because they can easily be adapted to any topic; we can discuss which is the most influential pop group (music), the relative merits of living in the countryside and the city (lifestyle), how to make diets healthier (food) or whether apes should have the same rights as people (ethics) as in the receptive skills lesson above. Debates tend to be more formalised discussions in which learners either choose or are given specific opinions and they have to defend these opinions. Choose your debate topic carefully and note that you may have to play Devil's advocate a little to get some debates going. While whole class debates are good fun, remember that they reduce the amount of speaking practice that each learner gets, so whenever possible use smaller groups. Be aware that there is some variation between cultures regarding how willing learners are to express personal views or disagree with classmates.

Speaking games

Games can be a great way to practise speaking skills. The most successful speaking games tend to be ones in which learners must use language in some way in order to win. Learners can play board games in which they have to answer questions to move, they could play card games in which they have to use the sentences on their cards during discussions, or they could play lying games in which they talk about something and their classmates must guess whether they are telling the truth or lying; see *Speaking Games* (Anderson, 2014) for more ideas. Competitive spirit not only encourages learners to try harder, but it also leads to lots of language use 'around' the game as learners negotiate turns, offer advice and congratulations, and even accuse each other of scheming, plotting or cheating!

Describing activities

Possibly not as intrinsically enjoyable as some of the other options, describing activities are nonetheless useful for practising certain areas of grammar (e.g. the present continuous aspect, or comparative adjectives as in the example grammar lesson above) or lexis (e.g. learners describe the contents of their fridge at home to practise lexis relating to food). We can make describing activities more interactive and motivating by turning them into 'describe and draw' tasks, in which learners must listen to their partner and try to draw whatever is being described.

Writing

While it tends to be the skill least practised in many communicative language classrooms, writing is not only an essential skill in itself, but also a vital scaffolding skill that can help learners to try out new grammatical structures, expand their vocabulary and even prepare for speaking activities, as in the comparatives lesson described earlier in this chapter. Writing may also constitute the main focus of a lesson, for example, if we want to teach our learners how to write informal emails or discursive essays. As we communicate more and more through digital media, writing is evolving rapidly, and many language learners today will need to learn not just about traditional genres such as reports, CVs and job application emails, but also how to interact through email or instant messaging services, and how to compose effective blogs and tweets. Features of spoken grammar are being used in text messages and tweets, and the speed at which we often find ourselves typing chat messages sometimes approaches the speed of spoken language use. Further changes are afoot with the rapid improvements currently occurring in voice recognition which is, paradoxically, a spoken form of writing.

Pause for thought

Make a list of the last 10 things that you wrote, either on paper or digitally. These may range from short text messages or post-it notes to longer emails and assignments for your CertTESOL. Identify any specific features of the different text types, such as degree of formality, use of specific functional language and possible alternative abbreviations or symbols used.

A key difference between written and spoken language use is the permanence of writing. Irrespective of how long or short a written 'text' is, it is almost always stored somewhere. This has two implications for teaching writing. Firstly, we can easily find and use such texts to help teach writing skills, and secondly, writing lessons can usefully focus on these specific text types or genres. Indeed, the text types that you listed in the previous *Pause for thought* task probably constitute specific genres, all of which may be useful for learners to study and practise. Here are some common text genres often practised in ELT writing lessons:

- postcards
- notes (e.g. notes on a lecture, notes for a talk or an essay)

- emails (both formal and informal, for various functions)
- CVs
- reviews (including arts, such as films, and consumer reviews on websites)
- blog entries (including 'blog dialogue' through comment chains)
- PowerPoint presentations (both academic and work-related)
- creative stories
- text messages and instant messaging
- reports
- essays and assignments

While writing lessons tend to focus on getting learners to produce complete texts, it's useful to note that writing activities can also be brief, like speaking activities. Learners benefit from practising the mechanics of writing phrases and sentences, especially at lower levels. This may include tasks such as writing example sentences, writing answers to text comprehension questions (many studious learners often do this by choice), or even making a note of their partners' answers during pairwork speaking tasks.

An example writing lesson: writing exam practice
Given the relative ease of obtaining examples of specific written text genres to study (compare this with spoken language), it makes a lot of sense if we begin writing lessons by providing examples of the text types that we're going to ask learners to produce later in the lesson and analyse these for aspects of structure, lexis and useful exponents of functional language; these are often called 'model texts'. Once more, our C-A-P mnemonic comes in handy. Table 2.13 shows a skeleton for a writing lesson for a class of upper intermediate (B2) learners who are all planning to take exams in order to study in English-medium universities next year:

Table 2.13: Lesson skeleton for a writing skills lesson	Context	After a lead-in discussion on the topic, learners read two example discursive essays, one strong (the model answer) and one weak, on the same exam question:
		Events like the Olympics are just a waste of money for the countries that host them. They only serve the interests of big multinational companies to sell their products.
		To what extent do you agree or disagree with this opinion? Provide reasons for your opinion. Write 150-250 words.
		Learners discuss the relative merits of the two essays.
	Analysis	Learners identify the model answer and focus firstly on the structure of the text (e.g. introduction, first argument, conclusion, etc.) and then on the language used. They pick out useful language used for justifying a point:
		One reason for this is... Another reason is...
		This has several advantages...
		They also underline any useful discourse marking adverbials, such as *however; nevertheless; what is more; therefore*; etc.
	Practice	Learners plan and write their own essay on a similar, but not identical, question:
		Sports play a vital role in improving relationships between countries and developing international understanding.
		To what extent do you agree or disagree with this opinion? Provide reasons for your opinion. Write 150-250 words.
		The teacher provides individual support to learners both during planning and writing.

Either at the end of the lesson or soon after, as in most writing lessons, the teacher would receive copies of the learners' work to read and provide feedback on. This feedback is an important part of the writing process and is discussed below.

As this is an exam writing lesson, the learners would typically work alone on the writing task. However, writing tasks can be made interactive by getting learners to work on them together. For example, a class of **general English** students may enjoy working in pairs on a story writing activity (see the *Pause for thought* task below). Alternatively, they could interact through IT-based media, such as What's App, Facebook, email or an instant messaging program (see below). They may also enjoy reading and writing comments on blogs, or submitting reviews to shopping websites, which can be done either in class or for homework. **Process writing** is an example of interactive writing in which learners work together to produce a number of drafts for a piece of writing for which they receive feedback from peers in their class, progressively improving their text as they do. It's so called because the process is seen to be at least as important as the product – the text.

Providing feedback on learners' writing
Another advantage of the permanence of writing when compared to speaking is that it allows us to provide much more detailed feedback on work produced by learners. This includes error

correction, possibly the most obvious area for feedback, but it also includes a number of other things, such as

- praise for strengths and for improvements made on prior action points
- an evaluation of overall structure, coherence and ideas
- possible requests for clarification if something is unclear
- comments on the range of language used, including the variety of lexis and grammar
- clear suggestions for further improvement

Pause for thought

Here is an authentic piece of writing produced by two learners in an upper intermediate (B2) level class. They were asked to write a story that included the sentence There's lipstick on this wine glass. *This was their second draft after receiving feedback and peer correction on their first draft from classmates. Imagine you are their teacher. What feedback would you provide on this story? Consider all the areas above, and check your ideas in the* Pause for thought Key *[16].*

"There's lipstick on this wine glass."

One day, a couple went to a restaurant. They were eating, suddenly the man fell over the floor and everyone in the restaurant went to help him. But the man died.

Next the people called to 911, When the police arrived to the restaurant, they asked "who was here with him", one waiter said "I saw a woman with him, but she left the restaurant after the man fell"

Then the police looked at the glass on the table and he said "there's lipstick on this wine glass" they took the glass to a lab. After that the glass was examine and the police through a fingerprint and saliva and they discovered the identity of two persons a woman (the deceaced man's wife) and the waiter who was the woman's lover.

the research deduce that the waiter put poison into the wine glass.

After a week the police caught the waiter and the woman in a pub.

Useful ideas for further help with writing

Using an error correction code

While it is possible for you to provide direct correction of learner mistakes in a text, it is potentially more useful if you highlight an error, provide a hint on the type of error and return the writing to the learner to encourage them to self-correct it, a bit like the prompting method of spoken error correction above. Here's an example:

> *One day, a couple went to a restaurant. They were eating, suddenly*
> *the man fell over the floor and everyone in the restaurant went to*
> *ww*
> *help him. But the man died.*
> *Pu*

Note three annotations have been added. The symbol after *eating* means there is a word missing (*when*), '**ww**' means wrong word (*onto*), and '**Pu**' indicates a punctuation error (no new sentence needed). Other symbols include '**wo**' – word order; '**sp**' – spelling; '**pr**' – preposition; '**gr**' – grammar; '**?**' – can't read or can't understand.

Error correction logs

Another useful suggestion for classes who do regular writing activities is to get the learners to keep error correction logs. These can be kept in the back of learners' notebooks where they record errors they made and the corrections provided. They can return to these logs periodically and test each other in pairs by taking their partner's notebook, reading out an error, and eliciting the correction. Alternatively, especially for classes who share the same L1 and make some of the same mistakes, an error correction log can be kept on a poster on the wall of the classroom. Here is an example from a secondary school class in Malaysia:

ERROR CORRECTION LOG

My Sentence	Correction	Rule/Note
The victim hands	The victim's hands	's refers to "kepunyaan"
The above procedure	The above procedures	Plural !!! add 's'
I will delivered a speech entitled....	I will deliver a speech entitled....	After modal mesti base form
to received	to receive	"to" base form :)
I couldn't	I could not	kalau dlm spm tidak buli guna ya contraction kecuali dalam ucapan; utama letak dialog
Already go	had gone	Sudah/belum → had/had not

Providing outlines or structures for text types

Many types of texts have quite generic structures, such as job application letters, reports or newspaper articles. These can be studied to elicit sequential components (introduction, description of context, statement of problem, etc.) which learners can keep for future reference when composing similar text types.

IT-based information exchange

Learners can practise writing skills by communicating with each other through email, social media or instant messaging, either during or after lesson time. One simple way of doing this is to use a role-play synopsis in which one learner requests information or advice and the other provides it. Another is for either you or a learner to post something on Facebook or a class blog and the others to reply through comments. Ideas for such exchange are evolving rapidly in tandem with developments in the media and apps themselves.

Translation activities (multilingual)

Any class of learners can do translation activities, irrespective of whether they share their L1 or not. One useful activity that can be practised is called 'reverse translation'. The basic idea behind it is that learners translate a specific text from English into L1, and then they translate it back again, usually later in the lesson or on a different day altogether. The time delay is important to help learners notice and recall features of language that they would otherwise forget. It can help them to notice similarities and differences between L1 and English, and is especially useful if key structures that you want them to learn are included in the original English text. It has the added benefit that learners can check their own work (in theory, accurate translation should lead to the original and final texts being similar). Another simple but effective idea is to get learners to choose a text that they like in their L1 and translate it into English to share with the whole class. This can be done, for example, with poetry, news stories, and even short stories (a class storybook is possible). Because they are individually responsible for bringing information and even culture into English from their L1 and sharing it with classmates, learners are often very interested in discussing nuances of meaning and differences between languages, all of which help both to raise language awareness and to develop this key skill that's likely to be useful in the future.

Translation activities (monolingual)

Classes that share a common language with each other and with their teacher can do a wider variety of translation activities. They can translate simple texts from L1 into English and more challenging texts from English into L1. This can be done with texts of almost any genre as a way of providing controlled practice of specific writing skills. Practical translation tasks are also very useful and might include translating their CV or a job application cover letter into English, translating documents from their field of expertise or work context into English (e.g. students can translate informational or promotional literature from their place of work). Students can take texts that they have written on personal interests and hobbies and translate these into English as well. An example of this I recall well is a student who, for a translation project, translated a website he had created in Italian into English. Through the English version website, he soon made friends with other English speakers who shared his interest and motivated him to learn the language further.

2.9 Integrating skills

While English teachers often plan lessons that focus on one specific skill, it is probably more common for us to integrate a number of these skills together in every lesson. Indeed, you may have noticed that the 'Context-Analysis-Practice' mnemonic used to plan the stages of the lessons above is essentially an integrated skills paradigm, with Context usually providing opportunities for reading or listening and Practice for speaking or writing. Other lesson structures also are possible, especially at higher levels where learners are less dependent on new language before they can practise using language. This includes the so-called 'Test–Teach–Test' paradigm in which a teacher may elect to begin a lesson with speaking or writing practice in order to notice how learners are already performing a specific function/sub-skill or using a specific area of language. After analysis and possibly error correction, the teacher might get the learners to perform the same speaking activity again, or something very similar. The 'testing' is, in reality 'Practice' during which the teacher carries out diagnostic assessment (at the start), and evaluative assessment (at the end). In *The Knowledge* at the back of this book, brief descriptions of a number of paradigms used to structure lessons are provided – many of these are flexible, and they allow us to describe lessons with any structure, both those that are skill-specific and those where skills are more integrated (e.g. ESA, ARC).

While lesson length varies in different contexts around the world, especially when teaching adult learners, lessons are likely to be over 60 minutes in length, and even up to three hours (with a break) on full-time English courses, as is common in UK EFL institutions. In such longer lessons, we inevitably find ourselves integrating skills in what Harmer calls 'patchwork' lessons (2007, p.56). These often follow the structure provided in EFL coursebooks, which themselves usually integrate work on all four skills in each unit.

Pause for thought

Choose a unit or chapter from an ELT coursebook (if you don't have any available, it's often possible to find sample units online from publishers' websites). Make a list of the activities in the order provided in the coursebook. For each activity in your list, make a note of whether you think its main aim is to develop a skill or sub-skill (SK), to provide a context for new language (CO), an opportunity to analyse new language (AN) or an opportunity to practise new language (PR). You will sometimes find that activities combine two of these.

Here is an example based on *New English File Intermediate* (2006), Unit 4C, which would probably take a class three or four lessons to complete:

Activity		Type	C-A-P cycle
1	Vocabulary input	AN	
2	Speaking practice	PR	
3	Reading – context for new grammar	CO	
4	Grammar – analysis of 'used to'	AN	1
5	Controlled practice of the grammar	PR	
6	Listening - mainly skills practice, but also involving 'used to'	SK/CO	
7	Pronunciation – /s/ and /z/	AN	2
8	Speaking - practice of 'used to'	PR	
9	Reading - context for new lexis	CO	
10	Lexis – analysis of phrasal verbs	AN	3
11	Listening – more phrasal verbs, but also useful skills practice	CO/SK	
12	Speaking – practice of phrasal verbs	PR	

This lesson is interesting because in stages 6 and 11, the listening practice provides more useful exposure to the target language analysed in the previous activity, thereby combining this with receptive skills practice. Notice also that it is nonetheless possible to identify three context–analysis–practice loops within the unit (see the last column), which many teachers might draw upon to structure individual lessons.

Activities that integrate skills

Skills may even be integrated in a single activity. An obvious example of this is a speaking activity. Although we perceive the main aim of such an activity to be to provide an opportunity for speaking practice, given that learners are hopefully doing this practice in pairs or small groups, the skill they are actually practising is 'discussing' or 'having a conversation', and listening (to their classmates) is an essential part of this skill.

Another example is writing. Although we don't always notice it, as we write we are constantly reading what we are writing. A process writing activity requires learners to work together to produce an initial draft of a text which their peers then read and provide feedback on. This gives learners practice of both writing and reading, and also speaking and listening as they discuss the drafts.

Project-based lessons also provide useful integration of all four skills, for example, if learners work in teams to research and present on specific topics or to produce a newsletter or blog. Such lessons typically involve receptive skills during initial research, speaking and listening during team interaction and productive skills during final presentations or in any written products that evolve out of the project.

An example of a shorter activity that integrates all four skills is the 'running dictation' described in *Practising pronunciation* above.

Reading Student A reads and tries to remember a sentence from a text stuck on the wall.

Speaking Student A tells student B what s/he remembers.

Listening Student B listens to student A.

Writing Student B writes what s/he heard.

Review of Unit 2
Understanding and teaching language

Match the terms to their definitions

Unit 2 includes a lot of new terminology. Select from the words or expressions in the box to complete the definitions provided. Be careful – there are more words than definitions!

> productive skills   receptive skills   implicit knowledge
> explicit knowledge   part of speech   parse   uncountable noun
> countable noun   intransitive verb   auxiliary verb   elicit   suffix
> collocation   phoneme   monophthong   drill   function   exponent

1 .... nouns which have no plural form (e.g. information)

2 .... type of word (e.g. nouns, adjective, verb, etc.)

3 .... analyse and identify the constituent parts in a sentence

4 .... a word combination that is useful for learners to learn

5 .... a verb that has no object

6 .... our instinctual knowledge that enables us to use a language without thinking

7 .... a purpose for using language, a reason for communicating

8 .... the smallest unit in the spoken language

9 .... an expression or phrase that can be used to perform a specific function

10 .... the two skills through which we get linguistic input (i.e. reading and listening)

11 .... get information from learners, rather than telling them

12 .... get learners to repeat a word, sentence or sound

If you need to, check your answers in the *Review Key* at the back of the book.

Now return to the learning opportunities provided at the start of the chapter. Check off the ones that you feel you have achieved and reread the relevant sections for any you're not sure about.

unit 3 Understanding learners

Learning opportunities

This unit will help you to...

- describe different levels of learner proficiency
- recognise how a learner's prior languages can influence their English
- understand how learners' needs, priorities and motivation affect what they expect from teachers
- develop an effective rapport with a class of learners
- understand how to manage differences between learners when we teach
- support learners as they develop greater learner autonomy
- understand the requirements of the Learner Profile
- teach your first one-to-one lesson successfully
- complete the different parts of the Learner Profile appropriately

Introduction

Unit 3 of the Trinity CertTESOL, The Learner Profile, is built around the most extensive assignment on your course. It provides you with a useful opportunity to find out about the background, needs and interests of one English language learner, then to prepare and teach a **one-to-one** lesson to this learner, and make recommendations for further study. The required **learning outcomes** are described clearly in the CertTESOL syllabus:

> *Successful trainees will demonstrate the following learning outcomes in the context of initial training:*
>
> 1 *be able to draw up a simple linguistic profile/analysis and needs analysis for one learner of English on the basis of interviews totalling a minimum of 60–90 minutes and a sample of the learner's written work which may include diagnostic tests. The interviews should include general discussion of the learner's language learning background and aims in learning English, preferred methods of learning, and the strengths and weaknesses of the learner*
>
> 2 *be able to prepare and teach (unobserved) one lesson of 45–60 minutes (this lesson does not count as one of the six hours of observed and assessed teaching practice)*
>
> 3 *be able to prepare a number of broad recommendations for the learner's study programme in at least one area of each of the four main skills, including grammar and phonology.*
>
> Trinity CertTESOL syllabus

Although Unit 3 requires less total work than Unit 1, it involves writing a fairly lengthy assignment that surprises many trainee teachers when they are introduced to it partway through an already intensive course! But this is for good reason; the Unit 3 assignment is extensive because it has a dual purpose. It is an opportunity firstly for you to show what you have learnt about your chosen learner, and secondly to demonstrate your ability to apply and document what you have learnt in other units of the CertTESOL, especially Unit 2.

We will look at this assignment in detail at the end of this unit. Before we do, let's take a careful look at language learners in general – they are the subject of this unit because they are the subjects of every language teacher's craft, and the learning that it is our job to facilitate must happen inside their brains. Without understanding them, their prior language knowledge, their interests, and their needs, we cannot expect to be competent teachers.

3.1 Learner language and learners' languages

> *It is a misconception to see a bilingual speaker as two monolinguals joined together.*
>
> Cameron & Larsen-Freeman, 2007, p.232

While many prior models of language learning tended to focus on the shortcomings of language learners, a model proposed by Vivian Cook (1995) chose to accentuate the positive resources that they bring to the classroom. Cook pointed out that all language learners are bilinguals – they have at least two languages, even if one of these is elementary English, and as such are developing a 'multi-competence' that involves all their languages, one that's necessarily different in its nature to the **monolingual** competence of some speakers of English. In this section of the chapter, we will look at two aspects of this multi-competence: their current proficiency in English, including their strengths and challenges (**learner language**), and their prior linguistic resources, which may include one, two or more languages and even more dialects within these languages, explored under *Learners' languages* below.

Learner language

While we all have our own unique way of using each language that we speak (called our **idiolect**), two observations regarding the development of learner language can nonetheless be made. The first is that certain patterns can be seen in the developmental progress of learners from a wide range of backgrounds as they learn English as a foreign language. The second is that learners who share a **first language** or related languages, often share characteristic features in their English. Let's look at these two features in a little more detail.

Describing levels of proficiency

There are several ways to describe general levels of learner proficiency in a foreign language. The two most common ones are shown in Table 3.1, and will probably be used by your CertTESOL course provider. Note that the mapping of the two frameworks shown is approximate:

Common European Framework (CEFR) Level		'Coursebook' level
A1	Basic user	1. Beginner
		2. Elementary
A2		3. Pre-intermediate ('pre-int' for short)
B1	Independent user	4. Intermediate
B2		5. Upper Intermediate ('upper int' for short)
C1	Proficient user	6. Advanced
C2		7. Proficiency

When we describe a learner as being, for example, 'elementary', or we say that she is at 'C1 level', we are making a very general assessment of their ability. The reality is that individual learners have significant variation in ability between the different skills. For example, my Russian speaking skills are close to C2 level, yet my Russian writing skills are probably at B2 level, and while my French reading skills are probably at B2 level, my French listening skills are probably somewhere in the B1 range. If I had to assess my Russian or my French in general, I would say they are currently at C1 and B1 levels respectively.

On your Trinity CertTESOL course you will teach learners at two or more of these levels. Course providers generally select levels from Elementary to Advanced. Here are some brief descriptions of the ability of typical learners at each of these levels, bearing in mind the likely variations within the specific skills of each individual learner mentioned above:

A1 – Elementary: Students usually (but not always) have basic literacy in English, meaning they can read and write the most common words in the language. Their vocabulary is very limited, and they may be struggling with basic word order when forming simple sentences (*I yesterday go.**). They will probably only be able to answer common formulaic questions such as *'How are you?'* or *'What is your job?'*. Their spoken English is likely to be strongly influenced by their **L1** accent.

A2 – Pre-intermediate: Students have a limited range of vocabulary at this level. They will know enough to read a simple text or write basic emails in English. They may have studied a lot of grammar but still make basic mistakes, for example, by using the present tense in the past (*Yesterday I go in school.**), or in formation of questions and negatives (*I not tell him.**). They can answer basic questions such as *'What do you do in your free time?'* or *'What did you do yesterday?'*, however they will make plenty of mistakes in their answers.

B1 – Intermediate: Students have a greater range of vocabulary, and will begin to understand simple newspaper articles, or follow simple conversations between native speakers of English if they talk slowly. They will have more control of grammar than pre-intermediate students, but there will still be frequent smaller mistakes in what they say (*On Saturday I went in the market for buy new trouser to present my friend.**). They can answer more complex questions such as *'What's your home town like?'* *'Do you come from a big family?'*

B2 – Upper Intermediate: Students will have a fairly wide vocabulary and be able to speak with reasonable fluency, although they will still make mistakes (*I'm really tired because I had to worked all the last night.**). They will probably have studied much of the important grammar of English, but may still have difficulty using it. They will be able to understand the basic content of a TV programme or a magazine article, although they may have difficulty evaluating the author's point of view or 'reading between the lines'. They can answer questions requiring opinion or specific vocabulary, such as *'What type of music are you into?'* or *'What's the best way to stay healthy?'*

C1 – Advanced: Students will be able to express most ideas with confidence, and only make mistakes with more ambitious language use, such as using idioms. They will enjoy reading books for native speakers, TV shows and film, often picking up on nuances of meaning, although they will not understand everything. They can attempt to answer almost any question, but will still be challenged by questions that require specific areas of lexical knowledge, such as *'What is your position on climate change?'* or *'What type of legal system do you have in your country?'*

Pause for thought

Look at the following two extracts from published teaching materials. Based on the information about the five levels provided above, see if you can guess what level the coursebooks have been written for.

Check your answers in the **Pause for thought** *Key [17] at the back of the book.*

Extract 1

---

1 **Read the newspaper article and answer the questions.**

Dangerous driving?

A top TV programme with over five million viewers features three presenters discussing cars. It is called *Top Gear* and is one of the most popular programmes on BBC 2. In this programme the presenters do not simply discuss the cars in front of a studio audience – they also test drive them and do outrageous stunts such as racing cars against trains, planes and speedboats. They are concerned with the fun and thrill of driving and certainly not with the environmental or safety aspects of driving, even mocking 'boring safe' drivers. The show has a huge following of fans who love speed and want to experience a vicarious thrill – given that they themselves do not have the opportunity to drive at speeds of over 70 mph in the UK. However, recently

the whole future of *Top Gear* and similar programmes has been called into question after one of the presenters only just survived a crash when travelling close to 300 mph while apparently attempting to break the world land speed record. Many issues have been raised concerning health and safety regulations and whether programmes such as this should be allowed to show people taking risks in this way. If such programmes are banned or toned down, it would be a huge disappointment to the viewers and yet another example of how 'the powers that be' are becoming far too overprotective and in the process cutting out a lot of what makes life fun. As a journalist recently remarked, many people believe that personal risk should be a matter between a man and his insurance company. Otherwise, where do you draw the line?

1 What happens on the programme?

2 Why do people enjoy watching it?

3 What happened recently?

4 What effect might this have on the future of the programme and others like it? Why?

5 What is the attitude of the writer of the article?

Extract 2

Checking into a hotel

Role Plays for Today

Read the dialogue and complete the questions with *do, does, is* or *are*.

Guest

Hello. 1_____ you speak English? ⟶

2_____ you have a double room for tonight?

Good. How much 3_____ it?

€40 per person or per room?

4_____ that include breakfast?

OK. 5_____ the bathroom en suite?

It means that it has a private bathroom.

Right. 7_____ it possible to see the room?

From England.

Yes. With my husband. He's in the car.

OK. This is fine. Shall I pay now?

Er... Isn't it €120?

Right. 10_____ you accept credit cards?

OK. Here you are. What time's breakfast?

Oh! 11_____ it possible to have it at 10?

Another €5! Per person?

Oh, all right! Here you are.

Hotel owner

A little, yes.

Let me see... Yes, we do.

€40.

Per person.

No. Breakfast is €10 extra, per person.

Sorry. What 6_____ 'en suite' mean?

Ah, yes! That's another €10, per person.

Yes. Come with me. Where 8_____ you from?

Really? 9_____ you on holiday?

Ah, I see. Here is the room.

Yes, please. That's €130, please.

Yes, and €10 for the car park.

No. Only cash.

From 8 to 9. My wife gets up early!

Yes. For an extra €5.

Per person.

And here is your key. Goodnight.

Extracts from:
Skills work by Lynda Edwards
© 2009 Delta Publishing;
Role plays for today by Jason Anderson
© 2006 Delta Publishing

> **❝ Pinpointing the difficulties experienced by learners allows you to understand the origin of the problem (e.g. L1 interference) and it is this understanding which allows you to anticipate errors and be proactive in dealing with them. ❞**
>
> Christa, CertTESOL trainer

Analysing learner 'errors'

Learners make both predictable and unpredictable errors when using English. Some of the most common ones seem to be the same, irrespective of the learner's nationality:

> *I am agree.* *

Others seem to be shared by speakers of a specific language, or related languages (sometimes called L1 influence or 'interference'):

> *Me, I think it is wrong because...* * (French)

And others may be shared by speakers of unrelated languages, because of similar features in these languages. For example, speakers of languages which do not have articles (*a, the*) are more likely to omit them than speakers of languages which do have articles, even though the rules for usage of articles may vary between such languages and lead to errors of their own:

> *I don't have pen.* * (omission of '*a*', common to speakers of languages including Farsi, Slavic and Arabic languages, which do not have an equivalent to '*a*')

> *I like the art.* * (overuse of '*the*', common to speakers of Latin languages before abstract nouns)

Another example of this is the distinction between the consonant sounds /l/ and /r/. While English and many western European languages have this distinction, a large number of languages worldwide do not, including entirely unrelated languages such as Japanese, Bantu languages of Africa, Korean and southern Chinese languages. This leads to a number of familiar errors:

> *I like /rɪsənɪŋ/ to music.* *

As we gain experience as language teachers, we become accustomed to many of the more common errors that our learners make. We are able to notice them, infer possible causes, and develop an instinctual awareness of how best to correct them, or whether to ignore them, recognising when a learner is likely to notice and respond to a correction and when they are not.

One of the inevitable implications of the influence of the first language on learners' English is that learners whose first language is more similar lexically, grammatically, phonologically or orthographically to English (e.g. French, German and Dutch) are likely to make fewer mistakes in English than learners whose first language is different in these respects (e.g. Japanese, Thai, Arabic), simply because fewer instances of first language influence on English turn out to be mistakes. Such similarities also mean that learners in the first of these two groups tend to make faster progress on average when learning English as a foreign language. In very general terms, speakers of Germanic and Latin languages, both of which are closely related to English, tend to be luckiest in this respect.

Extensive, practical information regarding the influence of learners' first languages on the use of English can be found in *Learner English* (Swan & Smith, 2001), a guide written specifically for language teachers – essential reading for CertTESOL trainee teachers!

Problematising the notion of 'error'
Before we finish this section on learner 'errors', you may have noticed the quotation marks I have sometimes used around this word. This is because a number of recent movements in language teaching theory and practice (such as the English as a lingua franca movement and the translingualism movement) have begun to question the meaning and validity of this word. We tend to presume that if language produced by learners diverges from that of native speakers, it is 'wrong', or 'erroneous'. However, recognising that English as a world language is no longer defined and controlled by native speakers of English (Widdowson, 1994) means that we should not necessarily presume that native speakers are authorities on what is right and what is wrong for non-native users. As such, it is argued that we should allow learners to decide whether they want to sound like native speakers, or simply to be understood before deciding what and how to correct. If their focus is primarily on being understood, it can be argued that the only 'errors' that should be corrected are those that impede understanding:

He live in London. (no interference with understanding – correction less important)

He /wɑks/ in London. (could be interpreted as 'works' or 'walks' – clarification required)

Learners' languages

> " Because our first language is used not only for communicative interaction but also to regulate our cognitive processes, it stands to reason that learners must necessarily rely on this language in order to mediate their learning of the L2. "
>
> Lantolf & Thorne, 2007, p.215

Contrary to the attempts of many approaches to language learning of the twentieth century (see 1.1. *Approaches to teaching* in Unit 1), learners are not, and can never be, blank slates. Attempts to mirror the process of child language acquisition with second language learning have never produced the same results, partly because it is impossible to replicate the environment and conditions of child language acquisition, and partly because of the prior resources that all learners (even children) bring to second language acquisition. This has important implications for teaching. While we do not need to be fluent in their prior languages (some may already be bilingual) to be able to teach them English (although the more a teacher knows about these, the more effectively she can teach such learners), we do need to acknowledge that these prior languages play an important role in all second language acquisition. This includes, but is not limited to, the following:

■ Difficult concepts are much easier to understand in our first language, so learners especially at lower levels of proficiency will benefit from accessing grammatical explanations in their first language whenever this is possible.

■ At lower levels of foreign language proficiency, most of us feel the need to think in our first language and translate our ideas, sometimes word-by-word into the language we are learning. As such, one of the most natural thoughts that language learners have is: *'How do I say 'X' in English?'*, where 'X' is a word in their first language (L1). While many teachers encourage learners to 'think in English', the reality is that it takes years to learn to do so. This natural phase of word-by-word translation is an important and useful intermediary stage that can help them to achieve this end goal, even if it does, at times, lead to some very original constructions in English! In fact, many learners will always have a need to translate words from one language to another, and they will find bilingual dictionaries and translation apps essential resources for helping with this.

■ Our choice of words, phrases and sentences is inevitably influenced by our first language, which leads not only to our choosing specific turns of phrase when using foreign languages, but also leads to errors that are often shared by speakers of the same first language. Understanding aspects of the structure of this language (e.g. features of the basic **syntax**) and features of its **phonology** (e.g. if it is tonal, like Cantonese or Thai) can help us to help our learners more effectively.

These observations are simultaneously grounded in sociocultural theory (Lantolf & Thorne, 2007), theorising in bilingual language teaching (Butzkamm & Caldwell, 2009), and the recent move to investigate ways in which the classroom can be more inclusive of the learners' prior languages (Cook, 2010). The implications for foreign language teachers are hopefully clear:

1   If you are teaching a class of learners who share their L1 and you don't speak it, you should work hard to learn this language as quickly as possible. You should also find out as much as you can about its grammar, phonology and lexis.

2   If you are teaching a classes of **multilingual** learners (as commonly happens in ELT environments in the UK, North America and Australasia), you should try to build up your general background knowledge of the most common first languages of learners in your classes. This doesn't mean trying to learn the languages, just familiarise yourself with the basics regarding their grammar, phonology and lexis. It will be of great use!

So how can we find out the basics regarding the grammar, phonology and lexis of our learners' first languages? The most useful resource for this is, once again, *Learner English*, (Swan & Smith, 2001), which provides reasonably short and fairly simple descriptions of learners' first language from the perspective of English language teaching.

The Trinity CertTESOL Learner Profile recognises the important influence of learners' first languages on both their English and the language learning process itself, which is why it requires you to analyse the features of your chosen learner's English in relation to this first language. This is discussed later in this chapter.

3.2   Learners' needs, priorities and motivation

In Unit 2 we looked at the content of language learning – the three features of the system (grammar, lexis and phonology) and the four skills (speaking, listening, reading and writing). We looked in some detail at how to teach aspects of each of these and even learnt a little bit about how learners are likely to learn them. When we talk about learners' needs in a generic sense, we can assume that most, if not all, need to study and practise using all of these elements, but that doesn't necessarily mean that they want to focus on all of these in their English lessons. Adult learners can obviously do some, possibly even a lot of learning independently of a teacher. So let's begin this section of the chapter with a provocative question:

Why do modern adult language learners need teachers or lessons at all? Especially in this day and age, when the Internet seems packed with language learning resources, free exercises, subtitled films and more reading than any individual could possibly expect to read in their lifetime.

Before reading on, spend a moment considering this question from a personal perspective. If you wanted to learn a foreign language (and hopefully you do), what would you need from a teacher to help you to learn it?

Let's ask several learners this very question: Why do you need a language teacher? Here are their answers. Note that all of the learners were on courses in private language schools in the UK:

Danijel (Serbian, intermediate/B1, general English student)

I can do many practices online but computer cannot answer my questions, and it cannot correct my mistakes, especially in grammar… My language, it is very much different from English in grammar, so I need teacher who explain very well, and then correct all my mistakes when I speak or I write something in English.

Dinah (Saudi Arabian, pre-intermediate/A2, general English student)

If you have very good teacher it makes motivation for study. This is important. I like teacher to organise and give student many works and practice for speaking and listening and writing… Reading less important to me.

Vinicius (Brazilian, advanced/C1, business English student)

I have no problem to understand colleagues at work or read emails in English, but I get a big frustration when I try to understand British, Indian or American people. The accents, and the speed, you know, it's so fast. I think a teacher is important to help with this – even if they are not native speakers, they can explain so you understand why it is difficult to understand all the accents in English, which is really useful for my work.

Marcia (Spanish, upper intermediate/B2, general English student)

Actually, to be honest, it's the class that I need more, less the teacher! Of course, the teacher is good, but I am so lazy so I never study at home. I came here to get the motivation, and to make friends with people who also study English. Together we have fun, we do mistakes and we learn from this, and this is most important for me.

Noriko (Japanese, advanced/C1, academic English student)

In my country we study the grammar a lot in school, but unfortunately we don't have speaking practice… there are so many students in the class and it is not normal in my culture for pupils to do conversation practice. So I think many Japanese people enrol for English classes to get this conversation practice and correction of their mistakes.

All of these learners would probably agree that they need practice of all four skills, and that they need to study lexis, grammar and phonology in order to learn English, but it's interesting to note what these learners have prioritised in their answers, because it is this that has caused them to enrol for English lessons:

- teachers can clarify tricky grammar and answer personal questions about grammar
- teachers can correct learners' mistakes when they practise using the language
- teachers can organise the learning and help to motivate learners
- teachers can help learners to decode and analyse the features of native speaker English
- the learning community can motivate learners to attend classes and study English and lets them know that they are not alone
- communicative lessons provide valuable opportunities for speaking practice, and correction

Motivation, organisation, explanation, practice and correction. These are perhaps the most consistent priorities in adult learners' reasons for going to English lessons. By providing these, we should be able to keep a class of learners happy, but we also need to do other things, such as create a social environment conducive to learning (see: *Developing rapport with classes of learners*, below), help them to develop their own ability to study independently of the teacher (see *Learner autonomy and learning strategies*, below). But we also need to find out about their individual needs, which may vary a lot, even in a **general English** class, and to do this we should conduct **needs analysis** assessment.

Needs analysis

As the above data from learners reveals, the simplest way to find out about learners' needs is to ask them. This constitutes perhaps our first objective when conducting needs analysis. However, it is also important to note that sometimes learners don't always know what they need. Just like doctors, who ask patients *'What seems to be the problem?'* before carrying out a comprehensive examination, language teachers should also examine learners' current skills, as well as their grammatical, lexical and phonological ability to build up a comprehensive picture of their needs. Such analysis is required for the Learner Profile on the CertTESOL. By doing this, we can find out exactly why they have chosen to enrol in a particular course, what their priorities are, and see if these coincide with their linguistic needs. We can also find out about their preferences and interests to ensure that we make our lessons as engaging for them as possible.

The most common means for conducting needs analysis in adult language teaching tends to be through a needs analysis questionnaire, which is usually accompanied by some kind of diagnostic language test (often called a **placement test**). Depending on the institute and the course, the needs analysis questionnaire may either be given to the learner for self-completion, or, as is usually preferable, completed by a teacher during an interview with the learner at the start of their course. In Section K.4 of *The Knowledge*, you will find a typical needs analysis questionnaire. Have a brief look at it now and do the *Pause for thought* task below:

Pause for thought

Look at the needs analysis questionnaire in The Knowledge *at the back of this book, and do the following:*

■ *Note how the questionnaire is organised, and where it attempts to find out about the learner's interests, priorities and perceived needs in language learning.*

■ *Look at the following description of an EFL learner from Korea and complete the first page of the questionnaire for her (copy it or use a pencil). If necessary, use artistic licence where the answers aren't given here!:*

Jin Hee Park is a 20-year-old Korean learner of English. She has recently arrived in London, after studying English at B2 level (upper intermediate) in Korea. Her spoken English is slow and careful as she doesn't like to make mistakes. Her listening is weaker. She speaks with a soft American English accent as she is very interested in American English and culture. She will be studying general English for another month, then she will be joining an exam class. Her 'official' long term plans, decided mainly by her parents are to study English language and literature at university in the UK, then to return to Korea to work as a translator. Her personal ambition is to be a travel journalist (and study journalism at university), but she hasn't told her parents yet.

When teaching a one-to-one lesson, needs analysis questionnaires of the type you have just looked at are essential, not only for building up an understanding of the learner, but also for planning the course of study that they will take. All good one-to-one teaching involves bespoke course preparation and teaching – a skill you will begin to learn about when you work on the Learner Profile (see later in this unit). When teaching a group of learners, the same information should inform our planning and teaching but must necessarily be balanced with the sometimes very different needs of other learners in the same class – which is perhaps one of the biggest challenges of teaching (see *Differences between learners* below).

Learner motivation

While there are many factors that affect success in language learning, it is likely that motivation is one of the most important, according to Zoltan Dörnyei, a leading authority on the topic (1998):

> *Motivation provides the primary impetus to initiate learning the L2 and later the driving force to sustain the long and often tedious learning process; indeed, all the other factors involved in L2 acquisition presuppose motivation to some extent. (p. 117).*

Not only are more motivated learners more likely to succeed in language learning, according to Rebecca Oxford, a leading authority on language learning strategies, *'more highly motivated learners use a significantly greater range of appropriate strategies than do less motivated learners'* (1990, p.13). In other words, the higher our motivation, the more effective and more successful we are as language learners. For this reason, understanding different types of learner motivation, why it often wanes during the language learning process and what role teachers can play in rekindling it are all an essential part of our job.

Early research into motivation identified a number of potentially useful motivating factors, presented below, that we are all likely to recognise in our own reasons for learning a language, or those of students we know. The first two ways of categorising motivation were developed by early researchers Gardner and Lambert (e.g. 1972), and the second two were proposed by Deci and Ryan (1985). Likely or typical examples of these are provided in Table 3.2.

Table 3.2:
Types of motivation

Type	Example
instrumental orientation	A desire to learn the language to achieve a practical goal (e.g. a Chinese learner who needs to pass an English exam to get onto a course at university in his home country).
integrative orientation	A desire to learn the language in order to interact and identify with others within a specific community (e.g. a Somalian refugee in the UK learning English in order to integrate into the local community).
extrinsic motivation	Motivation to do something not because of inherent interest in the activity, but because of external influences or future benefits (e.g. a learner who doesn't enjoy homework, but does it to perform better in the test tomorrow).
intrinsic motivation	Motivation to do something for the pleasure that accompanies the action (e.g. when a learner enjoys language learning, or being together in a learning community, like Marcia, earlier in this chapter).

A lot of this early research tended to identify integrative and intrinsic motivation as being more effective than instrumental or extrinsic, and, as a result, encouraged teachers to nurture them, perhaps through sparking interest in native speaker culture, or focusing on increasing enjoyment in the learning process. However, more recent research has uncovered a significantly more complex reality than either of these dichotomies was able to do justice to. We now know, for instance, that motivational factors are likely to gain and lose importance over time, even within a single lesson (Dörnyei & Skehan, 2003, p.121), and that success and motivation influence each other in a complex interdependent relationship. As Ellis & Larsen-Freeman put it:

Motivation is less a trait than a fluid play, an ever-changing one that emerges from the processes of interaction of many agents, internal and external, in the ever-changing complex world of the learner.

Ellis & Larsen Freeman, 2006, p.563

A more recent model, developed primarily by Dörnyei, called the L2 Motivational Self System (e.g. 2008) identifies three key influences on motivation during the process of learning a new language. I personally feel this model seems to better encompass many of the factors that influence my experience when learning a language than the dichotomies in Table 3.2 above (**L2** means the second language, English).

Table 3.3: Dörnyei's Motivational Self System		
1 ideal L2 self	The learner's (future) vision of him/herself as a successful (or unsuccessful) user of the language.	
2 ought-to L2 self	Qualities or attributes that the learner believes he/she should possess as a result of social pressure coming from the learner's environment (this includes the environment beyond the language classroom, such as the home).	
3 L2 learning experience	Situation-specific motivation that results from the immediate **learning environment** and experience, such as intrinsic enjoyment of an activity, or antipathy towards a test.	

According to Dörnyei, all of these sources of motivation can vary over time depending on a range of factors.

Pause for thought

Drawing on your own experience of learning languages, including at school, consider the following questions:

- *Which of the types of motivation shown in Tables 3.2 and 3.3 did you experience, or fail to experience?*
- *How did they affect your learning?*
- *Did they remain consistent, or change over time?*
- *What factors seemed to influence these changes?*

The extensive research that has been conducted into language learner motivation over the last 30 years has yielded disappointingly few practical recommendations for language teachers, although one useful exception to this can be found. Based on a survey of 200 Hungarian language teachers, Dörnyei and Csizér (1998) developed 10 macro strategies that they provocatively called 'The Ten Commandments for Motivating Language Learners', cited here with some additional notes in square brackets:

1 Set a personal example with your own behaviour.

2 Create a pleasant, relaxed atmosphere in the classroom.

3 Present the tasks properly.

4 Develop a good relationship with the learners.

5 Increase the learners' linguistic self-confidence [i.e. encourage them to believe in their own language ability].

6 Make the language classes interesting.

7 Promote learner autonomy.

8 Personalise the learning process [i.e. based on needs analysis, make the course relevant to each learner].

9 Increase the learners' goal-orientedness [i.e. help learners to identify appropriate and achievable goals in their language learning].

10 Familiarise learners with the **target language** culture [Given the rapid, recent evolution of English into a world language, the exact nature of 'target language culture' may have become somewhat more difficult to identify since this research was conducted.].

Dörnyei and Csizér, 1998, p.215

While most of these constitute what we might call 'common sense best practice', it's interesting to note that strategies 2 and 4 (and arguably others) relate directly to what language teachers often call **rapport** in the language classroom. Let's look at this now.

3.3 Developing rapport with classes of learners

One of the features most commonly commented on by trainee teachers when they observe the classes of effective experienced language teachers is what we might call 'classroom rapport'. By this, we mean the relationship between the teacher and the learners, including the friendship between the two parties, the trust the learners have in their teacher, and the knowledge that the teacher seems to have about the learners' emotional state and thoughts at any stage in the lesson. Contrast such a lesson with one of a less capable teacher who does not have the same rapport, and you are likely to agree – developing an effective rapport with learners is an essential teaching skill, valued highly by experienced teachers (Kassabgy et al. 2001), yet it is also perhaps one of the most difficult to 'teach' to trainee teachers.

Pause for thought

*If possible, watch a video of a class of an experienced language teacher (e.g. on YouTube). Make notes on any **soft skills** that contribute to improving the rapport within the learning community. How many of these are 'teaching-specific', and how many are transferable? Examples of these might include the use of learners' names, or praising positive achievement.*

The good news is that a large part of developing effective rapport is instinct, or some might say, common sense. It draws upon skills that most of us use on a daily basis to forge and maintain good working relationships with those around us. By being friendly, considerate, honest and working hard for our learners we can quickly build up the right kind of relationship that both fosters learning (as learners relax, gain faith in their teacher and enjoy themselves) and makes our lives as teachers easier. For this reason, it makes sense to work hard when you get a new class to build effective rapport with them. Table 3.4 shows some initial tips for how you can build rapport quickly with a new class of learners that you should find useful both on the CertTESOL and in your first teaching position.

Table 3.4:
Tips for building rapport
with new classes

What to do	Why?
1 Be very well prepared for your first lesson.	Your self-confidence will rub off on the learners; they will believe you know what you're doing. And obviously, first impressions count.
2 Get to the first lesson early, get yourself ready to begin and chat informally with the first learners who arrive.	This will calm your first-lesson nerves. It will calm theirs as well. Remember that learners are quite anxious when meeting a new teacher too!
3 Praise learners as genuinely as possible.	We can all spot false praise a mile off. Avoid exaggerating it, but whenever a learner does something praiseworthy, let them know how pleased you are, and try to be specific (e.g. *'Very clear pronunciation!'* rather than *'Excellent!'*).
4 Try to take a real interest in who they are, what they say and what they think.	There is something interesting in (nearly) everybody. By finding it, and finding out more about it, it's possible to quickly develop an individual rapport with each learner that can make both classroom discussions and individual chats much more meaningful.
5 Take the opportunity to chat informally with one or two learners after each lesson in your first week or two.	This will provide an opportunity for them to give informal feedback on how they (and possibly other class members) are finding you as a teacher. Ask simple questions like: *How was the lesson? Did you enjoy it?* Then probe any interesting leads.
6 Try to treat all learners equally…	Often, quiet learners get neglected by inexperienced teachers, but their needs and opinions matter as much as anybody's. They will appreciate you noticing them.
7 …but try to win over the class leaders.	This will make your job much easier! Such leaders are likely to lead on issues of praise and potential complaints.

Developing rapport with teenagers and children

Developing rapport with teenagers or children (often generically called **younger learners** in ELT) requires similar skills to building rapport with adults, however more patience is necessary, along with a little more control and consistency in your management of their behaviour. While the old saying of secondary school teachers at the start of the autumn term: 'Don't smile until Christmas!' is an exaggeration, it's a good idea to begin courses with teenage classes a little stricter than you would normally be, and then to relax as the rapport develops and the learners begin to trust you. With rooms full of younger learners, things can get quickly out of control if you don't set out some ground rules towards the start of a course, especially when you try to have fun with them, which you *can* do within clear routines and carefully negotiated rules!

Clear routines

Learners at primary and secondary ages tend to be used to routines, and if these are logical and consistent they often enjoy them and even find security in them. Here are some examples of appropriate routines for child and teenage learners, many of which encourage them to take responsibility, which can usually be increased as the class 'matures':

- Take the register, and share your intentions for the lesson consistently each day.
- Assign different 'monitor' roles each lesson. For example, a 'board monitor' (who cleans the white board/chalkboard), a 'homework monitor' (who collects in homework) and a 'resources monitor' (who hands out or collects in any resources used in the lesson).
- Organise **pairwork** and **groupwork** in similar ways each lesson, using familiar groupings that the learners are comfortable with.
- Give different roles to different learners for groupwork activities. For example: team secretary, team leader, group organiser, etc.
- Establish a clear system for rewards and sanctions.

There will of course be times and important reasons for departing from such classroom routines, so remember to explain these reasons to the learners whenever a departure takes place.

Clear rules

The number of predesignated rules appropriate for younger learner classes will depend on factors such as the size of the class, the maturity of the learners, how boisterous they are (which varies culturally) and even how much freedom you want to give the learners during activities. Perhaps counterintuitively, a teacher who wants to offer more freedom to learners for communicative activities will probably need more rules and will need to apply them more consistently than a teacher who offers less freedom to a similar class. One effective way to agree on rules of behaviour is to create a 'classroom contract' that both learners and teachers should abide by. This can involve negotiation with the learners and works particularly well with teenagers. A contract can be created as a class project towards the start of the course, and it can be displayed on the walls of the classroom for the duration of the course. If somebody breaks a promise on the contract, you can use it to elicit an apology, or provide a warning. Don't forget that if you break one of the promises on your side of the contract, you should also apologise and make up for this in future. Figure 3.1 shows an extract from an example classroom contract.

**Figure 3.1:
Example classroom
contract**

CLASSROOM CONTRACT - CLASS 4C

THE TEACHER

I agree to:

1. share lesson aims at the start of the lesson

2. be well prepared for every lesson

3. mark written work within three days

4. include at least one game in every lesson

THE LEARNERS

We agree to:

1. work together as a team and listen to each other

2. do our homework on time

3. ask questions if we don't understand something

4. learn 20 new words every week

3.4 Differences between learners

So far in this unit, we have noticed a number of differences between language learners, including differences between the generic level of different classes of learners, differences in how their prior language knowledge is likely to influence their English learning, and we have noticed how different learners prioritise different reasons for enrolling in English lessons. We have also focused in on the needs of a specific learner and reflected on how these can be evaluated and used to plan what we teach. Yet we haven't reflected on how the differences between individual learners affect what we do when teaching them as a group. Let's begin by looking some of the key differences and then we will move on to look at how we can best manage learning for a group of diverse individuals in the same class through a process called **differentiation**.

Within a typical group of adult English learners, differences in all the following areas are possible, and likely, even in a class at the same 'level':

1 age 2 personality 3 personal details (career, marital status, etc.) 4 interests and hobbies 5 knowledge about the world 6 values and beliefs	learner background
7 motivation for learning English 8 aptitude for language learning 9 prior learning history (including general education and English) 10 reasons for learning English 11 learning preferences (including preferred learning strategies) 12 ability in different areas of English (skills, lexicon, grammar, etc.)	the language learner

and in a class of multilingual learners we can also expect differences in:

13 L1 and other languages known 14 culture (including educational and classroom culture).	language and culture

Pause for thought

Before reading on, take a moment to consider what implications these differences have for how we should teach our learners as a group. Which differences are likely to have a positive effect on language learning, and which may make it more difficult for the teacher to provide for everyone's needs?

It is important to note initially that not all of these differences necessarily make them incompatible as a group of learners. Indeed, the fact that a class of multilingual learners do not share any other language than English is usually considered a significant advantage, because it forces them to communicate in English. The first six of these differences relate to what we might call learner background. In an English classroom these differences generally contribute to creating a colourful environment, involving information that learners can share (e.g. chatting about their interests, writing quiz questions for each other, etc.), differences that can create a dynamic rapport within a class of learners, or differences that can usefully fuel discussions and debates. And the final two differences, usually specific to multilingual classes, are likely to provide useful stimulus for communication in English, although they prevent teachers from making extensive use of the learners' L1.

The second group (7-12) relate to differences between the students as *learners*. Broadly speaking, differences in these areas are likely to increase the challenges that a teacher faces in ensuring that the needs and preferences of each learner are catered for. For example, learners who are more motivated are more likely to want more intensive instruction and more homework than those who are less motivated. Learners who have higher aptitude for an area of language learning (e.g. some learners pick up aspects of phonology very well, while others remember new vocabulary quickly) are likely to learn what we are teaching more quickly and become disengaged if we spend more time on an area of language for the sake of those who have lower aptitude in the area in question.

Balance

A number of these differences should be taken into account when planning our syllabus (such as the different interests in the class, or learners' reasons for learning English). However, because it is usually considered unrealistic to develop individual syllabi for groups of learners (and it rather defeats the object of putting them in a group), we should aim to achieve a careful balance – compromise even – to ensure that the syllabus content is as relevant as possible, and that the learning is as inclusive as possible for all the learners. For example, if all the learners in a specific group have expressed an interest in cinema, but only a few have an interest in cuisine, cinema gets priority in the syllabus. Or, if all the learners in a multilingual class are familiar and comfortable with a cafe as a context for a social English role-play, this would make a better setting than a pub, which some may not be familiar or comfortable with. Thus, balance can get us so far in our attempts to provide for the needs of all the learners in a diverse learning community.

Differentiation

However, while it is usually considered unrealistic to develop individual syllabi for learners in a group, there are a number of strategies and approaches we can adopt to make the learning content more relevant, more accessible and more tailored to the individual needs of learners in a group. Whenever we do this, and allow these differences to manifest themselves in a way that enables each learner to learn more effectively, we are *differentiating*, or allowing for *differentiated learning*. Let's look at some simple ways that we can differentiate in the language classroom, even if we intend to achieve broadly similar outcomes with the same group of learners:

Provide choice where possible

For example, we could organise a project in which learners select a personal topic or theme to focus on, or we could get learners to do mini-presentations (perhaps one a week) on their reasons for learning English. Alternatively, if a group of learners have particularly diverse needs with regards to grammatical challenges, we could introduce self-study periods into lessons when learners choose areas of language to focus on. If we are doing a jigsaw reading task, or a class debate, we can initially allow learners to choose which text they want to read, or which side of the debate they want to support, then negotiate if necessary to balance up any uneven groups.

Be flexible if possible

This is most likely to manifest itself in how learners prefer to do activities. For example, some learners may prefer to do a **controlled practice** activity individually, while others may prefer to do it in pairs. We can allow for this to happen either by making this clear in our instruction, or – with classes we know well – we can allow this to 'evolve' during a course of learning. Alternatively, for a global listening task, some learners may prefer to take notes in English as they listen, others may prefer to take notes in their first language, and others may prefer to close their eyes or stare up at the ceiling and focus on general understanding. Do, however, check with your TP tutor before giving differentiated instructions on the CertTESOL, as it can be difficult to do effectively.

Provide greater challenge for those who want it

If you notice either a significant difference in ability (this may be specific to one area of language use) or a difference in confidence or aptitude for language learning, you can allow for 'stronger' learners to be challenged more if they so desire. A common suggestion is to have backup activities for learners who finish an activity quickly to do while they are waiting. However, it can sometimes be time-consuming to plan supplementary activities, difficult to implement them in class and difficult to provide feedback. For this reason, I often prefer, especially with exercises that learners work on individually, to provide a slightly longer exercise (say 10 questions or sentences to complete) with the more challenging items at the end, and instruct learners to focus on the first five items only. As 'stronger' learners finish the first five items, they can be encouraged to work on the remaining ones. Feedback will then focus mainly on the first five items, and the 'stronger' learners can be nominated to feed back to the class on the more challenging items, thereby providing them with even more challenge. Alternatively, and very simply, for writing tasks, stronger learners can be encouraged to write more, or to achieve slightly more complex outcomes through a slightly different written instruction.

Provide more work for those who want it
If you find that you have learners who seem to be significantly more motivated to work harder in class, the simplest and most obvious way to keep them happy is to offer extra work for them to do in their free time. This may be in the form of free writing activities, self-study grammar exercises (which could be kept in a folder in the classroom), or opportunities to take on more responsibility (e.g. organising the end-of-term party, or searching on the Internet for an answer to a particularly difficult question, which they can then share with the class).

Learning styles?

One area of perceived learner difference not yet discussed is referred to generically as learning style. For some time a significant debate has simmered and occasionally raged regarding different models for describing learning styles and their impact on learning outcomes. The assumption is that a particular method or activity type is likely to suit certain learning styles (and therefore learners) more than others. If this is true, we need to be aware of this in our choice of methods and balance of activities, if necessary providing input and practice opportunities in a variety of different ways, to allow all learners to learn equally. However, the most objective and comprehensive reviews of the literature on learning styles have consistently failed to find a link between learning styles (including, for example, VAK, the Myers-Briggs Type Indicator, left brain/right brain differences, and the Kolb learning style inventory), choice of method and learning outcome (Coffield et al. 2004; Pashler et al. 2008). In other words, there is no evidence to support the idea that we need to teach the same learning content in different ways. Of course, this isn't saying that we should stop learners from trying to learn in different ways (preferred learning strategies), or that different learners don't enjoy different activities (personal learning preferences); given the influence of enjoyment on motivation and the importance of allowing learners individual agency, whenever possible, it makes sense to allow space for learners to choose activities and strategies that they prefer. However, whenever we are planning to do some 'whole class teaching' (e.g. presentations, explanations), one thing we don't need to worry about, at least on the weight of current evidence, is learning styles.

3.5 Learner autonomy and learning strategies

Learner autonomy, also called 'learner independence', refers to a learner's capacity to direct their own learning (Smith, 2008). As the main role of all teachers is to facilitate learning, one of the best ways we can do this is to help them to cultivate their own ability to learn independently of us. As such, learner autonomy is to some extent about teaching the learners to fish, rather than giving them fish! However, as Smith (2008) points out, before imposing any preconceived notions about how learners should study, we should engage with their existing autonomy and nurture it, mindful that a learner's preferences for how to study are likely to be influenced by, among other things, his/her age, nationality, culture and individual preferences (Oxford, 1992). Thus, rather than teaching them how to fish, we should attempt to understand how much fishing they are already doing, how effective their current fishing strategies are, and involve them in identifying ways in which they can make their own fishing more effective! As Rebecca Oxford observes:

> *A learning strategy cannot, a priori, be categorized as either good or bad. What makes a strategy positive for a given person? A strategy is useful if the following conditions are present: (1) the strategy relates well to the L2 task at hand; (2) the student employs the strategy effectively and links it with other relevant strategies for doing the task; and (3) the strategy coordinates with the student's general learning style preferences to one degree or another.*

Oxford, 2003, p.274

Pause for thought

Make notes on what you can do as a teacher to help learners develop useful learning strategies that meet the three conditions cited by Oxford. These may include suggestions relating to one of the three conditions only, or more general suggestions that will help learners with all three simultaneously.

While many teachers tend to conduct separate lessons on 'study skills' or 'self-directed learning', it is a good idea to also integrate reflection on learning strategies into the day-to-day teaching and learning process (Oxford, 1992), regularly cultivating learners' awareness of what we are doing and why, and encouraging them to reflect on what they learnt from it, how effective a particular activity or strategy was for them, and what, if anything, they would do to improve it. This helps them to develop an awareness of their learning that's likely to help them to **self-evaluate**, plan and organise their own study better in the future. This is known as **metacognitive awareness** and is a key feature shared by effective language learners (Oxford, 2011).

Here are a number of tips for helping you to help your learners to develop their metacognitive awareness and cultivate their learner autonomy. Some are appropriate for learners at all levels, and others will work better at higher levels of proficiency. Always be aware that these tips are also culturally dependent and will work better in some countries, schools and classes than others:

- Get learners to share language learning strategies and give them opportunities to try these out for homework.
- Get learners to evaluate their own learning at the end of each lesson or unit of study.
- Help learners to measure and notice their own progress and gain motivation from this.

- Involve learners in planning and organising classroom learning, for example, by getting them to prioritise elements from an upcoming unit or section of the syllabus.

- Empathise with learners' challenges in language learning and provide opportunities for them to discuss their challenges.

- Provide help with specific study skills, such as helping them to choose enjoyable and useful books to read and helping them to organise their vocabulary learning.

- Introduce them to apps and online resources for language learning that they can access and use independently of the teacher (e.g. Memrise, Macmillan Sounds, etc.).

- Encourage them to provide feedback on your teaching, whether this is informal discussions, quick Post-it notes, a feedback box or an end-of-course evaluation questionnaire – these all encourage learners to think carefully about the teaching process and its effect on their individual learning, as well as providing feedback that you can benefit from.

Perhaps the most important influence on our ability to help learners to cultivate effective study strategies is our own personal experience of using such strategies. Non-native speaker teachers, especially those who share their L1 with their learners, have important insights in this area that monolingual native speaker teachers do not share. They have been through the process of learning English, they recognise the challenges of the learners and are aware of what strategies were effective for them and how they helped. If they share the learner's L1, they will recognise the journey that learners have to take, empathise with the challenges on the way, and recognise how the L1 can facilitate learning the L2 (English). Hopefully, the implication for native speaker teachers of English is clear here – having experience in learning foreign languages will make you a more informed language teacher, and this is one of the reasons why Trinity allocates so much importance and devote a whole unit of the CertTESOL to the language learning experience (see Unit 5, *Experiencing learning*).

3.6 The Learner Profile

While there is some variation with regard to how different CertTESOL course providers administer different assignments, variations between course providers on the Learner Profile are fairly minimal due to quite specific guidelines from Trinity. As the assignment includes several stages, it is likely that your course provider will assign an **input session** or workshop to introduce you to it. They should also provide templates for the specific sections of the assignment, and will indicate approximate lengths for each section. Many course providers also make rooms or quiet spaces available for conducting interviews and one-to-one lessons. Figure 3.2 provides a summarised step-by-step overview of the assignment. The individual stages are discussed in more detail below.

Fig 3.2: Step-by-step overview of the Learner Profile	What to do	What to write in your assignment, and what to include in appendix
	1 Contact your learner and prepare for interview This should be someone reliable, ideally A2-B2 level, but not a relative. Select appropriate reading and listening texts. Prepare your questions, and writing task (if needed).	(nothing yet)

2 Interview your learner

Conduct one or more interviews (60-90 minutes in length). Discuss the learner's cultural and social background, his/her current use of English, reasons for learning English and likely future needs. Assess all four skills (reading, listening, speaking and writing) using pre-prepared texts for receptive skills and provide a writing task (unless you already have a sample of their writing).

Write:
Description of learner's background, future needs and preferences. Description of linguistic features of learner's L1. c. 15% of assignment.

Evaluation of learner's current linguistic proficiency, including all four skills, grammar, lexis and phonology. Include orthographic and phonemic transcription from interview. c. 50% of assignment.

Appendix:
Reading and listening texts. Example of learner's written English. Keep audio copy of interview.

3 Prepare the lesson
Based on the learner's needs, prepare a lesson plan including objectives, procedure and materials.

Write:
Reasons for choosing the lesson topic and content (rationale). Completed lesson plan.

4 Teach the lesson
Teach a one-to-one lesson to the learner, unobserved (45-60 minutes long).

Appendix:
Materials from the lesson.

5 Evaluate the lesson
Reflect on how the lesson went, and also compare teaching one-to-one and teaching groups.

Write:
Lesson evaluation and self-reflection. Lesson plan, rationale and evaluation constitute c. 20% of assignment.

6 Make recommendations
Make specific recommendations for five 45-minute lessons, based on the learning needs identified in Step 2, including lesson objectives and rationale.

Write:
Your recommendations in table format. c. 15% of assignment.
Bibliography.

Your Learner Profile should be presented in a folder including everything in the second column above. Pages should be numbered and there should be a Contents page at the front.

Let's now look at the key stages of the Learner Profile in more detail.

Conducting the Learner Profile interview

It's a good idea to choose a reliable learner who studies at the centre where you are taking your CertTESOL course because the learner in question will need to be present for both the interview and the lesson. Note that you are not allowed to choose a spouse or relative for the Learner Profile, and, if English is not your first language, Trinity recommends that you do not choose a learner who shares your L1, if possible. Be sure to organise a quiet room with a table and audio recording facilities for the interview. Remember to conduct some background reading about your learner's first language (e.g. *Learner English*, Swan & Smith, 2001) before the interview.

Interview checklist

During the interview, you should:

- ✓ Find out about the social and cultural background of the learner (age, nationality, first language, etc.), as well as their previous experience with learning English and how they use it at the moment.
- Find out about their interests, hobbies, and favourite activities in English lessons.
- ✓ Find out about their motivation for learning English and their perceived learning needs, including how they think they will use English in the future.
- Find out what challenges they have when using English, including specific difficulties with each of the four skills (reading, writing, speaking and listening).
- Record your interview so that afterwards you can analyse a sample of the learner's speech during natural conversation (not reading a text out loud).
- Get a sample of the learner's handwritten English. You may need to give a specific writing task for this. Keep the text for your assignment appendix.
- Notice and assess the learner's spoken interaction skills (for example, their speaking fluency, speaking accuracy, ability to communicate clearly, etc.).
- Notice and assess the learner's listening skills, both through their ability to understand you during the discussion and also through a listening comprehension task. Make a copy of the listening text tapescript for your assignment appendix.
- Provide the learner with a text and at least one appropriate reading task to enable you to assess the learner's silent reading skills. Keep the text for your assignment appendix.
- IMPORTANT: At the end of the interview, explain that you will prepare a one-to-one lesson for them. If possible, arrange a day and time for this lesson now, and stress the importance of it to the learner.

> *It's really important to make your learner feel at ease during the Learner Profile interview. They may be nervous at first, so get them talking about familiar topics and find out about their interests. This will give you plenty to work from when you analyse their speaking and writing skills.*
>
> Eva, CertTESOL trainer

Writing up your analysis of the learner

Description of the learner's background

The description of the learner's background should constitute about 15% of your total Learner Profile. Include details about the learner's cultural and social background, language learning experience, occasions when the learner currently uses English, reasons for learning English and contexts in which she/he is likely to use English in the future. Also include a description of the important linguistic features of the learner's L1.

Evaluation of the learner's current linguistic proficiency

The most extensive single section of the assignment is the evaluation of the learner's current linguistic proficiency based on data collected during the interview. It should constitute about 50% of your total Learner Profile, and must cover strengths and weaknesses in all four skills, and should make explicit reference to aspects of grammar, lexis and phonology, also making reference to the learner's L1 where relevant.

Receptive skills (reading and listening)

Trinity makes the following recommendations for writing up your analysis of the learner's reading and listening skills, suggesting about half to one page of A4 on each:

- indicate tasks set to assess these skills during the interview and describe how the learner responded to the tasks
- discuss the learner's general habits for reading and listening, in both L1 and English (this might include accessing news websites and blogs for reading, YouTube and TV shows for listening)
- describe any advice you provided for helping the learner to develop these skills
- for listening only, indicate the learner's ability to understand and respond to you appropriately during the interview

Speaking skills

Trinity requirements are quite specific here. First provide an initial introduction summarising the learner's general ability (e.g. fluency, communicative clarity, etc.) and key strengths and weaknesses. This must be followed by sections on the learner's phonology, grammar and lexis based on a transcription of an extract from the learner's natural speech, a task which constitutes probably the biggest challenge of the assignment. First you should write down in standard written English exactly what the learner says for approximately one minute of the interview (including mistakes), and then you should transcribe a 20-30-word segment of this (or several multi-word segments) into phonemic script. First transcribe it as it would be spoken in a 'standard' English accent, and then transcribe it exactly as the learner says it, so that differences between the two can be noticed. Trinity recognises that some of the sounds the learner produces may not be in the English phonemic set; try to find the closest equivalent if not. One of the skills to this part of the assignment is choosing a suitable stretch of the learner's speech which will provide enough fodder for the required error analysis, discussed below.

Here is an example orthographic and **phonemic transcription** for a pre-intermediate Turkish student called Ahmed:

Line	Orthographic transcription
1	I like in London. I go to cinema sometime – central London. I go with brother... London.
2	(unintelligible) I have two brother, the first one is name Ake, other is Tarik. But Tarik no in
3	London. He live Turkey. You went to Turkey?... If you like natural you can go to the north, many
4	nice place, and the weather is cool.

Phonemic transcription of how Ahmed said this (pauses in speech are indicated by spaces):

Line 1:   /aɪˈɡɒtuː ˈsɪnɪməsʌmtaɪm sentrəlʌnˈdɒn/

           I go to cinema sometime – central London.

Line 2:   /aɪhævtuː ˈbrʌdæ dəˈfɜːswʌnɪzneɪmˈæke/

           I have two brother, the first one is name Ake...

Line 3-4: /ɪfjuː ˈlaɪkˈnætʃrəl juːkæˈɡɒtuːdəˈnɒt meninaɪsˈpleɪs/

           If you like natural you can go to the north, many nice place...

To practise your phonemic transcription skills, try transcribing the same lines into a standard accent. Have a look at the **Pause for thought Key** *[18] to see how it would look in standard British pronunciation.*

Once you have completed your orthographic and phonemic transcription, you should then proceed with the analysis of phonological and grammatical/lexical errors from the transcriptions in table form. Examples of these are provided below, using the same Turkish student, Ahmed. Your course provider will provide a template for the tables that will be slightly different from those provided here.

Phonological error analysis

This should include at least two segmental errors (focusing on individual sounds) and two suprasegmental errors (focusing on features longer than the syllable, such as word stress and **intonation**) from the phonological transcription:

Line ref.	Student's utterance	Phonemic transcription	Description and cause of error	Correct utterance or transcription
1	I go to (the) cinema.	/aɪ gɒ tuː ˈsɪnɪmə/	Ahmed has used /ɒ/ instead of /əʊ/ probably because the /əʊ/ sound does not exist in Turkish, so Ahmed uses the closest sound /ɒ/. He also omitted *'the'*.	/aɪ gəʊ təː ðə ˈsɪnɪmə/
1	central London	/sentrəlʌnˈdɒn/	Ahmed has stressed the end of the word, replacing the /ə/ with a stronger /ɒ/. Final syllables are often stressed in Turkish.	/ˈsentrəl ˈlʌndən/

Spoken grammar and lexical error analysis

According to the Trinity syllabus, you should analyse between four and eight lexical and grammatical errors included in the orthographic transcription (individual course providers may have additional requirements). You may be able to explain some of the errors through your knowledge or background reading of the learner's first language. If this is not possible, an educated guess is acceptable. Note that some errors are likely to include both lexicogrammatical features as in the first example:

Line ref.	Student's utterance	Description of error	Possible cause of error	Correct utterance
2	the first one is name Ake	Wrong choice of verb. Passive voice incorrectly formed.	In many languages, the verb 'name' is used in such constructions. Turkish may be one of these. Ahmed has not yet learnt the passive voice in English, and rules for passive constructions differ from Turkish.	the first one is called Ake
2	other is Tarik	Omission of definite article *'the'*.	Turkish does not have definite articles. However, Ahmed uses one in a similar context in the previous phrase. He may be in the process of acquiring this area of grammar, applying the rule inconsistently.	the other is Tarik

Writing skills

Using the text obtained from the learner during the interview, analyse it with regard to the following two areas:

Part A grammatical accuracy, lexical range and accuracy, spelling and punctuation

Part B effective communication of meaning, appropriacy of register, organisation and handwriting

By 'register', we mean how formal and appropriate to the **genre** the text is. It is only necessary to analyse handwriting if the learner's L1 uses a different writing system. Remember that you should include both the original text from your learner (make a copy before you add any annotations) and a corrected version in your assignment appendix. Number the lines of the corrected text for easy reference.

Written error analysis

Your analysis of the learner's writing skills should also include an analysis of four to eight specific errors from the text using a tabular format as follows:

Line ref.	Student's written sentence	Description of error	Possible cause of error	Correct sentence
7	My family has two house.	Singular noun used instead of plural.	In Turkish, plurals are not necessary after numbers.	My family has two houses.
12	My brother's work is an engineer.	Misuse of *'work'* as a noun.	Ahmed is not aware that we use *'job'*, not *'work'* as the noun, possibly caused by the same word root used in his L1 for both the verb and the noun.	My brother works as an engineer.

Preparing and teaching the one-to-one lesson

Based on your evaluation of the learner's needs and interests and his/her strengths and weaknesses with using English, select appropriate **objectives** for the one-to-one lesson. A typical lesson might involve a combination of one or two skills and one or two grammatical, lexical or phonological areas. It is not appropriate to plan only to correct errors noticed in your learner analysis. Your course provider may request you use a specific lesson plan pro forma for this, which may be the same as the pro forma used for general English lessons.

You are usually expected to teach this lesson with little prior guidance on how to teach one-to-one classes. However, there are plenty of similarities between one-to-one lessons and group classes, and many differences are fairly commonsensical. Because you have only one learner, the lesson turns into more of a dialogue or conversation, and you can expect them to ask many more questions than you might expect from a learner in a group lesson. Here are some tips for preparing and teaching this lesson:

- Don't be too ambitious with your objectives – aim to achieve just one or two, and have backup activities just in case you achieve these objectives early.

- Let the learner know at the start that it's okay for him/her to interrupt you or ask questions at any point, especially if something isn't clear.

- Both parties can feel a little nervous at the start of a first one-to-one lesson, so begin with an informal chat or discussion activity to break the ice.

- While some teachers prefer to use a board in one-to-one lessons, you may find that pen and paper are more useful. Position a notepad between you and the learner, and use this as your 'board'. Make sure you keep your 'boardwork' as clear as you would do in a group class. The advantage of doing this on paper is that both of you can take away a copy at the end of the lesson, which is particularly useful for your assignment.

- Some learners can feel nervous about speaking in a one-to-one lesson. When you give them a speaking task, make it clear when you want them to begin and then 'pull back' and wait. Don't interrupt. They will ask you if they haven't understood the task.

- One-to-one lessons often have many tangents that will take you away from your planned lesson. Bear this in mind when you are planning, and be flexible during the lesson. It is often these tangents that the learner finds most useful.

- Try to have the opportunity to run over timewise at the end of the lesson. For example, if you've planned for 45 minutes, book the room and the learner for one hour.

- Don't panic if you don't get through everything you planned by the end. This is your first one-to-one lesson and you are not expected to have mastered this lesson type. But make sure you address this in your lesson evaluation in the assignment itself.

After the lesson you will need to complete a lesson evaluation and self-reflection for your assignment, in which you explain the rationale for your lesson, evaluate how well it went and reflect upon significant differences that you noticed between teaching group classes and one-to-one lessons, providing examples as appropriate. It's a good idea to do the self-evaluation soon after the lesson (or at least take some initial notes), and make sure you take away copies from the lesson of anything that would be useful for completing your assignment. For example, if you used the board or a notepad, take photos or photocopies respectively of what was written. Obviously you will need to put copies of the materials used with the learner in your assignment appendix.

Making recommendations for further study

Based on everything you have learnt about the learner, you should devise a scheme of work (this is basically a syllabus for specific lessons in a course) for five 45-minute lessons, and record details of these lessons in a table as in the example below. Note that grammatical, lexical and phonological focuses for all five lessons should be identified along with specific skills objectives. You should also provide a brief summary describing your reasons for choosing the lesson objectives and topics in question, drawing on your learner analysis earlier in the assignment.

Lesson no.	1	2
Functional/ structural objectives	To improve Ahmed's ability to use singular and plural noun forms appropriately.	To enable Ahmed to use common passive structures in English (e.g. *he's called…*).
Skills objectives	To develop reading skills using a text on statistics. To develop speaking skills describing facts about Turkey.	To develop writing skills, writing a short text about his family. To develop intensive listening skills through a short dictation activity.
Phonological objectives	To improve his ability to pronounce the three regular plural endings in English (/s/, /z/, /ɪz/).	To improve his ability to recognise and produce contracted forms of the verb 'to be' (*It's, We're,* etc.)
Lexical objectives	To increase vocabulary relating to shopping and markets (stall, barter, etc.).	To revise and add to Ahmed's active lexicon for describing family members.
Rationale	Ahmed often tends to forget to use plural forms, despite knowing how to form them.	Ahmed is often reluctant to contract the verb 'to be', and he makes frequent mistakes with certain passive structures (e.g. *I born in…*).

Passing the Learner Profile assignment

Course providers develop their own criteria for marking this assignment (although they are moderated by Trinity). These criteria should be available to trainee teachers, so ask if you haven't received a copy of them before beginning your assignment. Many course providers mark the different sections of the assignment separately, and you may be required to hand in the learner analysis section separately from the lesson plan, lesson evaluation and recommendations for further study. Other course providers require trainees to provide a first draft of the whole assignment, which is discussed before submission of the final draft.

Here is a set of example criteria that would be appropriate for this assignment:

Successful trainees will demonstrate:
1 The ability to compile an accurate profile of the learner, including relevant background details, reasons for learning English and specific learning needs and identifying the learner's perceived challenges when using English.
2 The ability to assess the learner's strengths and weaknesses with regard to the four skills (reading, writing, speaking and listening), as well as strengths and weaknesses with regard to grammar, lexis and phonology in English, including analysis of errors in all these areas and indication of possible causes.
3 The ability to prepare and teach a lesson appropriate to the learner's profile and needs, including appropriate resources, a clear rationale for choice of lesson objectives and content, and an honest, insightful self-evaluation of the strengths and weaknesses of the lesson.
4 The ability to compile appropriate recommendations for five 45-minute lessons, including relevant skills as well as aspects of grammar, lexis and phonology, providing a rationale for each lesson choice.
5 The ability to use clear, coherent English, not impeded due to ambiguity caused by misspelling, poor use of punctuation, grammar or aspects of discourse.

Some final tips

■ Your course provider may make available examples of past Learner Profile assignments. If they do, read at least one of these before you begin, to familiarise yourself with the structure of the assignment and what is required of you.

■ If possible, get your learner's contact details as soon as she/he has agreed to participate. This makes it easier to stay in touch and if, by chance, you forget to do anything during the interview or the lesson, you can always do this afterwards.

■ Make sure your writing sample has sufficient errors for analysis. If you are providing the task yourself, make sure it's fairly challenging, and if the learner is providing the sample, check it's got enough errors for you to work with.

■ As this assignment has many stages, and a large number of specific requirements, perhaps the most important tip is to check that you have done everything, and done it as required. In this regard, it's a good idea to check through everything carefully when finished, comparing it with the instructions you have received and any past Learner Profiles that have been provided as examples.

■ This is a complex assignment and it's okay to ask for guidance at different stages. If you don't understand anything, or are not sure about how to do part of the assignment, ask your co-trainees first, and if they don't know, you have a good reason for asking your tutors.

Review of Unit 3
Understanding learners

True or false

Decide if each of the statements below is true or false. Correct the false ones.

1 The Common European Framework describes different levels of coursebook.

2 Needs analysis questionnaires are used to test learners' English before starting a language course.

3 Highly motivated learners use more effective learning strategies than less motivated learners.

4 Younger learners usually prefer to have predictable routines during lessons.

5 All teachers need to provide different activities to cater for different learning styles in their classes.

6 A learner's capacity to manage and control their own learning is referred to as 'learner autonomy'.

7 For the Learner Profile, you will have to interview a learner, then prepare and teach a one-to-one lesson to this learner.

8 You should choose a reliable learner for your Learner Profile, but you cannot choose a family member.

9 Your TP tutor will observe your Learner Profile lesson.

10 The final stage of the Learner Profile assignment requires you to summarise the content of five future lessons with your chosen language learner.

If you need to, check your answers in the *Review Key* at the back of this book.

Now return to the learning opportunities provided at the start of the chapter. Check off the ones that you feel you have achieved and reread the relevant sections for any you're not sure about.

unit 4 Understanding and using materials

❝ Start thinking about your Materials Assignment as soon as you can. Reflect upon the effectiveness of the materials you use and consider the specific objectives of each activity. Think about how you could adapt them or create similar materials for your assignment. ❞

Dylan, CertTESOL trainer

Learning opportunities

This unit will help you to...

- understand the relationship between materials and language learning
- identify the specific objectives behind a set of materials
- evaluate off-the-shelf coursebooks
- become familiar with five different types of coursebook
- understand what resources are included in a published 'course'
- learn about the requirements of the Materials Assignment
- analyse and assess an example written Materials Assignment
- find out about the typical procedure for the spoken interview
- understand how the questions in the interview relate to the assessment criteria
- develop your own ideas for making and adapting materials

Introduction

Materials are the written resources that teachers use in class. The two most obvious examples are the coursebook and handouts. Materials can provide information about language, texts for skills practice, exercises, instructions or serve as prompts for communicative activities. Unit 4 of the Trinity CertTESOL requires trainees to create their own materials, use them in class and then evaluate the success of their materials afterwards. Unlike the other units of the CertTESOL, Unit 4 is assessed directly by the external **moderator**, not by your course tutors, although the tutors can provide guidance when choosing your materials and completing the Materials Assignment.

4.1 The role of materials in language learning

Let's look at a few examples of materials and how they help students to learn English. Notice how all of the examples below correspond to a specific activity and objective:

Type	Specific objective
Nine written statements or topics that learners read. They then listen to a conversation and identify which statements or topics are discussed.	To practise listening skills (listening for global understanding).
A list of words in three columns that learners must match to form expressions that they heard in a listening activity.	To help learners to notice useful vocabulary from the listening activity (verb-noun **collocations**).
A grammar explanation followed by examples and a **gap-fill** exercise.	To raise learners' awareness and provide **controlled practice** of an area of grammar.
A set of cartoons showing people breaking rules.	To provide learners with speaking practice describing the situations.
A list of three discussion questions.	To practise learners' speaking skills, giving their opinions on laws and rules in their country.

Table 4.1:
Examples of classroom materials and activities

Any of the above material types could have additional uses. For example, the nine statements in the first activity could include examples of grammar that learners study in a subsequent activity, or the gap-fill exercise could revise some useful vocabulary that learners need for a speaking activity later in the lesson. If we imagined that the above examples of materials were oriented around the theme of 'rules and laws', they could possibly be included in a course book in the same order as in Table 4.1 (as shown in the extract on page 151):

4.2 Coursebooks

A coursebook is basically a large set of ready-made learning materials stuck together in a particular order. The order reflects a learning syllabus that has been divided up into interlinked sections called 'units', 'modules' or 'files'. Each unit will normally introduce and provide practice of new language (grammar, vocabulary, **functional language**) as well as providing learners with practice in the four skills and opportunities to revise previous learning. Coursebooks are designed for use in a language classroom with a teacher present, unlike **self-study resource books**.

Most ELT coursebooks are generic commercial products. They are written for the widest possible range of teaching contexts, whether that be an Egyptian teacher teaching a **monolingual** class of Arabic speakers on an academic year course in Cairo or an Irish teacher teaching a **multilingual** class in a summer school near Dublin. The coursebook needs to fit both these contexts and many more, so it will have a number of characteristic features:

■ There will rarely be any definable 'lessons', because lesson length can vary between schools.

■ They are written for both monolingual and multilingual classes, so they are usually English-only and will tend to avoid translation activities.

LISTENING

You are going to hear three conversations about rules at work.

A Before you listen, work in pairs. Discuss these questions:
- Why do you think companies have the rules below?
- Do you think they are sensible and fair?

1 Women have to wear skirts or dresses at work.
2 We have to go outside to smoke.
3 We have to agree holidays with our boss. We can't take time off when we want.
4 We have to ask the admin assistant to make photocopies for us. We can't just do them ourselves.
5 We have to take our breaks at set times.
6 We have to wear a hard hat at all times.
7 We can't surf the web on company computers.
8 We can't call mobile phones from the office.
9 We can't talk to each other while we're working.

B ♫ 5.3 Listen and decide which of the rules in exercise A they talk about in each conversation.
Conversation 1 ......
Conversation 2 ......
Conversation 3 ......

C Work in pairs. Match the words used in the conversations. Then listen to check your answers.

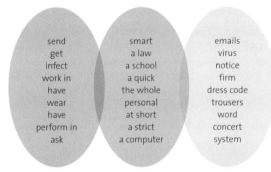

send	smart	emails
get	a law	virus
infect	a school	notice
work in	a quick	firm
have	the whole	dress code
wear	personal	trousers
have	at short	word
perform in	a strict	concert
ask	a computer	system

D Do you think the rules in exercise B are fair? Why? / Why not?

GRAMMAR Talking about rules

We sometimes use *be allowed to* instead of *can* to talk about permission. We use *be supposed to* and *should really* instead of *have to*, especially when the rules are often broken.

··

They have a strict dress code – woman *aren't* even *allowed to wear* smart trousers.
You're not supposed to use the company computers.
You should really arrange time off with me a month in advance.

A Choose the correct form in *italics*.
1 Sorry, *you're not allowed to / you don't have to* smoke in here. Can you go outside please?
2 *I'm supposed to / I don't have to* have my ID at all times, but nobody ever asks me for it!
3 I *can't / have to* start really early some days, but at least I *have to / I'm allowed to* go home early.
4 You're *supposed to / allowed to* dress smartly, but no one's said anything when I've worn jeans.
5 *We are supposed to / We are allowed to* belong to a trade union, but our manager doesn't really like it when we do.
6 We *shouldn't really / don't have to* come out here on the roof of the building, but it's a really nice place to have a break!
7 I know *I'm allowed to / I should really* turn off my phone before I come in, but I'm expecting a really important call!
8 *You can't / You're not really supposed to* eat or drink in the classroom, so please tidy everything up after you finish your coffee.

B What rules are being broken in the pictures?

C Work in pairs. Discuss these questions. Use *should / shouldn't really* and *(not) supposed to* where appropriate.
- Are there any rules where you work / study which you do not like? Do you follow them?
- Are there any laws in your country that people often break? How do you feel about that?
- Are there any other rules or laws you would like to see introduced at work / school / in your country?

▶ Need help? Read the grammar reference on p. 144

- Culture will be fairly international, meaning that regional accents will be slight, **non-standard forms of English** will be rare and they will avoid content that may be unfamiliar or controversial in some parts of the world (e.g. alcohol, religion or politics).

On your Trinity CertTESOL course, you will have an opportunity to work with a **general English** coursebook, but there are other types which tend to correspond to the different types of English that are taught. As well as the most common examples given below, there are also coursebooks for more specific fields of **ESP (English for specific purposes)**, including medical English, English for law and even English for teaching.

Type	Example titles	Who are they for?
general English coursebooks	Cutting Edge, English File, Headway, Total English, Inside Out	adult learners who need general English without a specific focus
business English coursebooks	Market Leader, Business Result, Business Advantage	adult learners who need English specifically for work
younger learner coursebooks	Kid's Box, Let's Go, Primary Colours, Chatterbox, Tiger Time	children and teenagers
exam class coursebooks	Oxford Trinity GESE, First Certificate Gold, Step Up to IELTS, Longman Preparation Course for the TOEFL Test	learners who are preparing to take an English language exam, such as GESE, ISE, IELTS, FCE or TOEFL
EAP (English for academic purposes)	Collins' Academic Skills, English for Academic Study, Oxford EAP	future or current undergraduate and graduate students studying in English

Pause for thought

Look at coursebook extracts A-D below. For each one, answer questions 1–3:

1   What type of coursebook is it? (choose from the five categories above, excluding general English)

2   What features make it appropriate for the learners it is aimed at?

3   What is the objective of the activity?

Check your answers in the **Pause for thought Key** [19]

Extract A

Study tip
When reading a text, many ideas on a topic may be presented. It is important to identify the importance of the ideas to the field in general. It is also important to recognize language that either supports or contradicts the ideas.

6 Match each theory (1–3) to an explanation of its importance (a–c).

1 the work of Lombroso
2 body-type studies
3 labelling

a These studies, whilst well known, have been shown to have little or no connection with the causes of crime.

b This work was important, as it formed some of the early basis for studying biological causes of crime.

c This theory is an important environmental study of the causes of crime, but so far has not been proven to be true.

Extract B

Try it first!

1 Before you study this section, try developing the theme of the previous section into the more abstract area of travel and tourism in general. Work in pairs. One person is the examiner, the other is the candidate. Here are some suggestions for questions from the examiner.

● Why do you think tourism is so popular and still increasing in popularity?
● Do you think people always get what they were hoping for on holiday?
● Why is tourism so important to some economies?
● What environmental problems can be caused by tourism?
● What can be done to reduce these environmental problems?

Extract C

Listening

2 (((11.1))) **Listen to a conversation between John Fletcher in London and Hina Sato in Tokyo in which they discuss arrangements for a visit by a senior executive. Decide if these statements are true (T) or false (F).**

1 The speakers use modal verbs like *could* and *may* to sound more formal.
2 Hina manages to slow John down.
3 Hina tells John when she doesn't understand something.
4 Hina asks for confirmation of the new arrangements by e-mail.

Extract D

Extracts from:
Delta Academic Objectives Reading Skills by Louis Rogers and Emma Kuhles © 2011 Delta Publishing;
IELTS Advantage Speaking and Listening Skills by Jon Marks © 2013 Delta Publishing;
Heads Up Level 2 by Mark Tulip, Louise Green and Richard Nicholas © 2015 Delta Publishing;
Practice and Pass Movers by Cheryl Pelteret and Viv Lambert © 2010 Delta Publishing.

2 **Look and write the words.**

buy   catch   drives   fly   ride   sail

1 My dad   _drives_   a car.
2 You can .... the bus outside the bus station.
3 We .... across the sea on a boat.
4 We .... to Australia in a plane.
5 Does your dad .... a motorbike?
6 You .... a ticket at the station.

drive + car, bus, lorry
ride + bike, horse, motorbike

Remember!

Coursebooks are often called simply 'courses' by publishers, as they usually consist of a range of books, video and audio files and online resources, of which the coursebook that the learners use in class (more correctly called the Student's Book) is the central item. Let's look more closely at what's available in most courses:

Resource	Who gets it?	What's in it?
Student's Book	the students	The Student's Book includes core lesson materials that learners study in class with the teacher. It's arranged into units with review sections throughout. At the back there will usually be listening 'tapescripts', grammar and vocabulary reference sections and sometimes further exercises.
Teacher's Guide	the teacher	The Teacher's Guide includes suggested lesson planning guidance for use with the Student's Book, including useful unit introductions, suggested procedure and all the answers to activities in the Student's Book. At the back you may find extra photocopiable resources for vocabulary, grammar or communicative activities and usually some tests based on the course content (although these are now often in the teacher E-resources).
Workbook (often with CD Rom or Student's Audio CD)	the students	In the Workbook you will find extra activities based on the Student's Book which are usually given for homework. Some versions have an answer key at the back.
Class Audio CD	the teacher	The Class Audio CD includes all the recordings for the Student's Book listening activities.
E-resources including CD ROM, interactive software, online resources, IWB materials and even apps for learners	the teacher and the students (depends on the resource)	E-resources tend to vary between courses. Some include a Teacher's CD ROM where editable tests and other printable resources are found. Others have extra resources on the coursebook website. Many also have online activities for the learners or downloadable apps (e.g. pronunciation chart, vocabulary games, progress tests) for mobile or tablet. Likely to develop more in the future, with some learning courses going completely online.
Video materials	usually the school	Short programmes or episodes in a series that often link loosely to the Student's Book units. On some courses this is now integrated with the Class CD or E-resources.

Given this wealth of resources in each course, it may seem surprising that most experienced teachers supplement this with their own materials or materials from other resource books. However, as mentioned above, because coursebooks and the syllabi they follow are generic, they will never provide the perfect balance of learning activities for any group of learners, nor for their needs as individuals. So the teacher must play an active role in adapting, supplementing, replacing, rearranging or even leaving out activities in the coursebook to create a series of cohesive lessons that fit the length of the course their learners are on. Being able to do this is critical to facilitating effective learning, and this is why Trinity requires all graduates of the CertTESOL to demonstrate the ability to create, use and evaluate their own materials.

4.3   The Materials Assignment

While many CertTESOL courses allow trainees to make use of materials from coursebooks or their own 'in-house' materials, others require their trainees to create all their own materials during their CertTESOL course. There are advantages to both approaches. While the learning curve is often steeper when you are creating your own materials, what you learn will help to prepare you for the Materials Assignment later in the course. The assignment focuses on one piece of material and a specific task you use it with in your assessed teaching practice lessons. You will either have to create these materials from scratch or adapt coursebook materials to: *'show evidence of imaginative and significant adaptation and exploitation of these'* (Trinity CertTESOL Syllabus).

There are two parts to the assignment – a completed pro forma of about 500 words and an interview with the course moderator where you expand on what you wrote on the pro forma. In both, you will be assessed on your ability to explain:

- why you created or adapted a certain set of materials for the class
- how effective they were in relation to your aims
- what you would/could do to improve them for future use

Remember that the materials assignment is *not* about creating perfect materials. It's about learning from your experience developing and using these materials. You should choose the materials for one activity only and talk primarily about the materials rather than the activity – your focus is always on the role of the materials in getting the learners to do what you want them to do. And if you've adapted them from published materials, you must acknowledge this by sourcing them (Harvard referencing format) clearly on the materials themselves as in the following example:

Oxenden, C. and Latham-Koenig, C. (2010). *New English File: Advanced Student's Book.* Oxford, UK: Oxford University Press.

Look back at the example activities in the coursebook extract on p.151 above. Which of them could most easily be adapted for the Materials Assignment? Which would you choose and why?

Compare your ideas with the suggestions in the **Pause for thought Key** *[20] at the back of the book.*

Completing the Materials Assignment pro forma

The assignment pro forma is a standardised document provided by Trinity. It should be completed carefully in line with the rubric (instruction) provided. The completed pro forma below is provided to exemplify a typical assignment and should not be considered a 'model' answer. In total there are three pages. You should write about 500 words for the second and third pages (called *the rationale* and *the evaluation* respectively). There is no word limit for the first page, but keep it clear and brief.

1st page

Number of learners:	14
Level of class:	Pre-intermediate (A2)
Monolingual/multilingual class – state majority language(s)	Multilingual – Chinese, Arabic, Turkish, Spanish
Type of material:	Two images of different cities with task instruction and extension question.
Type of activity:	Speaking activity, comparing images.
Point in lesson when used, noting preceding and subsequent activity:	It was the final activity of the lesson. It came after controlled practice of comparative adjectives, and before the lesson conclusion.

'A2' is the CEFR level.

Your two options here are monolingual or multilingual.

This should correspond to your lesson plan for the lesson in question.

Please show your word count for the rationale and the evaluation, excluding the Trinity rubric. The word count for the rubric is 143 words.

Try to make full use of the word count.

Word count: 478

2nd page

Rationale

Note the word 'linguistic'. Stick to aims related to systems (grammar, lexis, phonology) or skills practice.

What was the linguistic purpose of this material? What were the objectives for the learners' language development?

> To provide the students with an opportunity to use comparative adjectives (e.g. *busier, smaller, more modern*) to compare two places in a speaking activity. This fitted into my overall learning outcome for the students to improve their ability to describe and compare places.

'Specific' means 'the learners in your class'. Remember to link these needs to the materials.

How did you think this material was appropriate to your students' specific linguistic needs? Why was it appropriate?

> I have noticed that the learners spend a lot of time comparing their countries but tend to overuse *more* when doing this (*It's more big.**). I also noticed that some of them were forgetting to use *than* after comparatives, which was part of the grammar I was teaching. After studying this grammar, the material was necessary to provide an appropriate stimulus for them to activate what they had learnt in a speaking fluency activity and thus achieve the objective.

After you had prepared the material and before the lesson, what difficulties did you anticipate for your learners? What solutions did you identify for dealing with those difficulties?

Note that this box requires your 'anticipated problems' and solutions as part of your lesson planning.

My biggest concern was the vocabulary needed to do the activity. I was worried that they would try to name all the building types they could see. So I planned to remind them to focus on using the adjectives and nouns that they learnt earlier in the lesson and not to worry about any new words.

I was also concerned that some pairs might finish too soon. I planned to monitor carefully, and if this happened, I would move them on to the extension question: *Which city is more like your home town?* This allowed for differentiation between the different levels of English present in the class.

3rd page

Evaluation

Explain how you used the materials in the classroom effectively. What groupings did you use and why? How did the materials fit within the wider context of the lesson?

This trainee used an 'ESA' structure. You could also describe a lesson using CAP, PPP, a task-based learning framework or other structure.

While they were doing the activity, I monitored carefully, listening for use of the comparative structures and any errors to correct afterwards. The lesson structure was a typical 'ESA' (Harmer, 2007). The 'engage' phase involved the students describing their home towns. Then we studied the grammar of comparative adjectives. This was followed by controlled practice, after which these materials allowed for activation of the target language.

What reasons can you give for the success of your materials (or lack of)? How did you reach this conclusion?

Partial success is common. It is normally best to address both the strengths and the shortcomings in this box, providing evidence for your evaluation.

The materials were fairly successful. Firstly, all the pairs made use of comparative adjectives to describe the pictures, but only a few pairs managed 10 sentences. As I'd anticipated, others began describing irrelevant details and one pair spent more time writing their answers than saying them. I'd attribute the successes to the simplicity of the materials and a clear written instruction, and also to the fact that they enjoy speaking activities. The problems were caused by my not emphasising that they should speak, and perhaps my expectations were also too high for a pre-intermediate class.

157

How might the materials be improved for the same learners without changing the **learning objectives**?

Try to think of several points. Notice that bullet points are permitted and can reduce your word count. Focus on the materials, not your management of the activity.

- I'd add another line to the instructions emphasising that they should speak, not write.
- I'd include some prompt words around the pictures for ideas (e.g. age, size, temperature).
- I'd make the extension question at the bottom more central to the activity by moving it above the images. The pairs that did it used a lot of comparatives while discussing this question, and their communication was more natural.
- I'd give them colour pictures, rather than black and white. This makes the images clearer and more stimulating.

Here are the candidate's materials:

Comparing cities around the world

Work in pairs. Compare the two cities using comparative adjectives.
Think of at least 5 sentences each. (10 minutes)

If you have time, discuss this question:
Which city is more like your home town?

Pause for thought

Here are the assessment criteria for the written part of the assignment (there are separate criteria for the interview). How many of the 12 marks available would you award this candidate?

	The trainee is able to:	1 mark per criterion	1 mark per criterion
Written Communication Skills	identify a linguistic purpose and specific objectives	Identification of a linguistic purpose	Identification of specific objectives
	explain how the materials were appropriate to the students' linguistic needs	Identification of the class needs	Explanation of how the materials met the class needs
	identify potential difficulties of the materials for the learners and solutions for dealing with them	Identification of potential difficulties	Identification of potential solutions
	effectively discuss how the materials were used in the classroom	Discussion of groupings used	Discussion of the wider context of using the materials in the lesson, e.g. stages of lesson
	evaluate the success of the materials	Reasons for the success (or not) of the materials	Indication of how the conclusion was reached
	suggest how the materials might be improved	Suggestion(s) on how the materials might be improved in terms of relevancy to the linguistic needs of the students	Suggestion(s) of how the materials might be improved in terms of their design and presentation

Trinity CertTESOL Syllabus

The candidate in question scored 11 of the full 12 marks, making this a strong, but not perfect example. Did you manage to spot which mark was dropped?

Here is a clue; if the following sentence was added, it would score full marks. Where should it be added?

'I chose pairwork for this activity, so that everyone (even the quiet students) would get sufficient speaking practice.'

It should be added to the first answer of the evaluation, and would gain the mark for 'Discussion of groupings used'.

159

The Moderation Interview

The second part of the Materials Assignment is a 10-minute recorded interview with the course moderator about your materials. The moderation visit happens at the end of your course and is a compulsory part of all CertTESOL courses. As well as conducting the interviews, the moderator will look at a sample of the trainees' coursework and check that the course has been delivered according to the course provider's and Trinity's specifications. All Trinity moderators are current or former course trainers and English teachers. They've all been on similar courses to yours, and will be aware of the hard work required and the nerves that you may be feeling during the interview.

Before your individual interview, the moderator will already have spent some time looking at and assessing your completed pro forma. The interview will follow a similar order to the questions on the pro forma, beginning with your reasons for creating/adapting the materials, then moving on to evaluation and possible improvements. You will also be asked about your use of materials in general, including how you select or produce them, possible advantages and disadvantages of different types of materials and what you have

learnt from this assignment. Towards the end of your course, before moderation day, your course tutors will provide guidance on the moderation interview and allow you time to role-play the interview, usually in pairs or small groups with your co-trainees.

Here is a selection of the types of questions that may be asked during moderation interviews. Bear in mind that the questions that each trainee is asked will vary, depending on the materials, the lesson, the completed pro forma and the interview itself. The moderator will usually begin by asking you to summarise the rationale behind your materials and how they were used in class. They will then select questions to stimulate discussion and encourage you to demonstrate the required 'oral communication skills' (see the criteria below). Always listen to the question carefully, ask for clarification if you don't understand it, and then answer it directly and concisely.

Rationale

1 Were these materials adapted from or inspired by a coursebook activity?

2 What factors did you consider before creating the materials?

3 How relevant were your materials to your learners' needs?

4 To what extent did you anticipate that they would be interested in the activity?

5 When you were preparing the materials, what aspects, if any, of classroom management did you consider?

6 Did you anticipate any problems with the materials?

7 You wrote here that... Can you explain what you mean?

Evaluation and Adaptation

8 How effective were the materials in achieving your aims? How do you know?

9 Did the learners enjoy using them? How do you know? Did you expect this?

10 Did you have any problems with the materials / during the activity?

11 How did you respond to this problem?

12 How did the quality (e.g. quality of production, clarity, professionalism, attractiveness, etc.) of the materials affect their success?

13 You wrote here that... Can you provide an example of this?

14 What were the intended learning outcomes relating to the materials?

15 What changes would you make if you were to use the materials again?

General Issues and Learning

16 What factors should be considered when creating your own materials?

17 What factors should be considered when selecting materials from published sources / authentic sources?

18 What are the advantages of creating your own materials over using published materials / coursebooks? Are there any disadvantages?

19 What have you learnt from this assignment?

20 What challenges still remain for you in relation to materials design? How will you meet those challenges?

Useful ways of asking for clarification on questions

During the interview, if the moderator asks you a question that you don't understand, seek clarification before responding. For example, you may not be familiar with a term, expression or analogy they use. Here are some possible ways to do this:

Sorry, what do you mean by ... ?

Can you provide an example of that?

Could you rephrase the question?

Do you mean ... or ...?

Here are the assessment criteria for the interview. Read through them and match each criterion A-L to one of the questions above. For example, criterion A (Discussion of the suitability of the materials in terms of learner needs) would be elicited by asking question 3 (How relevant were your materials to your learners needs?). Then check your answers in the Pause for thought Key [21].

	The trainee is able to:	1 mark per criterion	1 mark per criterion
Oral Communication Skills	discuss the suitability of the materials both in terms of needs and motivation for learners	A. Discussion of the suitability of the materials in terms of learner needs	B. Discussion of the suitability of the materials in terms of learner motivation
	discuss what problems arose from the materials and how these were dealt with	C. Discussion of the actual problems that arose	D. Discussion of the solutions to these problems
	discuss how the learners responded to the materials and why the trainee thought this was the case	E. Discussion of the learners' response to the materials	F. Reason(s) for why the learners responded in this way
	discuss what the learning outcomes were from the materials and how the materials might be improved	G. Discussion of the learning outcomes	H. Discussion of the potential improvements to the materials
	demonstrate what they have learnt about the selection and production of English language teaching materials	I. Discussion of the point(s) made in relation to the selection of materials	J. Discussion of the point(s) made in relation to the production of materials
	demonstrate what they have learnt about teaching English using materials from different sources	K. Example(s) of what trainees have learnt	L. Justification for why using self-generated materials is beneficial

Trinity CertTESOL Syllabus

Passing the Materials Assignment

12 marks are available for the written assignment and 12 marks are available for the candidate's performance in the interview, making a maximum of 24 marks. To pass the assignment, candidates need to score 14 marks in total. It doesn't matter how these marks are divided between the two parts. No grades of pass are awarded, so there is only pass or referral. If you are referred you will have to retake the assignment (see *Referral* in *The Knowledge*). Moderators will give feedback to your Course Director on how candidates performed in the Materials Assignment at the end of moderation day.

How to develop your own Materials

While some trainees prefer to create their own materials from day one of their course, others find it useful to begin adapting coursebook materials. There are advantages to both approaches; the former will provide you with more opportunities to learn from your successes and mistakes and the latter will provide ideas and inspiration to get you started. If you are not sure, begin by looking in coursebooks and other resource books for ideas. You will often find an activity that's suitable, but not perfect for your learners. It may need 'tweaking', for example by removing a few difficult words, changing the number of questions, adding a clearer instruction or retyping with more space and some attractive images. Tweaking materials in this way is the first stage of resource creation and should lead naturally into further adaptation and original usage. As you progress through your course, you will begin to come up with your own ideas that will lead to resources based on the needs, interests and learning preferences of your students.

If you would like to use computer-based resources in your materials (e.g. an **interactive whiteboard** file, a video on YouTube, a website or Facebook page), make sure that it will be possible to print these and add them to your **Teaching Practice Portfolio** and Materials Assignment folder. Also make sure that the task that was given with the materials is clear to the moderator when they look at the materials. If you are not sure, talk to your course tutors about the use of such resources, or use hard copies in class.

When you are ready to begin creating your own materials from scratch, use the following three stages to help you through the process:

Before
Ask yourself these questions before you begin creating the materials:

1   What are my aims for the lesson? How will these aims be useful for the learners?
2   What are my objectives for the lesson stage when the materials will be used?
3   What activity do the students need to do to achieve these objectives?
4   What information (text or images) do the students need in order to complete this activity?

This should provide you with the basic idea for the materials.

During
Consider these questions while you are creating the materials:

1   How much time do you have for the activity?
2   Is the vocabulary and grammar at the right level for your learners?
3   Is the activity challenging, but not too difficult for your learners?

4   Is the content relevant to your learners? Is it appropriate for their ages/cultures?

5   Do your materials need a title?

6   Do they need a written instruction, or will you provide only a spoken instruction?

7   Is the design clear, easy to follow and professional?

8   Can you make the materials more attractive, or provide a visual context by using images?

9   Is your spelling correct and consistent (e.g. UK or US English)?

10 Have you sourced any adapted or copyright content using Harvard referencing?

After

Once you have finished creating your materials, do the following:

Get some friends or co-trainees to test out your materials for you and observe them carefully. Note firstly whether they achieve your lesson stage objective while using the materials. Also note whether they find the instructions clear, use the materials appropriately and how long it takes them to do it (obviously proficient English speakers will do most tasks faster than learners). After the 'test drive' you may need to 'tweak' the materials a little before they are ready to take into class.

Here are some final tips on resource creation from course trainers:

Ensure you have a clear understanding of why you used your material and how the students responded to it. Be certain about what it was for and make sure you can articulate this, both in the written and spoken parts of the assignment. It's invaluable to practise the interview at least once so that you know what to say, and understand explicitly what your material is for.

Samantha, CertTESOL trainer

As well as the language, it's really important to think about the design and 'mechanics' of your materials. If it's a game, for example, what are the rules? Why will students be motivated to play? What kind of materials have you used to create it and are they appealing and engaging? If your answer is yes, you're on the right track!

Sinèad, CertTESOL course director

The sheer volume of resources can be overwhelming, so, rather than reinventing the wheel, use a tried and tested coursebook and THEN try to be creative, e.g. changing the context to one which is relevant to your students.

Christa, CertTESOL trainer

Review of Unit 4
Understanding materials

Sentence completion

Complete the following sentences appropriately, based on what you have learnt in this chapter. Then, if needed, find the answers in the chapter above:

1   We can define 'materials' as ....

2   The main reason why teachers need to adapt coursebook materials is ....

3   *Market Leader*, *Cutting Edge* and *First Certificate Gold* are examples of ...., ... and .... respectively.

4   A published 'course' will often include Student's Book, ...

5   In the Materials Assignment, as well as describing why you created/adapted a set of materials, you should also .... and ....

6   The Materials Assignment has two parts. These are ....

7   In order to pass the Materials Assignment, trainees must score ....

If you need to, check your answers in the *Review Key* at the back of this book.

Now return to the learning opportunities provided at the start of the chapter. Check off the ones that you feel you have achieved and reread the relevant sections for any you're not sure about.

unit 5 Experiencing learning

> ❝ The Unknown Language Assignment is a wonderful opportunity to put yourself in your students' shoes and to experience the challenge involved in learning a second language as an adult. You'll learn not only about learning a new language from scratch, but also discover things about yourself as a learner you may never before have had the opportunity to consider. ❞
>
> Charlotte, CertTESOL trainer

Learning opportunities

This unit will help you to...

- understand the requirements of the Unknown Language Assignment
- find out about what happens in the unknown language lessons
- benefit fully from participating in these lessons
- complete your Unknown Language Journal effectively
- overcome any challenges presented by the assignment
- recognise the importance for a language teacher of also being a language learner

Introduction

Unit 5 of the Trinity CertTESOL requires you and your co-trainees to participate as students in four hours of tuition in an unknown language, experiencing what it's like to be a language learner at the beginner level. Trinity identifies three outcomes to this unit that you will need to demonstrate through the accompanying Unknown Language Assignment:

1 Awareness of the learning experiences and feelings of a learner being taught a new language, with little or no use of the learner's **first language**

2 Ability to identify the aims and **objectives** of the lesson and the ways in which these were or were not achieved through the methodology, materials and class management techniques employed

3 Awareness of a few of the main elementary contrastive features of the taught language and of English

Trinity CertTESOL syllabus

After each lesson you will complete a page in an Unknown Language Journal, a diary of your experiences for which your course provider will provide a pro forma. This journal will constitute the majority of your Unknown Language Assignment. You will also reflect on the overall learning experience in the assignment.

The majority of CertTESOL trainees enjoy this assignment and consistently report that they learn a great deal from it. However, it does present one significant challenge with regard to the three outcomes cited above. You will have to demonstrate the ability to analyse a lesson from the point of view of a language learner, a teacher and a linguist, wearing, as it were, three hats all at the same time! Like all assignments on the CertTESOL, Unit 5 provides an opportunity for you to demonstrate what you have learnt in other units. This includes reflections on the skills of the teacher and understanding of lesson aims and activities (Unit 1), observations on the nature of the language and its similarities or differences to English (Unit 2), insights into the experiences and challenges of the learner (Unit 3) and analysis of the specific role of materials in facilitating learning (Unit 4).

5.1 The Unknown Language Assignment

Let's look first at the two key aspects of the Unknown Language Assignment in detail, the lessons themselves and the Unknown Language Journal, analysing an example of how this has been completed by one trainee for her course provider. We will then discuss the assignment summary and look at some useful tips for ensuring that you pass what will probably be the first assignment on your CertTESOL course.

Pause for thought

*Make notes on specific ways in which the unknown language lessons are likely to benefit your own teaching during **teaching practice**. Think about specific skills in Unit 1 and areas of language teaching in Unit 2.*

Example: The lessons should provide useful models of how to present new language.

❝ Experiencing and reflecting on the language classroom as a student can be an incredibly eye-opening experience. Thinking about the things that worked for you and your colleagues (and didn't) can help you to make decisions in your own planning as a teacher. ❞

Sinèad, CertTESOL trainer

The language lessons

Your four hours of instruction will be divided up, usually into four separate one-hour lessons, and will start from the beginner level, presuming you have no prior knowledge of the language being taught. Your course provider will make every effort to ensure that the language really is new for all the participants, although this isn't an easy task, and on occasion it may be that one or two of the participants may have some prior knowledge of the language in question. Before the lesson begins, your course provider will have provided an introduction to the unit, and will have provided access to a pro forma document/template for your Unknown Language Journal, which you should check through carefully. Course providers will identify different things to focus on during each lesson, which will help to guide your observations (see *The Unknown Language Journal* below).

The methodology used in the lessons will normally be communicative, and as such, the lessons are generally useful examples of how to teach a foreign language at the beginner level. They should provide plenty of input and ideas for how to teach at higher levels as well. The lessons take place in the initial stages of your CertTESOL course, so they will provide a useful model regarding a number of the skills you will be required to demonstrate in your own teaching practice, such as

- coherent lesson structure and continuity between lessons
- awareness of the needs and interests of the learners
- general **classroom management** skills
- the ability to teach different skills and different areas of language
- specific techniques, such as **drilling**, praising learners, etc.
- the ability to communicate simply in the **target language**
- clear delivery of instructions
- appropriate **monitoring**
- integrated use of teaching and learning resources and materials

However, course providers are not required to teach 'model lessons', and you will not be required to 'copy' the practices of the teacher. It is quite possible that you will, as a developing trainee teacher, be able to identify weaknesses to the lessons, or challenges within your own learning that the teacher may have overlooked, and as such, you should reflect on these critically in your assignment.

While Trinity encourages the teacher to deliver the lessons mainly in the target language, recent changes in line with a move towards more L1-inclusive approaches to language learning in ELT allow the teacher: *'to make use of a shared L1 as appropriate and relevant to language and pedagogic objectives,'* (Trinity CertTESOL syllabus) depending on the context and the learners. If this happens, you should also reflect on what effect the use of English (as your L1) had on the learning.

As you are participating in the lessons, you should be mindful of your three objectives; to participate as a learner, to notice as a teacher, and to analyse as a linguist. As such, you will find it useful to take brief notes, but you should also endeavour to participate as naturally as possible as a learner. If you find it difficult to take notes during the lesson, make sure you do this as soon as possible afterwards, while the lesson structure, the lesson content and your own observations and emotions are still fresh in your memory. Some centres allocate time for discussion after each lesson, which may also help you to confirm and consolidate your observations.

Pause for thought

Read the following three extracts from published studies based on language learner diaries. For each one, consider whether the reflections provided are from the perspective of the learner, the teacher, the linguist, or a combination of these, and what can be learnt from the insight:

> *When it's my turn to talk, I stumble. I give out a short answer with no explanation or talk without my thinking together.*
>
> Lee & Lew, 2001, p.143

> *A rigid adherence to the audio-lingual method was followed in my Arabic class. The [target language] was used exclusively as the medium of instruction. Weekly lessons included full page dialogues followed by approximately 6-8 pages of drills. No translations, grammatical explanations vocabulary lists were given during the lessons nor did the text provide me with these supports.*
>
> Schumann & Schumann, 1977, p.244

> *I was surprised to hear myself say, 'A mi, me gusta' [I like it]. Where did that come from? I think it's right, because I'm sure I must have heard it (or did I invent it?). In any case, it came out so naturally that I can't imagine saying a bare 'me gusta' without the emphatic 'a mi.'*
>
> Carson & Longhini, 2002, p.140

Check your answers in the **Pause for thought Key** *[22] at the back of the book.*

The Unknown Language Journal

After each of the lessons you should complete an entry into your Unknown Language Journal, using the pro forma provided by your course provider. For each lesson you will be required to:

1   identify the grammatical/functional/lexical objectives of the lesson based on what happened in it and what you and the other participants learnt

2   describe the methods used by the teacher, reflecting on general lesson structure, choice of activities, the role of materials in these activities and how the teacher managed the learners and the learning

3   reflect on the learning experience, and on the degree to which the methods and attitudes suited the needs and preferences of everybody in the group (not just you)

In addition to this, you will be provided with a specific focus for each lesson. This is selected by the course provider, but may include tasks such as the following (this list is not exhaustive):

■   a focus on the teacher, what she/he does and how effective it is (e.g. whether instructions are clear, and if so, how they are made clear)

■   a focus on your own learning preferences and strategies (e.g. what you do to learn vocabulary, how you remember the pronunciation of words, etc.)

■   a focus on differences between learners in the class (e.g. motivation levels, aptitude for pronunciation learning, etc.)

■   a focus on a personal difficulty (e.g. an area of language that you found/are finding difficult to learn, or an activity type that makes you feel uncomfortable)

■   a focus on the syllabus, and how the lessons link and relate to each other (e.g. what revision occurs at the start of the lesson, how, and what effect this has on learning)

The extract below comes from a well-completed Unknown Language Journal for the second lesson in a course of Russian, with some comments added to indicate key features, strengths and a few weaknesses. As with previous example pro formas in this book, note firstly that it is not intended as a model answer, and also that different course providers will tend to structure the pro formas for the journal differently.

Unknown Language Journal – Lesson 2

> Here the trainee has estimated the intended learning outcomes. Keep this similar to how you describe your learning outcomes for your own teaching practice classes.

Perceived learning outcomes:

By the end of the lesson, the students will:

1   have learnt the meaning of key vocabulary associated with food and drink

2   have practised speaking (ordering in a restaurant and saying what you want)

> A thorough evaluation that provides a specific example

Evaluation of achievement of objectives:

At the end of the lesson the students seemed to all remember the meaning and pronunciation of the vocabulary. During the final exercise, language that was known from both this and the first lesson was being used freely, although two or three of the learners were still having difficulty with the word 'Zdravstvuyte' ['Hello'] in greetings. Apart from this, the lesson aims were well achieved.

Basic lesson structure:

Some course providers ask trainees to summarise the key lesson stages.

One aim has been omitted: To help learners understand the new question in context

Criticism of the lesson is welcomed, and should be backed up by clear reasons. This trainee has also provided a useful suggestion for improvement.

The reflections here on the trainee's own cognitive processes are interesting and insightful.

Stage	Procedure	Aim of the activity	Resources
1	Repetition of vocabulary learnt in previous session using ball nomination game. Students were each asked one of the dialogue questions from the previous lesson.	To revise previous lesson and recall any forgotten phrases.	A ball
2	Teacher showed a number of real objects on a tray (e.g. coffee, water, biscuits, etc.), saying the names in Russian, and then drilling pronunciation.	To introduce new vocabulary. To ensure meaning was clear.	Food/drinks items (realia), board
3	Teacher used objects to teach question 'Shto vi hotite?' ['What would you like?'].	To practise the new vocabulary.	Realia
4	Teacher and two learners role-play basic restaurant dialogue.	To use newly learnt language in practical context.	Realia, menus

Continues...

Focus on teaching:

Role-play was a key theme in this lesson, and the use of a few props (bow tie, menus and the realia) were effective in making the context for the role-play clear, and making it fun for everyone. I was surprised that at such an elementary level, something so practical and useful would be possible.

While the role-play activity was enjoyable, I think some of us found it difficult in only our second lesson. We couldn't remember all the questions, so we had to use our own notes quite a lot. A handout with these questions and possible answers on them would have helped at this stage.

Focus on learning:

I found that, rather than being a gimmick, the realia was really useful to me, and helped me to learn the words. When I forgot the meaning, looking at the object somehow helped me to remember the word, and even if I couldn't remember, pointing at least got the message across!

Towards the end of the lesson, the teacher encouraged us to translate the important questions and answers we had learnt into English, yet without speaking English himself. This was useful, because I hadn't understood the exact meaning of one of them, and I was now able to write it down in my notebook and learn it, sure of the meaning.

Focus on language:

We learnt that Russian has two words for 'you' ('vi' and 'ti'), and like French, one is plural and the other singular, with the plural form being appropriate for formal situations, even with just one person. The vowel sound in both these words (like /i:/, but shorter and further back in the mouth) had no equivalent in English and presented some problems for us.

The word 'pazhalsta' seems to have a number of uses, meaning 'please' and 'you're welcome'.

Specific focus for lesson 2: Revision

Make notes on how the teacher incorporates revision of the first lesson into this lesson, and how, if at all, this benefits the learners:

I found that due to the choral and individual drilling most of the learners remembered a lot of the phrases we had learnt in the first lesson, although some students hadn't, and the teacher was patient with them. He balanced his interaction with the different learners well, so that no-one felt left out.

The revision helped to speed up our recollection of the words so that we could begin our role-plays greeting each other with language we already knew before leaping into the unknown with the new language!

After noticing the problems one expression, 'Zdravstvuyte' ['Hello'], was still causing, I thought it was nice how the teacher decided to give us a simpler alternative, 'Privyet' ['Hi'], which many of us decided to use instead.

Summary of the unknown language experience

As well as the completed pro formas for each of the lessons in the Unknown Language Journal, you will also need to write a reflective summary of the experience as part of the assignment. This summary should include at least the following (your course provider may have other requirements):

- a description of the methodology used in the unknown language lessons and how effective you feel it was
- some reflection on what you and others in the group learnt from being in the role of the student
- your professional evaluation as a trainee teacher of the benefits of completing this unit
- an indication of what you have learnt from it and what you will carry forward into your own teaching

Some course providers will also require you to include your analysis of the language in this discursive section of the assignment, rather than in body of the journal, as is done in the example above.

Passing the Unknown Language Assignment

Like Unit 3 (the Learner Profile), the exact specifications for this assignment and criteria for assessment will be provided by your course provider, as Trinity encourages course providers to make these appropriate to the trainee teachers and learners on individual courses. As such, your assignments will be marked by your course tutors, and they will provide guidance and support as required. However, the following advice should also be useful:

Don't fall behind

Especially if you're on an intensive CertTESOL, there may be other concerns dominating your mind, such as your teaching practice lessons. However, if you don't take separate notes after each lesson you may find it difficult to recall exactly what happened, and what you felt in which lesson and why, and this can make writing the assignment much more difficult, more time-consuming, and will reduce the quality of your reflections. So stay ahead and make sure you plan a little free time in the evening after each lesson to complete your Unknown Language Journal.

Document the learning process in detail:

- keep accurate records of key details for each lesson to assist you when writing up your journal and assignment, including what happened in the lesson, how you coped and felt, how other learners reacted, and how the teacher responded to the learning
- keep an accurate notebook of the language content of the lessons, including vocabulary and grammar learnt and notes on areas of phonology
- keep copies of any materials used by the teacher, including handouts, cards and even boardwork (take photos of these if necessary)

Carry out additional research into the language

Although this is not a Trinity requirement, you will find it easier to understand and analyse a language if you know some important background details, such as the basic word order, whether the language is tonal or not, whether it has gender, etc. Once you have found out what language you are learning (and this may happen only after the first lesson), do some research on it either using *Learner English* (Swan & Smith, 2001) or on the Internet.

If you feel particularly challenged in the lessons, and find it difficult to learn what is being taught, as well as reflecting on this in your journal, you can always do a little bit of extra revision at home between lessons. This will enable you to relax a little more, and observe the lesson more with your teacher and linguist 'hats' on. And don't worry – slower learners often make more sensitive teachers!

Tick all the boxes

It's quite common for trainees to be asked to **resubmit** this assignment on small technicalities, such as on one or two specific omissions on pro formas, or not enough detail provided with regard to a specific requirement, so make sure you check your work carefully before submitting your journal for assessment. Make sure you have a copy of the assignment assessment criteria, and read through them, both before you begin, and after you finish your assignment to ensure that it has, to the best of your knowledge, fulfilled these criteria.

Seek guidance if you're not sure

As this assignment comes early in the course, you may be unsure of who to turn to for help if you find it difficult. You may not know other trainees very well, and may be anxious about the influence it will have on your tutors if you admit to having difficulty. However, remember that you're on a course run by teachers for teachers, and that they (your trainers) should take pride in making sure that their learners (you) understand what to do, how and why. They will feel personally responsible if you are confused or frustrated by any assignment, so ask at the first convenient opportunity if you are unclear about something. It's also a good idea to share contact details with at least one or two of the other trainees on your course, and to consult them, especially if you have difficulties at the weekend when your tutors may not be available.

5.2 Continuing to learn languages

One of the challenges that all teachers face in their continuing professional development is the danger of losing their ability to empathise with the challenges their learners face. Teachers of English as a foreign/second language vary significantly in this ability to empathise with learners. Non-native speaker teachers who learnt English as teenagers or adults have a significant advantage here (discussed in Unit 3, Section 3.4: *Learner autonomy and learning strategies*) as they are likely to remember many of the challenges of being a learner and will recall their long journey to proficiency. However, all native English-speaking teachers and any non-native speaker teachers who learnt English in early childhood are likely to have less ability to empathise with the challenges faced by someone learning English. Indeed, some will often find it difficult to see anything 'alien' in English at all – reading the very lines of this sentence, you may be unaware, for example, how many of the words in it are '*orthographically* opaque', not following any of the many, rather complex rules for English spelling-pronunciation relationships!

Yet we, as language teachers, are blessed with a wonderful advantage when compared to teachers of almost all other subjects. We can put ourselves in the shoes of the learner at any stage in the language learning process simply by trying to learn other foreign languages ourselves. This section of the unit explores a number of ways in which we can become more aware of the predicament of the learner, and more capable of predicting, understanding and empathising with their challenges – all through the practice of learning foreign languages ourselves.

Attrition

One of the first things that you will notice about learning foreign languages once you have completed your Unknown Language Assignment is exactly how quickly and effortlessly our brains seem able to forget words, phrases and even whole languages that we no longer need. This process is usually referred to as 'attrition' by researchers on language acquisition, and indicates an important reality about language learning – if you don't use it, you'll lose it. Despite having had reasonably fluent conversations in 10 different languages in my lifetime, I can profess to being a fluent speaker of only three… and a half… ish. This problem of attrition is something that many English students experience throughout their lives, including teenagers enrolled in 'intensive' summer schools each year who seem to forget the majority of what they've learnt between one year and the next, and adult professionals who change jobs, find they no longer need English (or a specific type of English) and gradually lose competence in it. If, like me, you have battled with this challenge yourself, you will be able to empathise with such learners and to suggest some simple, useful tips to help them to retain at least their passive understanding of English by, for example, watching a film once a week or using English news websites for their 'daily news fix', rather than first language websites.

Becoming a lifelong language learner

The Unknown Language lessons will doubtlessly have provided a useful taster of what it feels like to be a student in the language classroom, but given the intensities of the CertTESOL, it is usually only possible for you to experience the first four hours of a language learning course. Just to put that in perspective, learners at an advanced (C1) level in English are likely to have already studied the language for anything between 500 and 1,300 hours (Liskin-Gasparro, 1982)! What you have experienced constitutes the melting water on the surface of the tip of this prodigious iceberg.

So if you are not an experienced language learner, think carefully about how you can get more experience of being a language learner in order to become a better teacher.

Pause for thought

Consider how the following three teachers can usefully continue learning foreign languages after their CertTESOL course:

A   *a non-native speaker teacher from Germany planning to teach multilingual classes in the UK or Ireland*

B   *a monolingual native-speaker teacher planning to teach in China*

C   *a non-native speaker teacher from Spain planning to return to Spain to teach English to classes of Spanish students*

For teachers of multilingual classes, most likely to be working in the UK or other Anglophone countries, the simplest way to do this is to enrol in language classes yourself. This has the dual advantages of enabling you to gain experience both of learning a language and of being a long-term language learner. An important third bonus is that by enrolling you will increase your (extrinsic) motivation to study and attend, especially if you've paid for your lessons! Self-directed study is a much cheaper alternative, but lacks two of these advantages, and unless you are very disciplined and focused, your motivation to continue learning is likely to wane.

For teachers of classes who share the same language, if you do not speak that language, or only speak it to a limited level of proficiency, it's obviously a no-brainer that you should study this language, ideally in classes, for reasons mentioned in the previous paragraph. Not only will it provide you with the necessary experience of being a learner, but it will provide you with vital information about your learners' first language, and how it differs and contrasts with English. This will inform your planning, your teaching, and will even enable you, when you reach a higher level of proficiency to involve the L1 productively in teaching English.

But what about for teachers who already speak the first language of their learners fluently? What can you do to keep the language learning experience fresh? If you are gifted with complete bilingual proficiency in both languages, your only option is to study another language of your choice, as suggested above. And if you are a non-native speaker of English, even at C1 or C2 levels of proficiency, there are still options open to you for developing your proficiency in English. These include focusing on a specific area of English (e.g. English for business, useful for all English language teachers), or a specific variety of English (British,

American, Indian, Australian, Irish, Singlish, etc.). This is something you can realistically do with other colleagues (native or non-native speakers) that will help you to develop greater awareness of differences between varieties, expand your knowledge of idiomatic language use and slang, and will also provide a wider knowledge base from which you can decide which varieties and forms of English to draw into your own **idiolect**, and which you prefer to teach to your learners.

But whichever of these options you choose, you will find that you learn much more from being a student if you keep a diary of your experience. This need not be anything formal, and could even be a video diary. By completing diary entries after each lesson, it is likely that you will notice more through recollecting it and verbalising your emotions than if you participate in the lessons without keeping such a diary. In it you can reflect on your personal challenges, the challenges of other learners, the behaviour of the teacher, the choice of learning content, how this is structured into a syllabus, and the fascinating and often dynamic developments in classroom **rapport** that occur over a longer course of learning.

Review of Unit 5
Experiencing learning

Find the 'red herring'

Read the following requirements of the Unknown Language Journal. According to this chapter, you may be required to do all of them, except one. Can you find the 'red herring'?

1   work out what the objectives/aims of the lessons are

2   describe aspects of the lesson, such as the structure and activities used

3   notice the responses of your peers to the lesson activities

4   reflect on your own preferences as a learner

5   focus on a personal difficulty you have

6   analyse aspects of the language you are taught

7   remember the new language that you are taught

8   notice the behaviour of the teacher

9   comment on the cohesion of the lessons

10 reflect on the methodology used by the teacher

If you need to, check your answer in the *Review Key* at the back of this book.

Now return to the learning opportunities provided at the start of the chapter. Tick the ones that you feel you have achieved and re-read the relevant sections for any you're not sure about.

After the course

Learning opportunities

This unit will help you to...

- plan your first career moves as a CertTESOL qualified teacher
- prepare your CV and online presence to maximise job opportunities
- find the job you want
- pass the job interview
- deal with the initial learning curve when starting a new job
- understand your professional development needs as a newly qualified teacher
- make informed decisions about your long-term career path

Introduction

If you are reading this chapter upon successful completion of your CertTESOL, congratulations! More likely, you're reading it because you have already started thinking about your future life after graduation; if so, well done to you too! Having some idea of what you want to do will enable you to make the most of the course and the learning opportunities it provides.

The majority of people who enrol on a Trinity CertTESOL course usually have some idea of what they would like to do after the course. For some this may be a vague intention to work in a chosen country or part of the world, for others it may be an interest in a line of work or organisation, and for others still, prior experience and knowledge of a specific teaching context will inform your next career moves. Whether you fit into one of these categories, or you still truly have no idea of what you want to do after the course, this unit will help you to plan your next career moves, find potential jobs, evaluate the professionalism and commitment of different employers, and hopefully get the position you want.

But what then? Once you have been offered a job, you will initially need to work hard to prepare and deliver your lessons while keeping both learners and line managers happy. This is a steep learning curve and useful tips are provided below for how to manage it, and hopefully enjoy the learning. Then your mind is likely to turn towards your personal professional development and potential future career paths. Both of these are also discussed in detail in this unit.

A.1 Planning your next career moves

One of the first challenges you face is deciding exactly what type of English teaching you want to focus on. As Table A.1 shows, there are many options available, with EFL in non-Anglophone countries being by far the largest market and the most realistic prospect for CertTESOL graduates without prior teaching experience. While this sector of the industry offers work almost anywhere in the world, be aware that organisations vary significantly in their professionalism, and different destinations will have different advantages and disadvantages for different graduates. Many graduates prefer to start initially with a well-known chain/franchise (e.g. International House, EF, Bell), which may also offer opportunities to move between schools upon completion of contracts. Opportunities for online tuition are expanding rapidly and can provide useful initial experience to newly qualified teachers. Primary and secondary teaching may require qualified teacher status (QTS) and sometimes knowledge of the L1 of the learners, although volunteering posts in developing countries are less likely to require these and can be an immensely rewarding way to get valuable initial experience. CertTESOL graduates with prior experience stand higher chances of getting work in Anglophone countries (e.g. UK, USA, Australia, etc.) as competition here is stiff, except during the summer when many schools expand to offer additional classes or open residential summer schools. Starting work during the busy summer months or as a part-time teacher are good ways to get your 'foot in the door' of an organisation. Once you've proven your teaching ability, you may be offered a permanent post.

Table A.1: Career opportunities

Where?		
	In Anglophone countries (e.g. UK, Ireland) where English is the primary language	**In non-Anglophone countries ('overseas' for native speakers)**
What?	**EFL (English as a foreign language)** Mainly adult students on intensive (full-time programmes) except during the summer when opportunities for work in summer schools (mainly with teenagers) increase significantly. More competitive for the rest of the year, as many teachers have experience and higher level qualifications.	**EFL (English as a foreign language)** Adults, teenagers and children usually in private language institutes, and usually part-time students. High demand for teachers with initial certification and high chance of finding work. Professionalism of organisations varies significantly.
	ESP (English for specific purposes) Many learners require academic English (EAP) prior to starting academic programs. Significant numbers of business English students.	**ESP (English for specific purposes)** High demand for business English, often in company (you travel to the client). High demand for academic English, especially exam preparation (ISE, IELTS, FCE, TOEFL).
	ESOL/ESL (English for speakers of other languages / English as a second language) Mainly adult students, especially refugees and immigrants, many requiring literacy support. Competition for posts can be stiff, usually requiring experience, higher qualifications and specific skills, although volunteer posts may also be possible.	**Primary and secondary teaching** In medium and high income countries, teachers are usually required to have Qualified Teacher Status (QTS), and knowledge of first language may be necessary. In lower income countries, charities and volunteer organisations often offer positions (e.g. World Teach, VSO, Peace Corps).
	Online tuition An expanding international market, mainly involving **one-to-one** tuition, partly through VoIP (e.g. Skype, Google Hangout) and partly through discussion groups on platforms such as Moodle. IT skills, good Internet connection and fast typing speed are all prerequisites.	

❝ When you finish your course, ask your course provider about how to continue your development as a teacher. They may be able to put you in touch with a local graduate scheme or teaching association which aims to support newly-qualified teachers and which will give you access to local job and networking opportunities, as well as teaching and teacher development resources. ❞

Charlotte, CertTESOL trainer

If at this stage you are still flexible about where you want to go, ask the advice of your course tutors or other teachers at your training centre. Personal opinions are useful for obvious reasons, especially from someone who knows you. A number of course providers have links to schools or recruitment organisations that you may also be interested to pursue. If you are confident about your choice of country, it's a good idea to conduct more specific research on different organisations and areas in the country, and to try to link up online with teachers already working there. If you don't already speak the language, get learning – this will be a massive asset in your attempt to find work, even if you describe your level as 'elementary' on your CV.

A.2   Finding your first job

Conducting the job search

For most CertTESOL graduates, the job search begins online, and large TEFL employment databases (e.g. TEFL.com) offer a large number of opportunities all around the world with various organisations. Even if you're not thinking about applying at the moment, it's a good idea to have a look and see what opportunities are available. On many such websites you can also upload your CV and receive job alerts to your email inbox. Many of the larger organisations advertise positions on their own websites (e.g. http://careers.ef.com/), where you can often submit your CV. Certain recruitment organisations (e.g. Saxoncourt in the UK) often target graduates from CertTESOL courses, so these are also useful lines of enquiry. Developing your profile on LinkedIn is also a good idea (see below), as many recruitment organisations use it to search for graduates, post jobs and browse CVs.

If you are currently in the country where you are looking for work, you may also want to look up language schools on the Internet or in local advertisements and telephone directories and contact them directly, which can also be effective. Try to find out initially who is in charge of teacher recruitment. In larger schools this will be either a **Director of Studies** (DoS) or an Academic Director, who will usually be a trained and experienced language teacher. In smaller schools this maybe the school owner (who may not be a language teacher). Try to contact them directly with your initial enquiry. Sending a CV can be useful, or a friendly phone call enquiring about any possible positions can also work, but there is nothing like the face-to-face personal touch for making a solid first impression. Try popping into the school, well-dressed, on a day and at a time when they are least busy (Monday mornings are not usually a good idea!) with a copy of your CV, originals of important qualifications (including your CertTESOL certificate, obviously), your end-of-course report, and perhaps some evidence of your teaching skills through nicely prepared and printed materials, or documents providing positive feedback from your CertTESOL course (e.g. teaching practice feedback forms, assignment feedback, etc.). You may be turned away, but it pays to be ready in case you aren't. Make sure you are aware of local etiquette if you take this direct approach (see below); in some countries it may be frowned upon.

Look at the following two job advertisements, adapted from genuine postings on an EFL employment database. If you had to choose between the two employers, which would you choose and why?

Organisation A

Details of Position

12 positions available in private schools in Shenzhen and Hanghzou from February, teaching English to learners ages 12-16. Full induction and initial support provided by Chinese speaking colleagues.

Qualifications

- Competent, passionate teachers required
- Teachers from any countries encouraged to apply, but popularity with students a must
- Experience is preferable but not always necessary
- Initial teacher certificate (e.g. CertTESOL, CELTA or equivalent) is required. Degrees are also required due to working visa restrictions

Salary and Benefits

- Very competitive package of 12,000 RMB-16,000 RMB according to qualification and experience
- 20 contact hours per week
- Either free accommodation or housing allowance (in addition to above salary) provided
- Legal working visa and health insurance provided
- Air ticket allowance for return flight is available at end of contract
- Free lessons available in Mandarin and/or local language twice a week for all teachers

Organisation B

Details of Position

We require teachers for our extensive chain of schools in China – across the east of the country, all urban. 100 positions in 15 schools. Teenage students. Classes 30+ students. Enthusiastic!

Qualifications

- Native level speakers only
- ANY Bachelor's Degree
- TEFL / CertTESOL / CELTA certificate is advantage
- Without a degree – must have TEFL / CertTESOL / CELTA certificate
- Recent graduates with no experience are also welcome

Salary and Benefits

- Minimum 15,000 RMB
- Free accommodation – furnished studio apartment on school site
- 25 hrs per week guaranteed. Sometimes more
- One-year contract, visa provided
- One-way ticket reimbursement – Candidate gets ticket from home country to China and that amount is reimbursed
- Lunch provided by the school
- Basic Chinese language classes on arrival

Avoiding unscrupulous employers

Once you have found a position that you're interested in, check out the details carefully. As a rule of thumb, more scrupulous organisations tend to write more in their job advertisements, including specifics and details, and better schools will also try to sell their organisation in an attempt to attract the best candidates. Beware of organisations that do not disclose exact teaching locations, exact contract hours or remuneration details. While many organisations advertise for 'native (level) speakers', this practice has been outlawed as discriminatory by reputable ELT organisations such as IATEFL and TESOL. Hopefully you spotted some of these negative traits in the advertisement from Organisation B in the *Pause for thought* task above!

It's also a good idea to ask for more information when expressing initial interest in a position. Organisations that want good teachers are more than happy to send photos, details, brochures, website links (even if some of these are in a different language), all of which will help you to build up a better understanding of your potential future employer, position and location.

You can also ask for the full job description and more information about the application process. Any organisation that cannot provide these is unlikely to be very professional. And of course, any organisations that do not require you to attend a job interview (Skype or otherwise) are clearly not too concerned about quality in their recruitment process!

Your CV and your online profile

Your CV

You will obviously need to update your CV when you begin your job search, including details about your CertTESOL qualification. You may want to include an extended paragraph about the qualification in a prominent position on the CV, especially if it's the only relevant part of your CV for the position in question. This will highlight to any prospective employers that the CertTESOL is accredited and that it involved six hours of teaching practice (just in case they don't know). Here is such an example, which you may want to adapt or shorten as you see fit:

Trinity College London – Certificate in Teaching English to Speakers of Other Languages

Successfully completed the Trinity CertTESOL at [name of organisation]. UK NQF (National Qualifications Framework) Level 5. The course included the following:

- 6 hours of assessed teaching practice with learners of English as a foreign language
- 130 hours of supervised input
- 4 hours of guided observation of experienced teachers
- experience of planning for and delivering private one-to-one lessons

Skills / Competencies acquired:

- ability to assess learners' needs through detailed needs analysis
- ability to plan lessons based on learners' needs and interests
- ability to create/adapt original materials to meet learning outcomes
- ability to self-evaluate accurately and improve teaching practice as a result

In addition to this, or alternatively, you may want to include a personal statement outlining your current career plans as follows (again, you will need to adapt it to your personal circumstances):

Trinity CertTESOL qualified English teacher with…

- experience in *[add this if you've had a varied employment history]*
- a BA Honours Degree in *[add this if you've got a degree]*

Looking for a full-time teaching position in an English language school in [e.g. south-east Asia]. I'm interested in teaching both adults and younger learners… *[add any other course types you're interested in such as business English if you've got some previous work experience, or exam courses if you've got an academic background, etc.]*

Don't forget to also highlight any transferrable skills from previous jobs and responsibilities on your CV, such as public speaking, IT skills, positions of responsibility, etc.

Your online profile

You should also look carefully at your online profile before applying for any position. Employers can often find out a lot about you by Googling your name, searching for you on Facebook or through other social media. If necessary, remove any unusual or embarrassing images from your online profile, and consider adding other images as appropriate.

It's a good idea, if you haven't already got one, to create a LinkedIn profile for yourself. More and more employers and recruitment agencies are using LinkedIn both to find suitable candidates for positions, and for submission of CVs. The sooner you begin making your profile 'ELT relevant', the better. In this regard, it's a good idea to link up with your co-trainees on LinkedIn, join relevant teaching organisations (e.g. ELT Professionals around the World; iTeach English) and begin to build up your ELT profile. You can do this in a number of ways:

- co-endorse each other for teaching related skills (e.g. Teaching English as a Second Language; ESL; Intercultural Communication; International Education; Educational Materials, etc.)
- write recommendations for each other based on what you learnt from your colleagues during the CertTESOL course
- add images of you teaching or in 'end of course photos' with students
- read and participate in LinkedIn groups, start discussions and write original LinkedIn 'Pulse' posts, including for example, reflections on your initial training.

One final (hopefully obvious) tip – when sending a CV directly to an email address, don't forget to include a brief, friendly cover email saying a little bit about who you are and why you are interested in the position – anonymous CVs are not very attractive to potential employers for obvious reasons.

A.3 The job interview

It is highly likely that whatever position you apply for, you will be required to attend a job interview. This may happen face-to-face if you are in the country or applying through a recruitment consultant, or it may happen via Skype or telephone interview. Either way, the usual rules of etiquette and behaviour for job interviews apply. It is also a good idea to consider local cultural etiquette if you and your prospective interviewers have different cultural backgrounds (see below). While some of the guidelines provided here are common sense, others involve more industry-specific tips:

1   Research the organisation in advance, and prepare questions that show you've done your research – if you have a name for your interviewer, find out more about them online if possible.

2   Revise your knowledge of ELT coursebooks and materials that are likely to be relevant for the position in question – interviewers will be impressed if you can name books and identify one or two strengths and/or weaknesses.

3   Take along all required proof of qualification in the original, and also take along some evidence of your own work and ability, such as materials created for the Materials Assignment, or some of your more positive feedback from your teaching practice lessons.

4   Dress formally, but not drably – rightly or wrongly, many organisations expect English teachers to be 'lively' personalities.

5   Arrive at least five minutes early – punctuality is a must for language teachers.

6   Personality is important in interviews for ELT positions, so make sure you come across as friendly, interesting and most importantly, willing and ready to work hard and learn.

7   You should already know basic details about the position, but have a list of key questions relating to anything you don't know – a good employer will always give you an opportunity to ask these questions, and will answer them honestly.

8   Depending on how the interview goes, you may find you want to sell yourself more – if so, remember that you could offer to teach a trial lesson. While this is not a standard requirement, it does indicate willingness and confidence in your own teaching.

9   At the end, don't forget to thank your interviewer for their time, and summarise by telling them how much you would like to work for their organisation (unless of course you wouldn't!).

10 Follow-up the interview with a quick thank you email the following day – if there are many candidates for the post, this will help you to stand out from the crowd.

Additional tips for Skype interviews:

1   Think carefully about the positioning of your computer webcam so that anything seen in the background gives the right impression.

2   Try not to allow the webcam to be looking up your nose (this often happens with laptop computers) – if necessary raise the computer up on books so that you're looking horizontally at the webcam.

3   Have pen and paper ready and note down important details provided, especially names of interviewers – use these names during the interview.

4   Try to begin with a little chitchat (*'How's your day going?'; 'What time is it there?'*) to break any initial 'Skype-ice'.

5   At important points in the interview, look directly into the webcam – this will convey sincerity.

What questions are likely at the job interview?

This will, of course, depend on the position, the location, and any potential strengths and weaknesses they see in you as a candidate. However, to give you a flavour of the kind of things that directors of studies/academic directors often ask recent graduates at job interview, here is a sample compiled from colleagues working in such roles:

Specifically for newly qualified teachers

- Why did you decide to go into language teaching?
- Why did you take the CertTESOL?

Language awareness

- What do you know about the difference between… (e.g. present perfect and past simple)?
- If your student asked you a grammar question and you didn't know the answer, how would you deal with that in class?

Note that some employers may also administer a short language awareness exam, after which candidates are asked to comment on their answers to the task and questioned further as necessary. So swot up on your basic grammar knowledge the night before.

Lesson planning and admin

- How much time do you usually spend planning your classes on average?
- How important is admin to you?

Levels

- Is there a level that you prefer / have taught regularly?
- Which levels did you prefer teaching on your course? Why?
- What do you think are the main challenges to teaching low-level / high-level students?

Coursebooks, resources and materials

- Is there a coursebook you prefer / have used regularly?
- What coursebooks did you use on your course? What did you think of them?
- What resources do you enjoy using with your learners?
- How often do you adapt / develop your own materials for the class / learners you are teaching?

Learner satisfaction / needs / feedback

- How do you ensure the needs of all your learners are being met?
- What would you do if a learner told you your class was boring?
- How would you deal with a learner who is not participating much in your class?
- How would you deal with negative feedback?

Continued Professional Development

- How important is **CPD** to you? Why?
- What would you expect from us in terms of CPD?
- What areas of your own CPD are you prioritising at the moment?

Teaching

- What are your strengths and weaknesses as a teacher?
- Can you talk me through a lesson that you taught recently?
- What's your favourite activity? Could you describe it?
- What are your thoughts on teaching grammar versus teaching lexis?
- Choose three adjectives to describe your teaching style?
- Do you think teachers should use the students' language in class? Why/Why not?

Imagine you are at a job interview for your 'ideal ELT job'. Choose a selection of the questions above and think about how you would answer them. If you are currently preparing to attend a job interview, write down your answers; this will make you more coherent at the interview.

Alternatively, you could role-play a job interview with one of your colleagues on the course. You can select from the above questions, and add others relevant to the imaginary position your colleague is applying for.

Local culture and etiquette when looking for work

As mentioned earlier in this unit, if you do not share the culture of your likely interviewers (or even just one of them), it's a good idea to be aware of some basic cultural dos and don'ts. Even though many employers would not necessarily expect somebody from a different background to be aware of their culture, if you are, you're always more likely to impress, especially on a subconscious level. You can get a lot of useful information by Googling 'cultural etiquette in… (name of country)'. Examples of this include the following:

- In certain cultures, people may be uncomfortable if you stand too close (e.g. UK) and in others they may think you are unfriendly if you stand too far away (e.g. Brazil).
- In some cultures, handshakes are usually expected of all participants in an interview process, irrespective of gender or position in the organisation (e.g. Italy), in others physical contact may be socially unacceptable (e.g. between men and women in many Muslim countries).
- In some cultures, smiling is an important sign of friendliness and willingness (e.g. USA), and in others too much smiling can be frowned upon as a sign of stupidity (e.g. Russia).

Write down the names of the two countries or cultures you feel you 'know' well (these may be regional if you are only familiar with one national culture). Make notes on differences in the culture and etiquette between the two. To what extent do you modify your behaviour when moving from one of these countries/cultures to the other?

Finding work as a non-native speaker teacher

Research into differences between native English-speaking teachers (NESTs) and non-native English-speaking teachers (NNESTs) has revealed some interesting and important findings. Most importantly, students do not necessarily prefer native speaker teachers, and recognise complementary strengths in the two groups (e.g. Cheung, 2002; Lipovsky & Mahboob, 2010). While the often instinctual proficiency of native speakers is useful when it comes to knowledge of idiomatic language and low-frequency lexis, the more detailed understanding of the grammar rules and understanding of the learners' needs are just two of the useful strengths that non-native speaker teachers are more likely to have than native speaker teachers (Medgyes, 1994). Yet despite this important truth, non-native speaker teachers continue to suffer discrimination in the industry, especially by employers and recruitment organisations (Mahboob & Golden, 2013). Put simply, in many parts of the world there is a continuing bias towards employing native speaker teachers due to the naive presumption that they automatically make better teachers. It is important to be aware of this discrimination as you search for employment. Here are some suggestions for how *all* teachers (not just NNESTs) can help oppose it:

- Document and report any evidence of discrimination that you notice (e.g. job adverts for 'native speakers').
- Follow and contribute to online resources campaigning for non-native speaker teachers (e.g. teflequityadvocates.com).
- Join organisations that support and advocate for equal status for non-native speaker teachers (e.g. TESOL; IATEFL).

Advice specific to non-native speaker teachers:

- Promote your multilingualism and multiculturalism as a positive asset.
- Remember that NNESTs can effectively model and promote lingua franca varieties of English (Jenkins, 2000; Seidlhofer, 2011) in their own classroom practices, models that are potentially more appropriate to the majority of English language learners worldwide than native speaker models.
- Raise your own awareness of the comparative merits of native and non-native speaker teachers; *The NNEST Lens: Non-native English speakers in TESOL* (Mahboob, 2010) and *The Non-native Teacher* (Medgyes, 1994) are two useful books to read on this topic.
- Demonstrate your own expertise in English in the public forum (e.g. write a blog or LinkedIn post on an area of grammar and how to teach it).
- Highlight your own expertise in English and your teaching experience on your CV and LinkedIn profile prominently, including details of positions held and qualifications gained in English.
- Finally, remember that you have done something that no native speaker has done but all learners of English want to do – learn English as a foreign language!

For more advice, support and ideas, see: *Coping Strategies for NNES Teachers' Development* by Wu et al. (2010), from where several of the above suggestions are taken.

A.4 Starting work

The initial learning curve

It is possible that in your first day's teaching you will teach almost as many hours as you do on the whole of a typical CertTESOL course. Contact hours for full-time positions usually range from 20-30 a week, meaning 4-6 hours per day, although some organisations reduce this during the induction period of newly qualified teachers. You will cope (you have to), but you will have to develop a number of skills that are rarely taught on initial teacher training courses:

- planning a long lesson (up to 3 hours) quickly
- finding and preparing necessary resources quickly
- researching challenging areas of grammar, lexis and phonology quickly
- completing administrative documents quickly (e.g. records of lessons taught and materials used, class registers).

This may come as a shock if you feel you have already been doing things quickly on the CertTESOL, but it is likely that what you have been doing is preparing detailed lesson plans and professional materials quickly, while also dealing with assignments and other important course requirements.

What can I do to prepare for the initial workload?

Once you have accepted the job, a really useful tip is to find out as much as you can, as soon as you can, about who you'll be teaching in your first week, what materials you'll be using (you may be able to buy the coursebook and familiarise yourself with it, even if you're in a different country), and get examples of any admin documents you'll need to complete, especially lesson plan pro formas. Think about what's likely to happen in your first lessons and prepare materials for this. Here are some suggestions:

- an activity in which the learners find out about the teacher (e.g. write the answers to 10 questions about you on the board; the learners will need to guess the questions)
- a *'Find someone who…'* activity in which they stand and mingle to find out about each other and you (most useful if they are starting a new course together, less so if you are taking over an established class)
- a writing activity in which they inform you about their needs and preferences as learners (e.g. essay questions: *'Why are you learning English?'*, *'What makes a good teacher?'*)
- a project activity in which they contribute recommendations to a 'Welcome to our City!' booklet for you, their new teacher. Different pairs or groups can write articles about aspects of culture, transport, food, recommendations, etc.

It's unlikely that your future employer will require lesson plans for every lesson, or they will require brief plans only, so you will usually be able to 'rough prepare' your lessons. Here are some suggestions for how to do this:

- Read through any core course materials you will be expected to cover and make sure you understand how to do the activities and know the answers to any tricky questions.
- Make notes on how you will use the materials and prepare the first couple of activities in greater detail.
- Think about what kind of activities might complement these core course materials and

> *There's no need to plan lessons in as much detail as you did on your course. BUT, do plan and when you do, keep records of this. After the lesson, reflect on your planning by making notes on the plan. Not only will this help you build up a bank of lessons, it will also help you develop as a reflective practitioner.*
>
> Emma, CertTESOL trainer

either find these in photocopiable resource books or prepare them yourself – then make further notes on how you'll use them. After thinking carefully about student groupings, decide how many copies you will need, make these copies and cut up materials if required.

■ Think of one or two 'fall back' activities in case the students get through what you've prepared (e.g. a writing activity or discussion questions that require them to use the grammar, lexis and other language introduced in the lesson).

Many teachers find it useful to buy some pre-prepared materials that can supplement any coursebooks. This may come in the form of books offering useful ideas for activities and games (e.g. *700 Classroom Activities*, Seymour & Popova, 2003) or photocopiable resource books with ready-prepared activities for grammar practice (e.g. *Grammar Games and Activities for Teachers*, Watcyn-Jones, 1995), speaking practice (e.g. *Role Plays for Today*, Anderson, 2006; *Instant Discussions*, MacAndrew & Martinez, 2003) or longer whole-lesson activities (e.g. *Teamwork*, Anderson, 2004). Such books usually have grammatical and topical indexes where you can search for an area you are teaching and find useful materials.

After a week or two you should begin to get into the rhythm of your new job, and the preparation time will start to reduce. Keep working hard and remember that you're probably learning more now than you will at any other time in your career. After a couple of months, you will gain further confidence and, as well as beginning to find time for other things, your mind will turn towards your professional development as a newly qualified teacher.

Continuing professional development (CPD)

Within the broader field of teacher education, a distinction is often made between teacher training and teacher development (e.g. Freeman, 1989). While teacher training tends to focus on achieving specific, often predetermined and undifferentiated outcomes (like meeting the criteria on the CertTESOL), development tends to focus more on individual improvement, based on personal needs that are often achieved by means of supported enquiry and reflection (like the post-lesson feedback/discussion on the CertTESOL). As you begin to develop as a novice teacher, the support you require will naturally become more specific to your needs – what you find challenging, what you're most interested in and what you believe is important in teaching. You will hopefully find yourself questioning the rules of thumb and prescriptive frameworks provided on your CertTESOL. As Martin Parrott, an experienced teacher trainer, once advised me after watching me teach a CertTESOL-type lesson over a year after I'd graduated: *'You need to start breaking the rules.'*

Your first experience of developmental support is likely to come in the form of supervision, one or two lesson observations from your line manager. She or he will be firstly 'checking up' on you to ensure that you are meeting standards required of the school, but also (hopefully) helping you to develop personally – this combination of supervision and support is quite common in ELT. You may be required to produce a formal lesson plan, similar to those used on your CertTESOL, and after the lesson you should have an opportunity to discuss it, finishing with suggestions for personal improvement. This will hopefully be useful, but given the supervisory nature, you may feel nervous and this will often prevent you from experimenting much. For this, other provisions are more likely to be useful, such as discussion with peers, **mentoring**, **reflective practice** and **action research**.

> *Take five minutes at the end of every week to reflect on your teaching (ideally, over a celebratory piece of cake!). Make some notes on the successful moments in your classes. What worked and why do you think it did? Five-minute journaling can help you to identify some key moments in your practice.*
>
> Sinèad, CertTESOL trainer

While discussion sounds a rather obvious idea, research has shown that it is an effective means for helping teachers (especially newly-qualified teachers) to improve their practice (e.g. Villegas-Reimers, 2003). It can happen informally (over the photocopier or in the staff kitchen), or formally (in teacher development workshops) and involves teachers describing, comparing and evaluating their practice, something we tend to do naturally, often without thinking about it. For example, if you come back into the staff room after a weak lesson, start telling a colleague about it, and they offer some advice or criticise a coursebook you used, this is discussion. Or if a workshop requires you to discuss in pairs how you would set up an activity or deliver a piece of grammar, this is discussion and will help you to develop as a newly-qualified teacher.

A **mentor** is an experienced colleague who is able to afford a little time on a regular basis to help you to develop. They can also engage in discussion with you, but there are a number of other things a mentor can do that are useful:

- sit down with you to plan how you would like to move your professional development forward, identifying appropriate objectives and means to achieve these objectives
- observe your lessons (including the experimental ones) and discuss them with you afterwards
- let you observe their 'everyday' lessons and discuss these too
- share resources, ideas, activities and solutions that work in your current teaching context
- plan lessons together with you, enabling you to compare different ways of doing the same thing
- make recommendations, for example to read a book or article, attend a conference or visit a website

Reflective practice refers to a deliberate effort to examine your own teaching critically in order to improve. While this is something that many good teachers do naturally, we can make it more effective by employing specific strategies, such as keeping a teaching diary or writing a blog, evaluating our own lesson plans and materials after teaching in order to improve them, and also investigating important events that happen in our teaching to learn from them, what Brookfield calls 'critical incidents' (1990). A key advantage to reflective practice is that we can do it on our own if necessary, although it is likely to be most useful if it is combined with other professional development strategies.

Action research refers to a cyclical process of identifying a challenge or question important to your teaching, coming up with a possible solution, trying it out and then reflecting or evaluating how successful the solution is, so that you can decide whether to continue using it or to look for other potential solutions (see Figure A.1). Action research cycles can be conducted informally or they can be formalised into larger scale research projects that can be shared with colleagues or even published.

**Identify a challenge
or question**
e.g. My learners
never seem to do
writing homework.

**Come up with a
possible solution**
e.g. Perhaps they
need more guidance
on how to start.

Try out the solution
e.g. Devote the last
30 minutes of the
lesson to providing
such guidance.

**Reflect on or evaluate
the solution**
e.g. See how many
learners do the
homework, look at
quality of work and ask
their opinions regarding
the guidance.

CPD programmes

Every good language school should have an ongoing CPD programme of some sort, although this will vary in type, scale and degree of formality depending on the size and professionalism of the institution. For some schools, CPD means an observation by your line manager twice a year and a one-hour workshop for all the teachers every month. For others, you will have an opportunity to identify specific objectives that you want to achieve in a given year, support as you endeavour to achieve these objectives, and a professional development appraisal meeting at the end of the year to evaluate how well you have done, what you have learnt and what objectives you would like to focus on for the next year.

CPD workshops are probably the most obvious CPD activity that you can expect to participate in. Each workshop is usually led by a member of the teaching staff and attended by colleagues. Perhaps the most common type of CPD workshop is often called an 'ideas share' in which the teacher leading the workshop shows one or more activities for colleagues to discuss and try out in their own classes. Their choice of activities may relate to a specific personal interest, or something that they feel has worked well in their classroom. The emphasis in ideas share workshops is on the practical side of teaching, and they are often very useful to newly qualified teachers, less so to more experienced teachers who often know a lot of the ideas being presented. Discussion workshops are also common, in which a concept, question, article or opinion is introduced for discussion, which may happen either in small groups or in one larger group, depending on the size of the teaching staff and the nature of the activity. A third common topic for CPD workshops is presentations by colleagues, most commonly relating to areas of research or study of members of the teaching staff. Some larger schools may often also benefit from 'invited speakers' who conduct workshops on specific areas of expertise.

A.5   Teaching qualifications and career paths

As you settle into your first post-CertTESOL job, as well as starting to think about your professional development, you may also begin to think about further qualification or a specific career path. With regard to both of these, there are a number of options available to you.

Before reading on, try this short visualisation exercise:

> *Close your eyes (not yet) and imagine yourself in 10 years' time. Where will you be? What will you be doing? Most importantly, what will you have achieved by then, and what will you have learnt?*

Open your eyes and make a few notes. Don't worry if they are a bit sketchy or romantic at this stage – it's fun to dream! The next section of this chapter will hopefully help you to flesh out these ideas and get a clearer idea of how to achieve your goals.

Gaining further qualifications

While the Trinity CertTESOL provides you with 'certification' to teach, given the length of the course and the intensity of the experience, you are likely to have plenty of gaps in your professional knowledge, and a need for further, more extensive qualification. Let's look at some of the options:

Trinity DipTESOL and Cambridge English Delta	High level qualifications for EFL and ESL teachers that combine practical and theoretical aspects, both qualifications are designed to follow on from their initial counterparts later in your career. You will usually need two years' experience to be accepted on either course. Both are accredited at level 7 on the OFQUAL (Office of Qualifications and Examinations Regulation) UK Regulated Qualifications framework (RQF), and take from around 3 months (full-time, intensive) to 9-12 months (part-time) to complete.
MA (Master of Arts)	A large number of universities worldwide offer MAs in qualifications directly relating to language teaching. These include MA in ELT, MA in TESOL and an MA in Applied Linguistics. Also at level 7 on the UK RQF, MAs typically take one year (full-time) or two years (part-time) to complete. MAs tend to be more theoretical than DipTESOL or DELTA, although many MAs taken in the US and Canada will include a practicum element. Most useful if you plan to move into the academic field and/or higher education.
Teacher management qualifications	The Diploma in English Language Teaching Management (DELTM) qualification is designed for teachers or managers based in the UK and validated by Trinity College London. Courses run from September to June each year. The ELT Leadership Management Certificate Programme is run by the U.S.-based TESOL organisation, and is a shorter course, typically taking one month to complete.
QTS (Qualified Teacher Status)	If you are interested in working in primary or secondary schools in a specific country, it is likely that you will need Qualified Teacher Status. Paths to this vary, but can include full-time courses (such as the UK PGCE) and bridging courses through which you can add to your current qualifications to gain QTS. In some countries you may find you can gain qualified teacher status simply by having your current qualifications certified (e.g. a relevant BA plus CertTESOL).
Other qualifications for English language teachers	The Cambridge TKT (Teacher Knowledge Test) is a written test that demonstrates your knowledge of language (e.g. grammar, lexis, etc.), planning, methodology, resources and classroom management strategies. It does not have a teaching practice element. The Trinity TYLEC (Teaching Young Learners Extension Certificate) is an extension qualification for qualified teachers providing the skills and knowledge to teach younger learners aged 7-16. It involves course input, teaching practice and assisted lesson planning, an assessed Observation Journal and the completion of a reflective Teaching Practice Journal. The Cambridge ICELT (In-service Certificate in English Language Teaching) is an in-service qualification for experienced teachers (500+ hours) at a lower level than the Dip TESOL or the Delta, including three components: language for teachers, teaching, and methodology with a teaching practice element that you can usually do in your own classroom.
English language qualifications	If you are a non-native speaker teacher, you may want to gain specific English language qualifications, including the Trinity ISE (Integrated Skills in English) III (C1 level) and IV (C2 level), the Trinity GESE (Graded Exam in Spoken English) at levels 10 (C1) to 12 (C2), the Cambridge Advanced (C1) and Proficiency (C2) exams. Your choice of exam should be influenced both by your personal needs and knowledge about which exams are considered more prestigious in the country where you are seeking employment.

Your choice of qualifications should obviously be informed by your envisaged career path. If you intend to work within the private language teaching sector, the DipTESOL or DELTA are usually required for more senior teaching positions, or teaching positions in high-quality institutes such as the British Council and many language schools based in the UK. If you would like to move into management, any of the teacher management qualifications provided are obviously useful. MA qualifications are more important for anybody thinking about moving into the academic field, working at universities, and tend to be more widely recognised outside of the private ELT industry. Let's look at some possible career paths now.

Possible career paths in ELT

Figure A.2 shows a number of potential career paths within ELT. While these paths look quite organised on the chart, the reality is that many of us bounce about in different directions across this chart. And some of the best practitioners in our industry never feel the need to move beyond 'English teacher', simultaneously (in my opinion) the most important and the most difficult job of all to do well!

Figure A.2:
Career paths in ELT

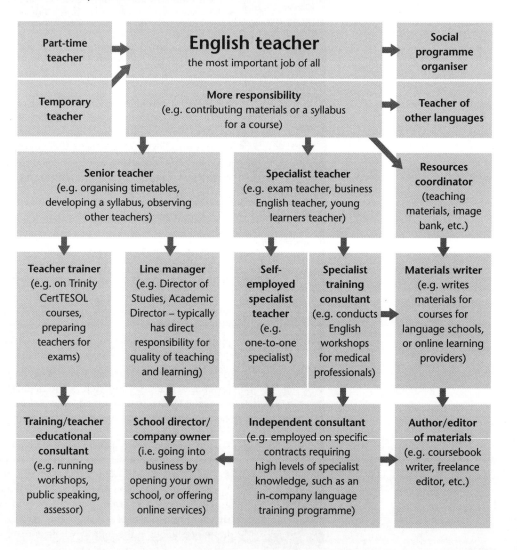

Taking on extra responsibility

Once you become a full-time English teacher and after having found your feet and dealt with the initial learning curve, the first step you will probably take in your career path will be to take on more responsibility, perhaps providing extra resources for courses, additional services for learners, etc. Schools often have social programmes and organising events can often include some of the most enjoyable extra responsibilities. Doing this can also be a great way to get to make friends with some of the students if you are new to the area.

Senior teacher

This can be an interesting and challenging end in itself for those of us who love teaching, as it provides a nice balance between teaching, supporting other teachers and possibly being involved in aspects of management (e.g. co-interviewing for a new position, designing a new course). In most schools it's likely to be accompanied by a higher salary, but also longer hours. Some senior teachers are expected to teach as many hours as their junior colleagues.

Teacher training

There are many ways to move into teacher training. The first step is probably to get a higher level teaching qualification such as the Trinity DipTESOL or Cambridge DELTA. Initial opportunities are likely to be found in larger schools which may need a senior teacher to observe and mentor new teachers, or to coordinate an in-school CPD programme. If you're interested in getting into initial teacher training (like your trainers on the CertTESOL) you will usually need to get a position at a school that runs such courses and train up gradually by shadowing the trainers before being approved by Trinity. Through teacher training, you may have opportunities to run workshops, do some public speaking or possibly get into teacher training assessment, all of which are rewarding. As with much of the other specialist work at this level, the biggest challenge if and when you go freelance is planning for, and managing a gradual but steady stream of work.

From line management to starting your own business

For those interested in management related work, the first stage after senior teacher is usually to become an Assistant Director of Studies, supporting the Director of Studies (DoS) and covering for them when they are away. When you have enough experience of this, you may get the opportunity to apply for posts as a DoS (look out for temporary DoS jobs at summer school camps). Larger schools may also have an Academic Director as well as a DoS, or instead of one. DoS's and Academic Directors primarily take responsibility for the quality of the 'product' of the school. It's their job to hire and support teachers, plan courses and deal with problems, complaints, etc.

If you have financial and/or entrepreneurial ambitions, you may think about opening your own business. The most obvious idea is to open a language school, but beware – markets are often saturated and profit margins can be small. Managing students and teachers can also make this a stressful career choice. Perhaps a less stressful option is to set up a niche business, such as developing a website or an app for language learning, starting a business that offers one-to-one teaching, or self-publish your own teaching materials.

Specialist teacher to independent consultant

This most commonly involves developing your skills in one specific area of teaching and gradually building up expertise within this domain. For example, prior experience in business can be a useful asset (but not a prerequisite) for those interested in becoming business

English teachers, some of whom go on to become 'international communication consultants' or 'cultural trainers'. Exams are perhaps the most common area requiring specialist teacher knowledge (knowing about a specific exam, how to prepare for and pass it). For many, such specialist work often leads into becoming a self-employed specialist teacher, possibly via one-to-one teaching; you can teach from home, or visit clients in offices. By building up a reputation, and possibly an online presence, this can lead to other work in either the public or private sector (e.g. developing an English language course for a bank or airline).

Resources development to materials writing

If you enjoyed the Materials Assignment, this career path may be for you. Many materials writers begin by developing their own materials and sharing them with others. You can do this now for free via online blogs or social networks – remember to get feedback from colleagues if you do. Another useful first step is to take responsibility for coordinating materials in your school. Today this is often 'soft' resources, including printable and photocopiable handouts and booklets prepared on a computer, although other resources such as posters for the classrooms, laminated colour images and a big box of useful **realia** are just as useful today as they ever were. As you begin to develop an understanding of what materials work and why, and of the role of materials in the teaching process, you can experiment with more extensive projects such as whole lessons, short courses, etc. Providing materials for online course providers and websites offering supplementary teaching resources can help to develop your skills further and to build useful contacts and familiarity with your name. You may be lucky and a publisher may take interest in a proposal idea you have. Alternatively, short projects will lead to specific contracts which themselves will get you into the publishing industry, writing supplementary resources, material for teachers or even coursebooks. While writing a coursebook sounds like great fun, be aware of the long hours of desk work required!

Review of After the course

Categorisation task

For each of the following pieces of advice, make a note of the section of the unit it refers to. An example has been provided:

Advice	Section?
1 Summer schools are great places to get some initial experience.	A.1 Planning your next career moves
2 Take along some ideas for warmers, games and language practice activities, in case you're asked.	
3 Try teaching an exam class if you want a challenge.	
4 Start learning the language before you go.	
5 Use Facebook and LinkedIn to make contact with teachers in the country where you would like to teach, and ask for advice.	
6 Prepare lesson plans for your first lessons in advance, using a 'Getting to know you' theme.	
7 Ask your tutors about countries where they've worked.	
8 Avoid employers who presume that being a native speaker is more important than being a qualified teacher.	
9 Don't be afraid to tell your line manager what you would like them to watch for when they observe your first lesson.	
10 Remember that you are an expert English language learner, unlike any native-speaker.	

If you need to, check your answers in the *Review Key* at the back of this book.

Now return to the learning opportunities provided at the start of the chapter. Tick the ones that you feel you have achieved and re-read the relevant sections for any you're not sure about.

The Knowledge

K.1 CertTESOL pass, fail and other outcomes explained

This section of *The Knowledge* helps you understand what you need to do to pass the Trinity CertTESOL, how you could fail the CertTESOL, and other possible options if you have difficulty meeting the required criteria. It is based on information provided on the Trinity CertTESOL syllabus. Always refer to the latest version of the Trinity syllabus if you are having difficulty, or need to check any of these details. The information provided here is intended as a summary only.

Passing the CertTESOL

In order to pass the CertTESOL, you must complete and pass all five units of the course. Usually this happens during the course, although on some occasions, units may be completed after the course (usually up to about a month later; see *Referral* below). Table K.1 summarises what you have to do for each unit and who assesses it.

Attendance

Obviously, you need to attend the whole course, although sickness and other reasons can sometimes cause trainees to miss a day or two. If you do, you will have to work hard to catch up, and must still complete all of the coursework to the required level. Course providers are likely to have minimum attendance requirements. If you do not meet these requirements for good reason, options for completing the course may include referral and deferral (see below). However, if you don't have a good reason for not attending, referral or deferral may not be possible. Your course tutors will discuss this with the external moderator.

a   some awareness of how to use reference materials and other sources of guidance as above

b   some ability to work collaboratively with peers and tutors in preparation of work and giving and receiving feedback on performance

c   some ability to produce journals and other assignments as above.

Deferral

In order to pass the course, trainees must be present on the day(s) when the external moderator visits the course provider, usually towards the end of the course. However, if you are absent on this day (e.g. due to illness or bereavement), as long as the course provider and moderator consider it appropriate, they can 'defer' you. This process is called deferral. If you are deferred, you will need to attend a moderation visit at some stage in the future. This may be with the same course provider, or if this is not possible, with a different course provider, at a different venue. This usually happens within two months of the end of the course.

Unit	What you have to do	Who assesses it
Unit 1: Teaching skills	There are three elements that you must pass in Unit 1: • Teaching practice (assessed by your tutors as you teach) • Teaching practice portfolio (the written record of your teaching practice, including lesson plans, materials, self-evaluation documents, etc.) • Guided Observation Journal based on lessons you observe and including the tasks that you completed during observation	All these elements are marked by your tutors and moderated (checked) by the external moderator.
Unit 2: Language Awareness & Skills	On many courses you take a written exam, which you will need to pass. On others you will have to complete a language awareness assignment to the required level.	Marked by your tutors and moderated by the external moderator.
Unit 3: Learner Profile	On all courses you will pass this unit by completing a Learner Profile assignment based on an interview and a one-to-one lesson with an English-language learner to the required level.	Marked by your tutors and moderated by the external moderator.
Unit 4: Materials Assignment	On all courses you will pass this unit by firstly creating and using some materials in your teaching practice lessons. You will then complete a written pro forma provided by Trinity, and then discuss the materials in a face-to-face interview with the external moderator towards the end of your course, meeting pre-specified criteria in both.	All elements assessed by the external moderator.
Unit 5: Unknown Language	On all courses you will pass this unit by completing an Unknown Language Assignment to the required level based on your experience of learning an unknown language, organised as part of your course.	Marked by your tutors and moderated by the external moderator.

Table K.1
Summary of
CertTESOL requirements

Failing the CertTESOL

Like all qualifications, it is possible to fail the CertTESOL. This happens if you finish the course but don't complete all the coursework, or you complete it but are not able to meet the required criteria. It is possible for you to fail without referral if your course tutors and the external moderator feel that it is not likely that you will be able to demonstrate the required knowledge, skills, awareness or attitude through referral (see below). Fail grades are more likely for candidates who are having difficulty on several units, especially Unit 1, as this is the most important unit on a course that qualifies you to teach. Trainees who are referred on one or more units must demonstrate the required criteria in the referred elements in order to pass. If they do not, they receive a fail grade. Fortunately, because all course providers are required to interview potential course candidates, and consider their suitability for the course before they begin, course providers are usually able to spot candidates who are likely to fail

197

in advance and recommend that they do not take the course. For this reason, failure is rare, but not because it's easy to pass the course. All candidates must complete the coursework as required by the course provider to the standards of the course provider.

In order to fail, you must complete the whole course. If you decide to leave the course before the end (of your own volition), you are considered to have withdrawn (see withdrawal below). If you have completed the whole course, there are two grounds for assigning a fail grade to a candidate. One is if you do not complete the required coursework on time (i.e. one or more of the internally assessed units is not submitted for marking before the moderation day). The other is possible if you complete all the coursework, but three or more of your assignments are below standard and you have demonstrated any of the following:

a an insufficient level of the necessary knowledge of language and language learning

b an insufficient level of the necessary competence in preparing for and teaching classes

c an insufficient awareness of how to use reference materials and other sources of guidance

d an insufficient ability to work collaboratively with peers and tutors in preparation of work, and giving/receiving feedback on performance

e an insufficient ability to produce journals and assignments

Withdrawal

If you do not complete the course (i.e. you stop attending) you are considered to have withdrawn from the course rather than failed it. Trainees who find the course too difficult, or perhaps are not enjoying teaching may choose to withdraw. If you withdraw you are not normally entitled to receive any refunds of any fees you have paid – for further guidance with this, see the Terms and Conditions of your course provider. However, a candidate who has to withdraw due to illness or other unavoidable occurrence may be able to transfer onto a different course, at the course provider's and Trinity's discretion.

Appeal

If you feel that you would like to appeal against your final grade, Trinity have an appeals procedure. Refer to the CertTESOL Summary document (called: A summary of course content and key information for course members) for the appeals procedure.

K.2 English language exams and tests

This section of *The Knowledge* provides an overview of some of the most commonly taught international English language exams available around the world.

While most exam teachers have prior experience, newly qualified teachers can also be asked to teach exam classes. If this happens to you, don't worry! While they are more challenging than teaching general English, exam classes have several advantages, including clear structure and course objectives, and often more motivated learners. Here are a number of useful tips in case you are asked to teach an exam class towards the start of your career:

1   Find the official website for the exam in question and investigate it carefully. There will often be detailed information about the exam contents, sample exam materials and links to resources for teachers.

2   Get hold of some past examination papers and study them carefully. The simplest way to become an expert on an English-language exam is to take it a few times yourself, which is useful even for native speakers of English. Then analyse it, working out which skills and areas of language each part of the exam is testing.

3   Make sure you have a good coursebook designed for the exam in question to use with your students. This may already have been chosen for you, but if not, research different coursebooks carefully and make sure you have both the Student's Book and Teacher's Book as well as other essential resources such as audio files/CD, Workbook and Resource Pack (if this exists).

4   Find out as much as possible about the students and the course in advance. You may be required to prepare them for an exam in quite a short time, in which case you will need to focus primarily on exam skills. Alternatively, you may have as much as a year (or even two) to prepare them, in which case you can balance the exam preparation with general development and improvement of the learners' skills, grammar, vocabulary and pronunciation.

5   If possible, talk to teachers who have prepared students for this exam, and get some advice.

Here follows some brief information about several of the most widely taken exams in ELT:

IELTS (International English Language Testing System)

IELTS is one of the most popular English-language tests in the world, originally developed primarily for students wishing to study in English (especially in the UK and Australasia), but now is increasingly also used for other purposes (e.g. visa and immigration purposes in the UK). It has two papers, an 'Academic' one for students and a 'General Training' one for other candidates, both of which test all four skills (reading, writing, speaking and listening). All parts of the academic exam involve tasks relevant to study, covering topics of general interest from both the natural and social sciences and the arts. IELTS can be taken at any level, and candidates receive a score rather than a pass or fail grade. As well as receiving an overall score, candidates receive a breakdown of scores for different skills. Scores range from 0 (lowest) to 9 (proficient user) and increments of 0.5 are possible. Typical scores required for study in the UK range from 5.5 (intermediate level; B1-2) to 8 (advanced level; C1).

TOEFL (Test of English as a Foreign Language)

TOEFL was initially offered as an exam to test the competencies of non-native speakers of English wishing to enrol in North American universities. Since then, it has expanded to become one of the largest international exams in the world, and is accepted by academic institutions in a wide range of countries. All parts of the exam have an academic flavour, including lectures in the listening exam, academic papers in the reading exam and a discursive essay in the writing task. Like IELTS, candidates receive scores. Tests can be taken online (iBT) or on paper, and confusingly, scores are different for the two versions. For the iBT a total score out of 120 points is calculated by adding together scores for the four skills (reading, writing, speaking and listening – 30 marks each), and for the paper-based test, scores range between 310 and 677. Typical scores for entry into university range from 60 to over 100 on the more common iBT.

Trinity Graded Exams in Spoken English (GESE)

GESE exams are some of the most popular spoken English language exams taken by learners of all ages around the world. They test both speaking and listening skills, and include 12 exams at four different stages (Initial stage – Grades 1-3; Elementary stage – Grades 4-6; Intermediate stage – Grades 7-9; Advanced stage – Grades 10-12). GESE exams are taken face-to-face with a trained examiner, and include realistic tasks such as conversation, interactive tasks and listening tasks.

Trinity Integrated Skills in English (ISE)

ISE exams are available at five levels (Foundation, I, II, III, IV), which correspond to the Common European Framework levels (A2-C2) and aim to test skills in an integrated fashion (with two exam modules: Reading & Writing; Speaking & Listening). ISE exams are taken by many students who wish to enter higher education in the UK, where they are accepted by the vast majority of institutions.

ESOL Skills for Life

Offered by a number of organisations (Trinity, City and Guilds), Skills for Life are UK-oriented exams based on the UK adult ESOL core curriculum. Typically taken by learners studying in ESOL classes, Skills for Life exams are oriented towards immigrants (so not normally taken by EFL students). They are designed with a practical focus to help candidates gain basic skills that will enable them to integrate into, and work in UK society effectively. They are linked to the UK Regulated Qualifications Framework, with exams at five levels (Entry 1, Entry 2, Entry 3, Level 1 and Level 2). Because many ESOL learners have quite varying profiles (some may have very good speaking skills but weak writing, or good reading and writing but weak speaking and listening), candidates can sometimes gain qualification in different skills at different levels. The speaking and listening skills are normally assessed together in one exam, and the reading and writing each usually have their own exam.

Cambridge General English exams

Often called the 'Cambridge Main Suite', these exams range from A2 to C2 level. The Cambridge General English exams can be passed or failed, and as well as testing all four skills they usually have a paper oriented towards use of English that tests aspects of grammar and lexis. The First (previously called 'First Certificate in English') is the most popular; a pass mark indicates an approximately upper intermediate (B2) level of English. The Cambridge Advanced and Proficiency are considered valid for entry into many universities in the UK, and to a lesser extent in Australasia and North America. The exams are also accepted in some countries for immigration purposes. For all of these exams, the speaking test is taken in pairs, which has the advantage for teachers of encouraging learners to work in pairs more during lessons. Versions of the KET, PET and FCE are also available for schools:

1   Cambridge English Key (KET) – A2 level

2   Cambridge English Preliminary (PET) – B1 level

3   Cambridge English First (FCE) – B2 level

4   Cambridge English Advanced (CAE) – C1 level

5   Cambridge English Proficiency (CPE) – C2 level

Cambridge Young Learners exams

These three exams are designed as counterparts to the General English exams, but with papers and questions that are 'child friendly'. Like the General English exams, candidates can pass or fail:

1   Cambridge English: Starters (YLE Starters) – beginner level

2   Cambridge English: Movers (YLE Movers) – A1 level

3   Cambridge English: Flyers (YLE Flyers) – A2 level

Cambridge Business English Certificates

This set includes three general business exams ranging from B1 to C1 level. Marketed to both individual professionals and companies, these exams prepare candidates to work in international business environments, and follow similar formats to the Cambridge General English exams. For example, candidates take the speaking exams in pairs:

1   BEC Preliminary – B1 level

2   BEC Vantage – B2 level

3   BEC Higher – C1 level

Other exams

APTIS: A recently developed exam offered online by the British Council. It is targeted mainly at companies and organisations, who may tailor it to their own needs. Involves a grammar and vocabulary paper, and any or all of the four skills, depending on how it is used.

BULATS – Business Language Testing Service: The English exam in this international series is developed by Cambridge and offers a score, rather than pass or fail grades. It typically provides services for companies rather than individuals.

International English for Speakers of Other Languages – I(S)ESOL: Offered by City and Guilds. The spoken exam (ISESOL) is offered separately from the IESOL exam, which is written and includes listening, reading and writing.

Pearson PTE: Offers academic or general exams, developed by Pearson Language Assessments, appropriate for both study abroad and immigration purposes in some countries.

TOEIC – Test of English for International communication: A U.S.-based international exam, popular also in the Far East. Like IELTS and TOEFL, TOEIC candidates receive a score rather than a pass or fail.

Different exam qualifications mapped onto the CEFR

Table K.2 provides a summary of how the different exams map onto one another using the Common European Framework (CEFR) for comparison. Be aware that because the different exams use very different systems for assessment, and even different constructs of proficiency, this mapping is only approximate.

Table K.2
Main ELT exams
mapped onto the CEFR

CEFR	Level	Trinity	Cambridge	Scored exams
–	Beginner	Trinity GESE Grade 1	Cambridge YLE Starters	–
A1	Elementary	Trinity GESE Grade 2	Cambridge YLE Movers	–
		ESOL Skills for Life Entry 1		
A2	Pre-intermediate	Trinity GESE Grade 3-4 Trinity ISE Foundation	Cambridge KET Cambridge YLE Flyers	–
		ESOL Skills for Life Entry 2		
B1	Intermediate	Trinity GESE Grade 5-6 Trinity ISE I	Cambridge PET Cambridge BEC Preliminary	IELTS 4.0-5.5 TOEFL iBT > c. 60*
		ESOL Skills for Life Entry 3		
B2	Upper intermediate	Trinity GESE Grade 7-9 Trinity ISE II	Cambridge FCE Cambridge BEC Vantage	IELTS 5.5-6.5 TOEFL iBT c. 70-90*
		ESOL Skills for Life Level 1		
C1	Advanced	Trinity GESE Grade 10-11 Trinity ISE III	Cambridge Advanced Cambridge BEC Higher	IELTS 7-8 TOEFL iBT c. 100-115
		ESOL Skills for Life Level 2		
C2	Proficiency	Trinity GESE Grade 12 Trinity ISE IV	Cambridge Proficiency	IELTS 8.5-9 TOEFL iBT c. 115+

*Below C1 level, there is a lot of variation in opinion as to how TOEFL maps onto the other frameworks.

K.3 Lesson structures and paradigms

This section of *The Knowledge* describes some of the models (often called 'paradigms') commonly used to structure lessons in ELT. It is likely that your tutors on your CertTESOL will introduce one or more of these paradigms to help you to plan and describe the structure of your lessons. Different paradigms tend to reflect different approaches to teaching and underlying philosophies about how languages are learnt. On your course, you will need to follow the advice provided by your tutors, but you may also have the chance to learn by experimenting with different paradigms. Each is likely to suit certain learners, certain levels, certain areas of language, certain types of course, certain cultures and even certain teaching styles.

PPP – Presentation, practice, production (Byrne 1976)

The oldest and the most enduring paradigm within communicative language teaching. Originally developed by Donn Byrne in *Teaching Oral English* (1976), it is still used on some CertTESOL courses today, although it has been criticised for being restrictive and teacher-centred by some. While Byrne (1986) argued that the steps could be used flexibly, it is typically used in the *Presentation-> Practice-> Production* order, and generally only suitable for describing lessons where new language (lexis, grammar and functional language) is introduced. *Presentation* typically involves the teacher presenting (or helping learners to notice) new language, *Practice* typically involves controlled practice (e.g. gap fill activities, spoken drills, etc.), and *Production* typically involves freer activities where learners are encouraged to use the new language in more natural communicative contexts.

OHE – Observe, hypothesize, experiment (Lewis 1993)

Michael Lewis's paradigm for describing how learners acquire new structures, and associated with his Lexical Approach. While it is undoubtedly 'learner-centred' (it describes exactly what the learner does when they learn new language), because it focuses on individual, internal processes, it is arguably of less use to teachers who need to plan and organise lessons as social events.

ARC – Authentic (practice), restricted (practice), clarification (Scrivener 1994)

Jim Scrivener's planning paradigm introduced in the first edition of *Learning Teaching*. The three elements are flexible in order. *Clarification* is similar to *Presentation* in PPP, but does not presuppose that the teacher leads this stage, *Restricted practice* is pretty much the same as *Practice* in PPP, and *Authentic practice* involves using language in ways that emulate real-world language use, and can potentially include receptive skills, like Harmer's *Activate* (below). One potential problem with Scrivener's model is the notion of 'authenticity' which, some writers have argued is a poorly defined construct, or even impossible for language learners in a classroom (e.g. Widdowson, 1998).

Task-based learning (e.g. Willis 1996)

Task-based learning (TBL) is more an approach than a specific paradigm, and a wide number of writers from the mid-1980s to the present day have described different models for task-based learning. One of the most commonly used TBL models in ELT teacher training is Jane Willis's *Framework for Task-based Learning* (1996). Willis's model typically involves three elements that take place in the following order: *Pre-task*, in which learners are introduced to the task and the topic, *Task cycle*, in which learners do the task then report on how it went and *Language focus*, in which learners analyse and practise language. Leaving the language focus towards the end of the lesson may seem counterintuitive, although there is some evidence from research that learners may be more receptive to analysis after trying to do the task. Task-based learning has been criticised for a number of reasons (see, e.g., Swan, 2005b), but it continues to interest many teachers who feel it is effective, especially at higher levels of proficiency.

ESA – Engage, study, activate (Harmer 1998)

Jeremy Harmer's planning paradigm first introduced in *How to Teach English* (1998) is one of the most popular on CertTESOL courses. The three elements are more flexible in order than PPP. The *Engage* element emphasises the importance of learner involvement in the learning process. The *Study* element includes both the *Presentation and Practice* from PPP, although it is less prescriptive as to how learners should 'study' language. *Activate* is similar to *Production*, but also can potentially include receptive skills (if learners are engaging with a reading or listening text to understand the content rather than to focus on the language). One potential criticism of Harmer's model is that arguably all stages in a lesson should engage learners, including *Study* and *Activate*.

TTT – Test, teach, test (anonymous)

Test Teach Test is a paradigm used to provide learners with focused instruction that enables them to see the progress they are making in an individual lesson. It begins by providing an opportunity for the learners to try out doing something in English, or possibly to use an area of language. While the learners are doing this, the teacher monitors to notice any issues they have or mistakes they are making. The teacher then teaches the learners about this area of language, focusing specifically on areas where difficulty was observed. Afterwards, the learners do another task (or possibly repeat the same one) that requires the same language or the same outcome, and the teacher monitors again to (hopefully) notice improvement. An interesting model, but the use of the term 'test' is problematic, as learners are actually using language, not being tested on their usage of it.

Receptive skills lesson paradigm: Pre, During and Post (e.g. Scrivener 2011)

Although this paradigm does not have a memorable name or acronym, it is perhaps the most universally taught one on initial teacher training courses like the CertTESOL (Harris, 2015). It is applicable usually only to receptive skills lessons, and is described in detail in Unit 2 under *Receptive Skills* (reading and listening). Because it is logical, easy to implement and reassuring for learners, trainee teachers often find it useful for structuring lessons. However, it is not without its critics, and those who dislike it argue that it is not very realistic (we never get preparation or two listenings in real life), not challenging enough (the comprehension tasks used are often superficial) and doesn't necessarily improve the sub-skills it is designed to improve. Nonetheless, it makes an accessible starting point, after which experimentation with other ways of teaching receptive skills can take place.

K.4 Learner needs analysis

Needs analysis is an essential part of all good teaching. While it is not too difficult to find out about a learner's basic needs (as required in the Learner Profile assignment of the CertTESOL), it is more challenging to understand and tease apart the separate, but closely related elements of needs, preferences and aspirations. However, perhaps the biggest challenge with regards to needs analysis is working out how to manage the needs of many different learners within the same class. A number of important skills are required for this (e.g. developing rapport, managing demanding learners, dealing with cultural expectations), and these are only likely to develop with experience.

One of the things that you will quickly learn when you start teaching (if not before) is that, depending on the learner, the learning context and the type of class, you will need to modify how you collect data in order to assess the learner's needs. To provide an obvious example of this, the needs analysis questionnaire that we might use with one-to-one learners is rather different from the questionnaire that we would use with group learners. In the former context, the learner can pretty much dictate the syllabus, so it is useful to collect as much information as possible regarding what they want to study. However, in the latter context, given that the learner will be studying in a larger class, where the syllabus is already predefined, it is useful to focus the interview more on other aspects of the learner's needs.

Figure K.1 provides a generic Needs analysis questionnaire that you should find useful when you begin teaching. It should also help you to develop your interview questions for the Learner Profile, although please note that it has not been designed specifically with that assignment in mind, and will require adaptation (see Unit 3). The questionnaire has two pages. The first page is likely to be useful with all general English learners, including those learning in a class. The second page relates to syllabus design and is likely to be useful mainly for teaching one-to-one students.

Learner needs analysis questionnaire

Name:	Nationality:
Occupation:	Other languages spoken:

Part 1 – General Information

1. Why are you studying English?

2. Which areas of English do you think you are weak (W), average (OK) or strong (S) in?
   ▢ vocabulary   ▢ grammar   ▢ pronunciation   ▢ speaking
   ▢ writing   ▢ reading   ▢ listening

3. When do you use English at the moment? (tick any)
   ▢ Socialising with friends   ▢ Talking to colleagues/customers at work
   ▢ Writing (e.g. emails) at work   ▢ Chatting online with friends
   ▢ Using English in shops, cafes, etc.   ▢ Accessing written information (e.g. on the Internet)
   ▢ Other: please specify   ▢ Studying: specify area of study

4. When do you think you will need to use English in the future? (tick any)
   ▢ Socialising with friends   ▢ Talking to colleagues/customers at work
   ▢ Writing (e.g. emails) at work   ▢ Chatting online with friends
   ▢ Using English in shops, cafes, etc.   ▢ Accessing written information (e.g. on the internet)
   ▢ Other: please specify   ▢ Studying – What?

5. What kind of lesson do you think you learn more from? (tick any)
   ▢ grammar   ▢ vocabulary   ▢ reading and discussion
   ▢ writing and correction   ▢ listening   ▢ speaking and correction

6. How do you like your teacher to correct your mistakes? (tick one)
   ▢ correct everything   ▢ correct most of my mistakes
   ▢ only correct major mistakes   ▢ note down the corrections and tell me afterwards

7. How often do you prefer to do homework? (tick one)
   ▢ every day   ▢ 3-4 times a week   ▢ 1-2 times a week   ▢ never

8. What are your main interests when you are not working?

9. What qualities do you think make a good language teacher?

10. Do you have any specific needs that you would like to discuss (e.g. a disability or impairment)?

Part 2 – Syllabus Planning

11. In a typical one-hour lesson, how much of the following would you like? (specify in minutes)
    a) Discussing the latest news
    b) Talking about a specific subject
    c) Intensive correction of spoken English
    d) Study and explanation of grammar
    e) Spoken practice of grammar
    f) Study and explanation of vocabulary
    g) Spoken practice of vocabulary
    h) Listening practice (audio/video based)
    i) Reading practice (from course books or authentic sources)
    j) Writing practice (based around what you may need to write)

12. How interesting are the following subjects for discussion for you?
    Write from 1 (not interesting) to 5 (very interesting):

    ☐ Travel, tourism, holidays   ☐ Free time, sport, leisure
    ☐ Food, restaurants, diet   ☐ Jobs, work, CVs
    ☐ School, education, university   ☐ Socialising with friends
    ☐ Relationships, family, marriage   ☐ Theatre, the arts
    ☐ Science, technology   ☐ Computers and IT
    ☐ Crime, the police, law   ☐ Television and film
    ☐ Money, banks   ☐ The news, current affairs
    ☐ Business, politics   ☐ Health, doctors, the body
    ☐ Geography, weather   ☐ Culture, traditions
    ☐ Environment, animals, plants   ☐ Home, furniture, architecture
    ☐ Describing appearance   ☐ Describing personality and emotions
    Others – Please Specify

13. How important are the following areas of grammar to you?
    Write from 1 (not important) to 5 (very important):

    ☐ Tense grammar – Present   ☐ Tense grammar – Past / Present perfect
    ☐ Tense grammar – Future   ☐ Articles – a / the
    ☐ Countable and Uncountable Nouns   ☐ Question forms
    ☐ Word order in sentences   ☐ Comparatives / Superlatives
    ☐ Modal verbs   ☐ Verb patterns and structures
    ☐ Prepositions   ☐ Conjunctions
    ☐ Conditional structures   ☐ Relative Clauses
    Others – Please Specify

14. Is there anything else that you would like to study that hasn't been covered in Part 2?

K.5 Grammar reference

Sentence structure

Sentences can vary in their length and complexity. The simplest sentences in English contain only one finite verb form (a finite verb is a verb in a specific tense, not including infinitives or gerunds), and are called, logically, 'simple sentences'. Here is an example:

The dog — subject *ate* — verb *the bone.* — object

In order to make this a more complex sentence, we need to link it to other actions/verb forms. Perhaps the most common way that this is done is to use a conjunction (e.g. *but, when, if,* etc.). The following example shows how two simple sentences are linked together to become 'clauses' within a new, complex sentence:

The dog ate the bone, — clause 1 *but* — conjunction *he didn't eat the fish.* — clause 2

Parts of speech

Notice that the structural elements of a sentence can each contain a number of parts of speech:

definite article	adjective	noun	preposition	definite article	noun	auxiliary verb	adverb	main/ lexical verb	quantifier	indefinite article	noun
The	old	dog	in	the	corner	was	greedily	eating	half	a	bone
subject (noun phrase)						verb (verb phrase)			object (noun phrase)		

The long noun phrase at the start of the sentence also includes a prepositional phrase (*in the corner*), and that prepositional phrase includes a shorter noun phrase ('the corner').

If you have difficulty working out which type of word it is, try this:

- To find the adverb, ask HOW? e.g. *How did he eat?* Answer: *greedily*
- To find the object, ask WHO/WHAT? e.g. *What did he eat?* Answer: *half a bone*
- To find the subject, ask WHO/WHAT (did it?) e.g. *Who/what ate the bone?* Answer: *the dog*
- To find the verb, ask WHAT did he DO? e.g. *What did he do to the bone?* Answer: *he ate it*

Different parts of speech and areas of grammar are dealt with below in alphabetical order. While this is a good initial overview, more detail and more examples can be found in pedagogical grammars such as Michael Swan's *Practical English Usage* (2005a), and Martin Parrott's *Grammar for English Language Teachers* (2010).

Adjectives

Adjectives describe nouns, e.g. *the greedy dog*

- **Comparative adjective:** *Rover is a greedier dog than the others.*
- **Superlative adjective:** *Rover is the greediest dog of them all.*

Notice that the comparative and superlative form of longer adjectives take 'more' and 'most' respectively:

- *English is more difficult than Italian.*
- *Chinese is the most difficult language.*

Adverbs

Adverbs qualify verbs (i.e. they describe how the verb was done) e.g. *The dog ate greedily.*

These familiar adverbs are called adverbs of manner and usually end in *'ly'*. They answer the general question: How? Example adverbs of manner are: *slowly, lazily, well, badly*, etc.

However, there are several other types of adverbs, many of which do not end in *'ly'*:

- Adverbs of frequency: *sometimes, often, never*
- Adverbs of certainty: *possibly, maybe, definitely*
- Adverbs of comment: *fortunately, surprisingly*
- Connecting adverbs: *then, next*
- Adverbs of time: *yesterday, now, soon*

Adverbs can also consist of more than one word. For example: *five minutes ago* is an adverb of time. If they consist of more than one word, we sometimes call them 'adverbials' or 'adverbial phrases'.

Articles

1   **a/an** = indefinite article – used for a non-specific item, or an item not mentioned before.
2   **the** = definite article – used for a specific thing mentioned before, or when there is only one of something (e.g. *the Queen of England*).
3   **ø** = zero (i.e. *'no'*) article – we don't use any articles in some situations or expressions (e.g. *in hospital, for breakfast*).

Example:
I had a cup of tea and a sandwich for lunch. The tea was nice, but the sandwich wasn't.

Conditional Structures

A conditional sentence typically includes two clauses, with one clause stating the condition and the other the result:

Example 1: *If I were you, I'd apologise.*

Example 2: *I'll go to the park unless it rains.*

We use a conjunction to introduce the conditional clause (*if, unless*). Notice how the conditional clause can come either first or second in the sentence, and if it comes first, we usually use a comma to separate the two clauses, as in Example 1 above.

We can identify four basic types of conditional structure, although in reality, especially when speaking, we may mix different structures quite regularly. Each structure tends to have specific verb forms, and conveys subtly different meanings to other conditional structures that can make them tricky for language learners to understand and use. Here are the most commonly identified types in coursebooks and pedagogic grammars:

- **Zero conditional** – present tense/present tense; implies something is always true:

  Example: *If you press this button, it scans the document automatically.*

- **1st conditional** – present tense/future tense (or modal); implies a real future situation:

  Example: *If it rains, I'll take my umbrella.*

- **2nd conditional** – past tense/*would* (or other modal) + infinitive; implies a hypothetical situation:

  Example: *If I won the lottery, I'd give up this job.*

- **3rd conditional** – past perfect tense/*would have* + past participle; implies a past hypothesis, something that is not possible, but can be imagined:

  Example: *If I hadn't missed the bus, I would have made it to the concert on time.*

Conjunctions

Conjunctions are one of several types of words we use to link ideas together. Conjunctions link ideas within a sentence. Examples are: *and, but, although, if, when, because, so.* Three types are commonly identified: coordinating conjunctions (*and, or,* etc.), subordinating conjunctions (because, if, so, etc.) and correlative conjunctions, which come in pairs (*both… and…, rather… than…,* etc.).

Generally speaking, conjunctions can link two clauses together to make a longer sentence.

Example 1: *I'll go <u>if</u> you go.*

Example 2: *I went home <u>because</u> I was tired.*

Determiners

Determiners often begin noun phrases, and there are several types: **articles** (*a, the, ø*), demonstratives (*this, that, these, those*), possessive determiners, also called possessive adjectives/pronouns (*my, your, his, her, its, our, their*) and **quantifiers** (*several, a little, the whole*, etc., see *Quantifiers* below).

Gerunds

Gerunds are verb forms that operate as nouns. They all end in *-ing*, but so do a number of other parts of speech such as *-ing* verb forms (participles), common nouns (lightning) or adjectives (boring).

> Example 1: *Living in London is expensive.*

> Example 2: *I can't stand waiting.*

Nouns

Common nouns are 'things' (real or abstract) which can be preceded by an article:

> Example: *the dog, an apple, a cat, the problem, an idea,* etc.

Proper nouns are names of things (words you wouldn't find in a dictionary, but in an Encyclopaedia), and usually start with a capital letter:

> Example: *Luton, Helen, the Amazon,* etc.

Prepositions

Prepositions are a type of linking word. For example, we can use them to link verbs to pronouns/nouns (e.g. *It depends on you.*), or link two nouns together (e.g. *the old dog in the corner*). Because English does not have many prepositions, each one often has a range of different uses. While they may seem logical to native speakers, many of the uses of a specific preposition cannot be predicted and need to be learnt by students. Here are some of the common classes of prepositions commonly taught in ELT coursebooks:

- prepositions of location: *under the table, near the door*
- prepositions of movement: *through the tunnel, up the stairs*
- prepositions of time: *at 4 o'clock, on Tuesday*
- dependent prepositions (typically follow verbs or adjectives): *depend on, good at*

Pronouns

Pronouns are used instead of nouns:

Subject Pronouns	I	he	she	it	we	you	they
Object Pronouns	me	him	her	it	us	you	them
Personal Pronouns	mine	his	hers	its (no apostrophe)	ours	yours	theirs

(for possessive pronouns see *determiners*)

Quantifiers

Quantifiers include words such as: *many, a few, several, all, half,* etc. As their name implies, they indicate how much or how many of something we're talking about. They are a type of **determiner**.

Relative Clauses

Relative clauses are one of the areas of syntax most commonly studied in ELT coursebooks. Learners need guidance with them because there are specific rules for usage in English. Relative clauses provide information about a noun in the sentence, and usually come directly after that noun. In some cases, the relative clause provides additional information that's interesting, but not necessarily essential for understanding the sentence. The relative clause is underlined in the following sentence, and the noun that it is describing is in bold:

> **Hamlet**, <u>*which many critics think is one of Shakespeare's greatest plays*</u>, *is set in Denmark.*

Notice how the relative clause is embedded within the main clause from which it is separated by commas. Relative clauses often start with relative pronouns; *which* in the above sentence. Other relative pronouns include *who, whom, whose* and *that*. Sometimes a relative pronoun can be omitted, but only in certain types of sentences:

> **The book** <u>*(that) I bought last week*</u> *was better than this one.*

That can be omitted in this sentence, because it is the object of the verb (*bought*) in the relative clause (*I bought **the book***). Notice that in the following sentence, the relative pronoun (*that*) is the subject of the verb, so it cannot be omitted (***the book** helped me*):

> *This is* **the book** <u>*that helped me*</u> *to overcome my depression.*

ELT coursebooks often describe two types of relative clause, 'defining' and 'non-defining', also called 'identifying' and 'non-identifying' by some authors. There are important differences between the two types and how they are used. Consult a more detailed grammar reference book if you are planning to teach them.

Verbs 1: Transitive & intransitive verbs

Verbs are words which describe actions, states or feelings (e.g. *wonder, walk, hate,* etc.). Verbs are usually preceded by a subject (except imperatives such as *Stop!*), but they are not always followed by an object.

Transitive verbs require an object: *The dog <u>ate the bone</u>.*

Intransitive verbs don't require an object: *The dog <u>barked</u>.*

Some verbs can be used transitively or intransitively (e.g. *eat*):

> Example1: *The dog <u>ate</u> hungrily.* (no object)
> Example 2: *The dog <u>ate</u> the bone.* (with object)

Verbs 2: Verb Forms (morphemes)

In English, most verbs have four forms, although some irregular verbs have five:

Infinitive / base form	Present simple 3rd person	Past simple	Past participle	Active participle ('-ing' form)
eat	eats	ate	eaten	eating
work	works	worked		working

Verbs 3: 'Tenses' Overview

The following chart shows all the possible 'tenses' in English. Technically speaking, this table combines tenses (past and present), aspects (perfect and continuous) and a modal form (will), but they are commonly referred to as 'tenses' in coursebooks and among English language teachers. Common contractions are shown in brackets (e.g. *doesn't*).

		Present	Past	Future
Simple		**Present simple**	**Past simple**	**Future simple/*'Will'* future**
	+	she eats	she ate	she will (she'll) eat
	-	she does not (doesn't) eat	she did not (didn't) eat	she will not (won't) eat
	?	does she eat?	did she eat?	will she eat?
Continuous		**Present continuous**	**Past continuous**	**Future continuous**
	+	he is eating	he was eating	he will be eating
	-	he is not (isn't) eating	he was not (wasn't) eating	he will not (won't) be eating
	?	is he eating?	was he eating?	will he be eating?
Perfect		**Present perfect (simple)**	**Past perfect (simple)**	**Future perfect (simple)**
	+	she has eaten	she had eaten	she will have eaten
	-	she has not (hasn't) eaten	she had not (hadn't) eaten	she will not (won't) have eaten
	?	has she eaten?	had she eaten?	will she have eaten?
Perfect continuous		**Present perfect continuous**	**Past perfect continuous**	**Future perfect continuous**
	+	he has been eating	he had been eating	he will have been eating
	-	he has not (hasn't) been eating	he had not (hadn't) been eating	he will not (won't) have been eating
	?	has he been eating?	had he been eating?	will he have been eating?

Note that many more contractions can be used to shorten the above, especially when speaking. Example: *She'll have eaten. She'll've eaten.* etc.

Verbs 4: Auxiliaries (including modals)

In order to conjugate some of the tenses/aspects above, we often need to use extra 'helping' verbs. We call these helping verbs 'auxiliaries'. For example, the following present perfect simple verb form consists of two verbs: *eat*: the main verb in the past participle form, and *have*: the auxiliary verb required to make the perfect aspect:

> *I have eaten lunch.*

Three verbs are used as auxiliaries to make main verbs into negatives, questions and different aspects:

- *do (do/does/did)* – used with simple forms
- *have (have/has/had)* – used with perfect forms
- *be (be/am/is/are/was/were/been)* – used with continuous forms

There are a number of modal verbs (full name 'modal auxiliaries') in English (e.g. *may, might, will, must, should*), all of which come before the main verb. Modal auxiliaries modify the meaning of the main verb to express a range of functions such as obligation (*must*), possibility (*might*), ability (*can*), etc.

> Example 1: *You must stop smoking.*

> Example 2: *I can't see anything.*

Verbs 5: Passives

Compare the two sentences:

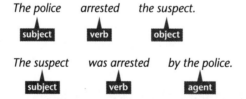

In both sentences the police *do* the verb (i.e. they are the agent), but in the second, we have chosen to put *the suspect* at the front of the sentence, perhaps because it's the main focus of interest. In order to do this, we change the verb form, into the 'passive voice': *was arrested*. The passive voice is used for a variety of reasons, especially style, but it may also be used when we don't know the agent, or aren't interested in it:

> Example 1: *Seven people were injured in the accident.*

> Example 2: *This chair was made in Switzerland.*

There is a passive form for every tense and aspect in English. They're made by adding the verb *'to be'* to the past participle of the main verb. Here are some examples. The passive verb forms are in bold:

	Active	Passive
Present simple	The police catch criminals.	Criminals **are caught** by the police.
Past simple	They arrested him last night.	He **was arrested** last night
Future simple	They will charge him tomorrow.	He **will be charged** tomorrow.
Present continuous	They are holding the suspect at the police station.	The suspect **is being held** at the police station.
Past continuous	They were holding the suspect at the police station.	The suspect **was being held** at the police station.
Future continuous	They will be charging him tomorrow.	He **will be being charged** tomorrow.
Present perfect	They have caught him.	He **has been caught**.
Past perfect	They had caught him, but he escaped.	He **had been caught**, but he escaped.
Future perfect	They will have sentenced him by tomorrow evening.	He **will have been sentenced** by tomorrow evening.

Note how in the passive sentence, the auxiliary verb *'be'* is modified into the same tense/aspect of the active sentence, and the main verb is always in past participle form. Also note that some of the above (e.g. future continuous passive) are very rare in actual usage.

Pre-course preparation tasks

The following tasks are included to help future CertTESOL trainees prepare effectively for their course. If you have already begun your course, you may also find the tasks useful. The tasks require you to demonstrate understanding of the content of this book, for example by applying theory to practice, thinking up useful ideas or drawing on prior experience to solve problems. You may also want to read more widely to help you to research your answers, which is always a good idea. The tasks are provided in the order of the units in the book. No tasks are provided for two of the Units: *Before the Course* and *After the Course*.

Your course provider may decide to incorporate some of these tasks into their own pre-course preparation. If they do, they will collect in your completed tasks at the start of your course and provide feedback soon after. Answers are not provided as most of the tasks require personal perspectives, and for those that do not, the answers can be found in the units themselves.

Unit 1 Understanding teaching practice

1   Which of the approaches described in Unit 1.1 have you experienced in the past, either as a pupil at school or learning (or teaching) as an adult? Describe how you found them, and identify features that could have improved your learning (either from your own ideas or from other approaches described).

2   Choose one of the three example lessons outlined in the section on lesson planning on page 33. Write a brief lesson plan for your chosen lesson, including the following:

   ■ aims/learning outcomes of the lesson

   ■ main lesson stages, including stage aims, procedure and estimated timeframes

3   Choose two of the activities from your example lesson plan and write down the instructions you would give exactly as you would say them. Remember to follow all the guidelines provided in Unit 1.

4   Considering your previous experience (e.g. your own learning, your experience of teaching others something, public speaking, presenting to colleagues, etc.), what do you think your biggest challenges are likely to be during the teaching practice element of the course? Try to identify at least three, and for each one, indicate why you chose it, and how you will try to overcome it.

Unit 2 Understanding and teaching language and skills

5 Identify the advantages and disadvantages of being a native speaker of English with regard to language awareness, contrasting this with the specific advantages that non-native speaker course participants are likely to have in this area.

6 Choose one of the following sentences, and parse it:

A 'Teachers can change lives with just the right mix of chalk and challenges.' (Joyce Meyer)

B 'I have never let my schooling interfere with my education.' (Mark Twain)

C 'A teacher affects eternity; he can never tell where his influence stops.' (Henry Adams)

7 Record a short extract from a natural spoken conversation between friends (50-100 words only). Transcribe it into written English and then identify any features of spoken grammar that are present in the extract.

8 Listen again to your short extract from the conversation between friends. Select a short passage of 10-15 words (this may include more than one speaker) and transcribe this into phonemic script (see *3.6 The Learner Profile* for help with this). Add word stress to any words that have more than one syllable. Then see if you can identify any features of connected speech in the extract.

9 Analyse the following extract from a famous TV comedy sketch for different aspects of lexis (e.g. affixes, collocations, idioms, etc.):

A: Now that's what I call a dead parrot.

B: No, he's stunned! You stunned him, just as he was waking up!

A: Now look, mate, I've definitely had enough of this. That parrot is definitely deceased, and when I purchased it, you assured me that its total lack of movement was due to it being tired out following a prolonged squawk.

B: Well, he's probably pining for the fjords.

A: Pining for the fjords? Look, why did he fall flat on his back the moment I got him home?

B: The Norwegian Blue prefers kipping on its back! Remarkable bird, isn't it, squire? Lovely plumage!

A: Look, I took the liberty of examining that parrot when I got it home, and I discovered the only reason that it had been sitting on its perch was that it had been nailed there. If you hadn't nailed him to the perch he'd be pushing up the daisies!

(Chapman et al., 1989)

10 Choose a short, interesting text from a newspaper, magazine or website (300-500 words), and develop a reading lesson based on the receptive skills lesson structure provided in Unit 2. Describe the basic stages of your lesson using a similar format to the one provided on page 99. Don't forget to include your text and provide its source.

Unit 3   Understanding learners

11 Using the descriptions provided in Unit *3.1 Learner language and learners' languages*, list three languages that either you or a friend/family member know, and indicate the level of proficiency in each, providing a brief description of ability in each of the four skills.

12 Imagine yourself in a year's time, as you were asked to do in the *Before the Course* unit. Choose a language that will probably be useful to you then. Photocopy and complete the needs analysis questionnaire on pages 206-207 (both pages) for yourself in this imagined context. Then compare yourself with the learner described on page 127. What significant differences do you notice that will influence the type of language learning course you need?

13 Which do you think you will be better at and why: teaching multilingual classes of learners, teaching monolingual classes of learners or teaching one-to-one lessons? Provide reasons for your answers.

Unit 4   Understanding and using materials

14 Look at the coursebook extracts on page 153. Choose one of the activities (each activity is lettered A, B, C or D) and provide three or four suggestions for how you could 'lift this activity out of the coursebook'. For example, think about how you could make it more stimulating, more useful or more enjoyable.

15 Task 10 above suggested that you choose a specific text appropriate to a reading skills lesson. Now consider how you would make such a text more suitable for the Materials Assignment and briefly do the following, drawing on the advice given for the Materials Assignment:

   A   Describe how you would use the text in class.

   B   Describe how you would present the text to make it look professional and appealing.

   C   Identify two problems that the learners could have with your chosen text.

16 Imagine you are the candidate who created the materials for the example assignment pro forma provided on pages 156-158. Read the pro forma again and make brief notes on possible answers to the following moderation interview questions:

   A   What was the linguistic purpose of your materials?

   B   How relevant were your materials to your learners' needs?

   C   How effective were the materials in achieving your aims?

   D   What problems did you have with the materials during the activity?

   E   What changes would you make if you were to use the materials again?

Unit 5   Experiencing learning

17 Identify three similarities and three likely differences between the unknown language experience that you will undergo on your CertTESOL course, and your prior experience of language learning. These differences may relate to the learner (you), the teacher, the lesson, or the 'learning community'.

18 Do you think such beginner lessons should be conducted without any use of the learners' first language (in this case English)? Give reasons for your answer.

19 Look at the Unknown Language Journal pro forma extract on pages 169-171. Read it carefully and identify five things that the trainee who wrote it probably learnt from the lesson. For each of these five points, identify which area the learning related to. For example:

A   the needs of language learners

B   the challenges of learning a foreign language

C   how to structure lessons

D   useful teaching skills, strategies, techniques, etc.

E   preparation and effective use of resources

F   the challenges of managing the learning process

G   aspects of language and language use in the target language

20 Imagine you are moving to a country where you don't know the language to teach English in one month's time. List five things you could do to begin learning the language before you leave.

Answer Keys

Review Key

Before the Course Review Key

1 EFL students...

2 She teaches only EFL learners.

3 ...at level 5.

4 It refers to a class that contains students of mixed nationality – the class is multilingual rather than the individuals.

5 Part-time courses should involve approximately the same amount of study.

6 Applicants without A-levels or degrees can still be accepted if they demonstrate the required academic study potential needed to complete the course.

7 All applicants have to attend an interview, either face-to-face or via Skype.

8 Your assignments must be your own work.

9 Non-native speakers usually have less difficulty with explaining grammar to learners.

10 The more background reading you do before the course the better.

Unit 1 Review Key

1 False. All teachers can improve their practice by reflecting carefully after each lesson.

2 Basically true. The communicative approach has changed surprisingly little since the 1980s.

3 False. They also help you learn.

4 False. It's probably best if you start by thinking about what you want the learners to do and achieve (your intended aims or outcomes).

5 False. The standard required increases gradually.

6 True.

7 False. It's less appropriate for lessons focusing on receptive skills.

8 True.

9 False. It's integrated.

10 False. Commentating should be avoided.

11 False. Guided Observation is when you observe qualified teachers, and peer observation is when you observe your co-trainees on the course.

12 Generally true. Each learner is likely to get more speaking practice during a pairwork activity than groupwork.

13 False. Specific and measurable aims are often impossible due to the incremental nature of skills development in language teaching.

14 False. This is a good idea if possible, but sometimes it is necessary to give the materials earlier in the instruction (e.g. if they need to see an image, example or table to understand the instruction).

15 False. You should try to be as objective as possible.

Unit 2 Review Key

1 uncountable noun

2 part of speech

3 parse

4 collocation

5 intransitive verb

6 implicit knowledge

7 function

8 phoneme

9 exponent

10 receptive skills

11 elicit

12 drill

Unit 3 Review Key

1 False. The Common European Framework describes learner proficiency at different levels.

2 False. Needs analysis questionnaires typically collect data on a range of aspects of the learner (see the example in *The Knowledge*).

3 True.

4 True.

5 Probably not true. We still have no evidence to support the need to cater for different learning styles in the language classroom.

6 True.

7 True.

8 True.

9 False. The one-to-one lesson is unobserved and unassessed.

10 True.

Unit 4 Review Key

Suggested answers:

1 … the written resources that teachers use in class.

2 … because coursebooks are generic products and never designed to cater for the needs of your learners.

3 … business English coursebooks, general English coursebooks, exam class coursebooks.

4 …Teacher's Guide, Workbook, Class Audio CD, E-resources, Video materials.

5 …say how effective they were and what you would/ could do to improve them for future use.

6 …a completed written assignment and an interview with the course moderator.

7 …14 marks.

Unit 5 Review Key

The 'red herring' is number **7**. You will not be expected to, nor will you be assessed on your ability to remember what you are taught in the Unknown Language lessons.

After the Course Review Key

2 A.3 The job interview

3 A.5 Teaching qualifications and career paths

4 A.1 Planning your next career moves

5 A.2 Finding your first job

6 A.4 Starting work

7 A.1 Planning your next career moves

8 A.2 Finding your first job

9 A.4 Starting work

10 A.3 The job interview (*Finding work as a non-native speaker teacher*)

Pause for thought Key

1 An example of a simplified instruction is: *'Read the text and answer the questions below it.'*

2 One possible solution is to remind them that discussion activities are not a race, and that the aim is to try to speak for the full five minutes. You could ask them to try again bearing this in mind, or get them to think of three more questions on the same topic that they could discuss.

3 YouTube videos and website articles could easily be used to teach listening and reading skills. These same raw materials should provide a useful context for analysing the three systems (grammar, vocabulary and pronunciation). Using Skype, you could engage the learner in speaking practice and also provide further listening practice and pronunciation support.

As for a whiteboard, Adobe Connect enables you to show and write on slides in real time, so that other conversation members can read what you have written. As a much simpler solution, Skype messaging can be used simultaneously with a Skype conversation for writing basic words, sentences, etc.

The key potential advantage is convenience for both you and the learner. You can both work from home, reducing travel costs, time and impact on the environment. The biggest disadvantage is probably the quality of video and audio, which is dependent on both of you having a good connection. Occasionally, if it breaks down altogether, you may need to reschedule a lesson.

4 *got out* – phrasal verb
and – conjunction
we – pronoun
under – preposition
angrily – adverb
stealing – gerund
silver – adjective
Peugeot 206 – proper noun
other – determiner
've – auxiliary verb
so – conjunction
quiet – adjective
may – modal auxiliary verb
as – preposition

5 **1** I spoke English.

    2 I had been speaking English …

    3 I have spoken English …

    4 I will be speaking English …

6 Base form/infinitive: *play* (tennis)
Past simple form: *played* (tennis)
Continuous/active participle: *playing* (tennis)
Past participle: *played* (tennis)

    1 Past simple and past participle forms are the same for regular verbs.

    2 by adding *-ed*

    3 Regular: *work, live, remember*
Irregular: *do, eat, swim*

    4 Many courses teach the verb 'to be' first at elementary level, even though it's an irregular verb, because it's so important. Then they usually teach the regular verbs, because one basic rule enables learners to do a lot with the language. Irregular verbs will usually come next.

7 **1** Present perfect continuous.

    2 *Then; so; when the car broke down* (this whole phrase acts like an adverb); *down*

    3 *We won't be taking …; Will we be taking …?*

    4 Question tag.

    5 The learner is trying to count an uncountable noun in English (*bread*).

    6 The tense is past simple for both verbs, and the adjective is in the comparative form.

8 There are of course many implications – here are two: firstly, as teachers we shouldn't get frustrated if learners don't necessarily learn things as we teach them. Secondly, the more we understand about this natural order, the more we can help to move learners along it more quickly by anticipating and providing help with the next phase.

9 **T** Look at this adjective. [Points at *expensive*] How many syllables does it have?

    Ss Three.

    T That's right. What do we add to it to make the comparative form?

    Ss 'more'

    T Exactly. And do we add it before or after the adjective?

    Ss Before.

    T What do we use comparative adjectives for?

    Ss To show a difference / to compare.

    T Yes. And when we use a comparative, how many things are we comparing?

    Ss Two.

    T Do we use it just to compare objects?

    Ss No. Also to compare people or places.

10 **1** Sentence jumble

    2 Sentence transformation

    3 Error correction

    4 Matching

    5 Controlled writing

    6 Spoken transformation drill

11 Collocations include: *unforgettable laugh; great sense of humour; hear rumours; unbelievable charm.*

    Idiom: *quite a card; talk his way out of it* (this is also a multi-word verb)

    Multi-word verb: *warm to somebody; pull over*

    Words with several morphemes: *description* (*describe + tion*); *unforgettable* (*un + forget + able*); *policemen* (*police + man*); *unbelievable* (*un + believe + able*)

12 **1** Useful to distinguish from *producer*.

    2 Useful to distinguish from *actor*.

    3 Less useful, but may also distinguish from *producer / backer*.

    4 May be useful, although the fact that directors often say '*Action!*' in English may not be shared in other cultures, and students may not know the word in English.

    5 Useful. Examples help to crystallise a concept.

    6 An interesting question, but does not check the concept.

13 **1** 12; **2** 8; **3** 24; **4** 9;
    5 /iː/ 'thr<u>ee</u>'; /uː/ 'tr<u>ue</u>'; /ŋ/ 'bri<u>ng</u>'; /ɜː/ 'b<u>ur</u>n';
    /θ/ '<u>th</u>ink'; /ʃ/ 'wi<u>sh</u>'

14

●	●•	•●	●••	●••
jeans	*monkey*	*unique*	*detective*	*photograph*
	trousers	*abroad*	*computer*	*calculate*

15 **1** Time permitting, I would deal with this immediately. I'd write the two words on the board and model the correct pronunciation. I'd get the learners to notice the vowel sound in each word, and then I'd drill it, starting with the vowel and building up to the full word.

2 I'd leave this for a future lesson, and have a look on YouTube for some examples of this accent. If I found a good example, I'd probably arrange a listening comprehension activity around it.

3 I'd leave this for a future lesson, and possibly choose either a role-play activity for a situation in which sounding warmer and more interested was important (e.g. job or university interview).

16 I'd attach a note to the piece of writing as follows: 'Well done! This is a really nice story. I like the twist at the end that brings the waiter into the crime. Some nice vocabulary, and a nice range of sentence structures. I thought it finished a little bit suddenly – could you turn that last sentence into a paragraph perhaps? Also, check the difference between *fall, fall over, fall down,* and *fall onto.* I'd also provide some correction of the mistakes in the text itself.

17 Extract 1: upper-intermediate;
Extract 2: pre-intermediate.

18 Here is one possible rendition in fairly slow, careful RP, with the errors corrected:
Line 1: /aɪˈɡəʊtəðə ˈsɪnəməˈsʌmtaɪmz ɪnˈsentrəlˈlʌndən/
Line 2: /aɪhəvtuː ˈbrʌðəz ðəˈfɜːstwʌnɪzˈneɪmdˈæke/
Line 3-4: /ɪfjə ˈlaɪkˈneɪtʃə jəkənˈɡəʊ təðəˈnɔːθ
ˈmenɪˈnaɪsˈpleɪsɪz.../

19 **1** Extract A: EAP coursebook
Extract B: exam class coursebook
Extract 3: business English coursebook
Extract 4: younger learner coursebook

2 Extract A: It uses academic language, and provides advice for reading academic texts.
Extract B: It provides an opportunity for learners to practise part of the speaking exam.
Extract C: It covers a topic and skills that business English students may find useful.
Extract D: The text is larger, the contexts, images and layout make it attractive and clear to younger learners.

3 Extract A: To help learners to understand three theories presented in a text (not shown);
Extract B: To practise a section of the speaking exam;
Extract C: To improve listening skills. It also probably models and helps learners to notice new language (e.g. for making arrangements);
Extract D: To help the learners to remember (or revise) and practise common collocations.

20 While any of the activities could be adapted for the materials assignment, Exercise C under Listening and Exercise B under Grammar provide perhaps the best opportunity for creative adaptation. For example, the words in Listening Exercise C could be copied onto flashcards for learners to work with on their desk – different coloured flashcards could be used for the 3 different columns. The pictures provided for Grammar Exercise B could be blown up and learners could add their own captions, speech bubbles or sentences, which they could then display on the walls of the classroom.

21 Note that these are approximate matches:
1 A
2 A, B
3 A
4 A, B
5 A, B
6 C
7 Depends
8 E, F, G
9 E, F
10 C
11 D
12 I, J
13 Depends
14 G
15 H
16 J, L
17 I
18 I, J, L
19 K
20 K, L

22 First quote: the learner
Second quote: the linguist and the teacher
Third quote: the learner

Glossary

Units in which the terms occur are indicated in brackets (e.g. **A** – After the course; **1** – Unit 1).

action research (A)	Research that a teacher carries out in her/his own classroom, typically to develop understanding about teaching and learning.
activity cycle (1, 2)	A cycle that typically includes three stages; Preparation, Activity, and Feedback. These stages are usually followed in this order each time we do an activity, exercise or task in class.
aspect (2)	Grammatical term. Alongside **tense**, the aspect of a verb form provides information about its completion or duration (e.g. the continuous aspect).
assimilation (2)	Feature of pronunciation. When a sound in one word influences the pronunciation of an adjacent sound in another word (e.g. *'ten people'* may be pronounced *'tem-people'*).
authentic text (1, 2)	A text from the 'real world' that is used in the language classroom largely or wholly unchanged (e.g. a news website article, a radio interview or an extract from a novel).
auxiliary (2)	Grammatical term. An auxiliary verb is often added to a main verb to form different tenses, questions and negatives (e.g. *be, do* and *have*). Modal auxiliaries include *can, should* and *will*.
blended learning (1)	A combination of digital/online learning and more traditional face-to-face learning.
boardwork (1)	The teacher's use and organisation of the whiteboard/chalkboard space.
bound morpheme (2)	Contrasts with **free morpheme**. Part of a word that cannot exist on its own (e.g. the 's' in a plural: books).
business English (B, 4)	The learning and teaching of English specifically for use in business/ work-related contexts.
CAP (1, 2)	Context, Analysis, Practice. A 3-stage model for structuring new language lessons.
catenation (2)	Feature of pronunciation. Describes how words join together in fast speech (e.g. *an apple* may sound like one word to a language learner).
chesting (1)	Showing a handout or piece of material to learners while giving an instruction, by holding it in front of your chest.
choral drill (2)	When the teacher gets all the learners to repeat a word, short phrase or sentence together in unison.
classroom management (B, 1, 5)	A general term used to refer to everything that contributes to the organisation and management of a lesson (e.g. giving instructions, organising groupwork, monitoring, etc.).
CLIL (1)	Stands for 'Content and Language Integrated Learning'. Refers to an approach to teaching in which a foreign language is used to teach school subjects (e.g. history, science), based on the assumption that the learners will learn both the subject and foreign language at the same time.
collocation (1, 2, 4)	A common or habitual combination of two or more words in a phrase (e.g. *hard work* or *run a business*).

commentate (1)	When a teacher tells learners unnecessary information. Often caused by the teacher thinking out loud rather than giving concise instructions or information.
Communicative Approach / communicative language teaching (1, 2)	Refers to an approach to language teaching in which the ability to communicate (especially in spoken form) is the goal, and communicative interaction is a key part of the learning process.
communicative competence (1)	Linguistics term. Refers to a language user's ability to communicate effectively (typically made up of grammatical, sociolinguistic, strategic and discourse competences).
concept check questions (CCQs) (2)	Questions a teacher asks students to check their understanding of a concept (e.g. *Is it past or present?* checks the time reference of a verb tense).
contrastive analysis (2)	When aspects of two languages (e.g. the learner's L1 and English) are compared and analysed.
controlled practice (1, 2, 3, 4)	Practice of an area of language (e.g. a grammar point) through an activity that restricts learners' choices or freedom (e.g. a pronunciation drill or a gap-fill exercise). Contrasts with **freer practice**.
countability (2)	Grammatical concept. Refers to whether a word can be pluralised and counted. For example, *water* is usually uncountable, but *bottle* is countable (e.g. *two bottles*).
CPD (A)	Stands for 'Continuing Professional Development'. Refers to the process of improving, developing and expanding our knowledge as teachers through, for example, workshops, observations and career progress.
differentiation (1, 3)	Pedagogical term. Refers to how a teacher responds to differences between the learners in a class to provide for all their needs as effectively as possible.
Director of studies (A)	Job title, especially common in private language schools. The director of studies is usually responsible for organising classes, recruitment and management of teachers and quality control of the teaching process.
discourse (2)	Written or spoken communication or debate. In linguistics, the term is used to refer to units of language use longer than a sentence.
discovery learning (2)	A constructivist approach or technique in which learners are actively involved in the learning process, typically finding out something for themselves rather than being told it or shown it.
Dogme ELT (1)	An approach to English language teaching that rejects the use of coursebooks in order to focus on the relationship and interaction between learners and teachers.
drill/drilling (1, 2, 5)	A language teaching technique in which learners repeat a word or phrase in order to improve their pronunciation, often, but not always, after the teacher has modelled it.
e-learning (1)	Learning conducted through, or with the support of electronic media, such as the Internet, apps, etc.
EAP (4, A)	English for academic purposes. The learning and teaching of English specifically in order to study in an academic environment (e.g. at university).
ELF (1)	English as a lingua franca. Refers to the use of English in communication between non-native speakers of English (usually of different **first language** backgrounds), and the study of how English is used in such contexts.

elicit (1, 2)	When the teacher uses questions and prompts to get the learners to provide information or an answer rather than the teacher providing it.
elision (2)	Pronunciation term. Refers to the disappearance of some sounds, especially in connected speech, that might otherwise be pronounced in slower speech. For example, the *'t'* in *next* may be elided in the phrase: *next please*.
emergent language (2)	Language that arises naturally during the learning process, often produced or needed by learners, that is then focused on through clarification with the support of the teacher.
ESP (4, A)	English for specific purposes. Contrasts with **general English**. Refers to the teaching and learning of English for a narrower context of use. Examples include **business English**, **English for academic purposes** or English for law.
explicit knowledge (1, 2)	In linguistics, this refers to conscious, declarative knowledge about language (e.g. the ability to name a verb tense), and contrasts with the instinctual **implicit knowledge** that enables all native speakers to use a language.
exponent (2)	An expression or phrase that can be used to perform a specific function in a language. For example, the exponent: *Would you mind if I…?* is used to perform the function of making polite requests.
extensive (reading/ listening) (2)	Contrasts with **intensive reading/listening**. Reading or listening to a longer text such as a book or a film.
false friend (2)	A word or expression in one language that looks or sounds like an expression in another language, but actually has a different meaning. For example, the word *librairie* in French means bookshop, not library.
false start (2)	In the analysis of spoken language data, a false start refers to when we begin a sentence, but don't finish it, often abandoning it and choosing a different sentence structure instead.
filler (2)	Common, short, fixed expressions in spoken language that are used primarily to allow a speaker time to think. For example: *you know, I mean*.
first language (B, 2, 3, 5)	Also called **L1**. Usually refers to the first language learnt during childhood, although some people grow up with two or more such languages, making the term essentially problematic.
fixed expression (1, 2)	A combination of words often used together, and often with a specific meaning. For example: *on the other hand, Merry Christmas, pleased to meet you*, etc.
flashcard (1, 2)	A piece of card or paper with a word, phrase or image written large enough on it for the learners to see it when shown by the teacher or displayed on the board.
form (B, 2)	When referring to the analysis of grammar and lexis, form refers to the written element that may need to be studied, such as the spelling of a noun, or the combination of words in a verb tense.
formative assessment (1)	Contrasts with **summative assessment**. Refers to any assessment that provide useful data/ feedback for the teacher or learner. Also called 'assessment for learning'.
free morpheme (2)	Contrasts with **bound morpheme**. Refers to a word or word element that can stand alone. In the word: apples, apple is a free morpheme, and '-s' is a bound morpheme.

freer practice (1, 2)	Contrasts with **controlled practice**. Practice of an area of language (e.g. a grammar point) through an activity that enables learners to use language more freely as might happen outside the classroom, for example in a role-play, discussion or a blog entry.
function / functional language (1, 2, 4)	The function of a piece of language is its communicative purpose. For example, giving advice is the function performed by the sentence: *You should see a doctor.* Functional language refers to language that is analysed and practised with a focus on this communicative purpose.
gallery activities (1)	Any activity in the classroom in which a number of images, texts or bits of language are stuck on the walls for learners to move about, look at and respond to.
gap-fill (1, 2, 4)	A common controlled practice activity, in which learners must complete gaps in written sentences or a text, often used to demonstrate understanding of new language.
general English (B, 1, 2, 3, 4)	Contrasts with **English for specific purposes**. Refers to the learning of English with no particular field or context in mind, and focuses on developing lexis, phonology, grammar and skills for any potential future context.
genre (2, 3)	In linguistics, 'genre' refers to specific modes of language use. Common written genres that language learners may study include emails, newspaper articles, etc.
groupwork (1, 2, 3)	An interaction pattern in which learners do an activity in groups of three or more.
idiolect (3, 5)	The language choice and way of talking of an individual person.
implicit knowledge (1, 2)	In linguistics, this refers to the instinctual, unanalysed knowledge of a language that all native speakers of that language have. It contrasts with the conscious, **explicit knowledge** about language (e.g. the ability to name a verb tense), that language learners often study.
individual drill (2)	Pronunciation term. When a teacher asks individual learners to repeat a word or phrase to improve their pronunciation of it.
information gap (1,2)	An activity common in **communicative language teaching** in which learners are given different information and a task that requires them to communicate to share and compare that information. For example, a 'spot the difference' activity in which learners can't show their pictures to each other.
input sessions (B, 3)	Workshops and seminars in which your trainers teach you about language and language teaching.
instruction check questions (ICQs) (1)	Questions asked by a language teacher to check that learners have understood an instruction. For example: *'What do you talk about?' 'Do you write down your partner's answers?'*
intensive (reading/ listening) (2)	Contrasts with **extensive reading/listening**. Refers to the study of shorter texts, or text extracts, in order to understand or analyse them in detail.
interactive whiteboard / IWB (1, 2, 4)	A whiteboard with IT capability, typically including a computer display and touch sensitivity, such as a Smartboard™.
intercultural competence (1)	The ability to communicate effectively and appropriately across cultural boundaries.
intonation (2, 3)	Changes in pitch in spoken language – the 'music' of language.
intransitive verb (2)	A verb that requires no object. For example: *die: He died.*

L1 (B, 1, 2, 3, 5)	See **first language**.
L2 (3)	Second language. Usually refers to the language being learnt, even if this is the learner's third or fourth language.
language awareness (LA) (B, 2, A)	Somebody's conscious knowledge about grammar or vocabulary that enables him or her to identify composite elements, tenses, uses, **parts of speech**, etc.
learner autonomy (3)	A learner's ability to direct her/his own learning.
learner language (3)	The language used by a language learner or group of language learners, including abilities, changes and errors. Also called 'interlanguage'.
learning aims (1)	The aims of a lesson or lesson activity, often required on lesson plan documents.
learning environment (1, 3)	The situation in which the learner is learning a language. This may include the language classroom, an online environment, or the learner's social environment.
learning outcome (1, 2, 3, 4, 5)	ˌalternative term to lesson aim, a statement that describes what the learners will be able to do by the end of a lesson or course.
learning style (B, 1, 3)	A term that has historically been used to refer to different ways of learning that different learners appear to exhibit. However, research has yet to establish that 'learning styles' exist.
Lexical Approach (1)	An approach to language teaching developed primarily by Michael Lewis in which key aspects of **lexis** are emphasised and given priority over grammar (Lewis, 1993).
lexical chunks (1)	A group of words that are commonly found together including **collocations**, semi-fixed and **fixed expressions**.
lexis (B, 1, 2, 3, 5)	Vocabulary. The word **lexis** is preferred in linguistics, and also used in the CertTESOL syllabus.
liaison (2)	Pronunciation term. Refers to the different ways in which words or sounds can be linked together in connected speech, including both linking sounds (e.g. /r/) and intrusive sounds (e.g. /w/).
linking (2)	Pronunciation term. Used as a synonym for liaison by some authors, or more specifically to refer to certain sounds use to link two words together in connected speech (e.g. linking /r/).
meaning (B, 2)	One of several components of grammar or **lexis** that is often analysed and clarified when teaching English. The others include use, **form** and pronunciation.
mentoring (A)	When an experienced teacher provides support to a novice teacher, for example by planning together, conducting peer observations, etc.
metacognitive awareness (3)	Pedagogical term. Refers to a learner's awareness of their own language learning, including chosen strategies, personal aims and awareness of own learning.
mingle (1, 2, A)	An interaction pattern in which learners move around the classroom, conducting brief interactions with other learners before moving on, much like mingling at a party.
minimal pairs (2)	Pronunciation term. A minimal pair is a set of two words that has only one phonological difference between them. For example, *pin* and *bin* are a minimal pair.

model (1, 2)	When a teacher demonstrates or shows something. In language teaching, this usually refers to the demonstration of pronunciation of a word, phrase or sentence or of how grammar is used in a clause or sentence. Also used as an adjective 'a model answer', and a noun 'a model' in the more general sense meaning a good example to follow.
moderation (visit) (B, 4)	At the end of every CertTESOL course, an external assessor (called a **moderator**) visits the course as part of the assessment process. The moderation visit includes sampling of portfolios and conducting of interviews with trainees for the Unit 4 assignment.
moderator (1, 4)	The external assessor who visits a CertTESOL course at its end. Moderators are experienced CertTESOL trainers who have been appointed their role by Trinity.
monitor (1, 2, 5)	What the teacher does when the learners are working either individually, in pairs or in groups. Monitoring involves moving around the classroom, checking all the learners are on task, offering help, providing correction, etc.
monolingual (B, 3, 4)	Contrasts with **multilingual**. A monolingual class is a class of learners who share a common language, which may be the **first language** for most of them. A monolingual person is an individual who only speaks one language.
morpheme (2)	Linguistic term. Any part of the word that can combine with other morphemes. For example: *play* and *-ed* are both morphemes that can combine together. See also **bound morpheme** and **free morpheme**.
morphology (2)	The study of the form of words, especially in English language teaching with regard to how different **morphemes** combine. Compare with **syntax**.
mother tongue (B)	Another word for **first language/L1**. Usually refers to the first language that monolingual learners acquire during childhood.
multilingual (B, 1, 2, 3, 4, 5)	Contrasts with **monolingual**. A multilingual class is a class of learners who do not share a common language other than the language being taught. A multilingual person is an individual who speaks more than one language.
multi-word verb (2)	A verb consisting of two or more parts, especially phrasal verbs such as *take off, put up with,* etc.
native speaker norms (1)	Language use habits, conventions and beliefs regarding appropriacy and correctness of usage that are based on the practices of native speaker users of a language.
needs analysis (3)	The process of finding out about a learner's language learning needs (and also often their preferences, strengths and weaknesses). Can be conducted through an interview, a questionnaire or a combination of the two.
non-standard forms of English (4)	Forms of English that do not conform to the standards or expectations of established varieties of English. This may include slang, unusual spellings, and unconventional uses of grammar.
noun phrase (2)	Grammatical term. Either a noun on its own or a group of words containing a noun and functioning as the subject or object of a sentence (e.g. *The lazy cat...*).
one-to-one (B, 1, 3, A)	Teaching one-to-one means teaching one student alone in a private lesson.
objective (B,1, 3, 4, 5)	(alternative to lesson aim) A statement of the goal or intended learning of a lesson, often more specific than an aim.

orthographic (3, 5)	An adjective that means 'written. In language teaching 'orthographic script' is often contrasted with **phonemic script** to indicate normal written script.
pairwork (1, 2, 3)	When learners do an activity working in pairs.
paraphrasing (1)	This means simply saying (or writing) something using different words. Paraphrasing is a useful skill for language learners as it enables them to communicate even if they don't know a specific word.
parse / parsing (2)	To analyse a sentence, phrase or text for its composite grammatical elements.
part of speech (2)	Category or type of word. For example, noun, verb, preposition or adjective. Means the same as 'word class'.
pedagogical content knowledge (2)	A teacher's knowledge of how to teach the content of a subject. In language teaching this goes beyond our knowledge of *what* we are teaching to include our understanding of *how*, for example, to help learners to understand it or get them practising it.
peer correction (1, 2)	When a student corrects another student's mistake.
peer feedback (B, 1)	On the CertTESOL, peer feedback is when trainees provide feedback to each other on their lessons.
peer observation tasks (1)	Tasks that your CertTESOL tutors ask you to complete while observing your co-trainees.
phoneme (2)	Pronunciation term. A phoneme is a sound that has meaning in a language (either on its own or when combined with others).
phonemic chart (B, 1, 2)	A chart that shows all of the sounds of a specific language (English in our case), and can be used in class.
phonemic script / transcription (B, 2, 3)	A way of writing the sounds of a language. English phonemic script includes both standard letters and letters from the International phonetic alphabet (e.g. /θɪŋk/ is the phonemic transcription of the word *think*).
phonology (B, 1, 2, 3, 5, A)	The study of meaningful sounds in a language.
placement test (3)	A test that is given to learners primarily in order to put them in the right class, usually according to level of proficiency.
post-lesson reflection (1)	Often called simply **TP feedback** on many CertTESOL courses. Post-lesson reflection is the discussion between trainees and trainer that happens after **teaching practice** on the CertTESOL.
prefix (2)	Part of a word that can be added to the front of another word to create a new word. For example, the prefix *'un'* can be added to *happy* to make *unhappy*.
process writing (2)	An approach to writing that focuses more on the process than the product, recognising that especially when done collaboratively (e.g. students working in pairs), the act of planning, drafting and responding to feedback on a text provides useful opportunities for communicating and learning.
productive skills (1, 2)	Contrasts with **receptive skills**. The two productive skills usually recognised in language teaching are speaking and writing.

professional awareness and development (PAD) (1)	One of the assessment criteria specified in the CertTESOL syllabus that encourages trainees to behave professionally (e.g. being punctual, following institutional guidelines, and working together with co-trainees effectively as a team).
rapport (B, 1, 3, 5)	A teacher's rapport is her/his relationship with learners. We often talk about 'establishing a good rapport' in class as an important part of quality teaching.
realia (1, 2, A)	Real things brought into class (or even found in class) to support language learning. For example, a teacher might bring in cooking utensils for a lesson on kitchen vocabulary and recipes.
receptive skills (1, 2)	Contrasts with **productive skills**. The two receptive skills usually recognised in language teaching are reading and listening.
reflective practice (A)	A teacher's ability to examine her/his own teaching critically in order to improve.
register (3)	Two basic registers are often taught in language teaching, formal and informal. However, register can also refer to conventions of language use in specific situations and contexts (e.g. legal register).
remedial grammar teaching (1)	Teaching an area of grammar after noticing the learners have difficulty with it.
resubmit (1, 3, 5)	Submit something again. On the CertTESOL if a trainee's assignment does not pass on first submission, the trainee may be given an opportunity to resubmit it after receiving feedback.
scaffold / scaffolding (B, 1, 2)	Understood simply, scaffolding means supporting or helping learning. Within sociocultural theory, scaffolding refers to the specific guidance and/or support needed to enable a learner to solve a problem, complete a task or gain a new piece of knowledge.
schemata (2)	Plural of 'schema'. An organisation or representation of knowledge in the learner's brain. Often in ELT, lead-in activities provide opportunities to activate learners' prior schemata (i.e. background knowledge) before texts or the introduction of new language.
scripting (1)	Writing something down in full. In language teacher education, trainee teachers are often advised to script instructions if they are having difficulty making them clear.
self-evaluate / evaluation (B, 1, 2, 3)	Evaluate one's own performance. On the CertTESOL, trainees are expected to provide both written and spoken self-evaluation on their own teaching after each assessed lesson.
self-study resource books (4)	Books designed for learners to access and read on their own, e.g. a grammar practice book with exercises and an answer key.
sentence stress (2)	Pronunciation term. Refers to how some words receive greater stress in a sentence and others are weaker. Also referred to as 'utterance stress'.
soft skills (3)	A general term used especially in work-related and training contexts that refers to the social skills, common sense and awareness of appropriacy that enable us to interact and work effectively with others.
sub-skills (1, 2)	In language teaching, sub-skills refers to the skills that together make up one of the four main skills (reading, writing, speaking and listening). For example, letter recognition is a sub-skill learnt early on in the process of learning to read a language.
suffix (2)	Part of a word that can be added to the end of another word to create a new word. For example, the suffix *'ness'* can be added to *happy* to make *happiness*.

syntax (2, 3)	The ordering and arrangement of words within the grammar of a specific language. Compare with **morphology**.
tablet chairs (1)	A type of chair often used in classrooms that have small tables on one of the arms.
target language (1, 2, 3, 5)	This term has two meanings in language teaching. It can either refer to the language being learnt (i.e. English in our case) or a specific area of language that a teacher is intending the learners to learn in a specific lesson (e.g. *'will'* could be the target language in a lesson on future predictions).
task-based learning (TBL) (1)	Also called task-based language teaching. A specific approach, usually recognised as part of **communicative language teaching**, in which meaningful tasks form the focus of the learning process. There are both strong and weak versions of TBL.
teaching practice (B, 1, 2, 4, 5)	On the CertTESOL, teaching practice is the part of the course when you teach real language learners English. It's also the primary focus of Unit 1 of the CertTESOL.
Teaching Practice Portfolio (1, 4)	On the CertTESOL, your Teaching Practice Portfolio is a file in which you keep all your lesson plans, materials, feedback from tutors on your teaching and self-evaluation documents. Part of your assessed portfolio.
TP feedback (1)	A more common, informal term for **post-lesson reflection** on the CertTESOL. Refers to the discussion that happens after **teaching practice** between trainees and trainer.
tense (1, 2, 3)	Alongside **aspect**, the tense of a verb form provides information about when the activity was completed (e.g. past tense).
timeframe (1)	An indication of time allocated to a specific activity or lesson stage either on the lesson plan or when indicated to learners during an instruction. A timeframe provides rough guidance, not a strict time limit.
time management (1, 2)	Refers to a teacher's ability to manage time effectively during a lesson.
usage (B, 1, 2)	A description of how an item of language (e.g. a grammar point) is typically used.
utterance(s) (B, 1)	A unit of spoken language. As we do not speak in sentences, the term utterance is often preferred by linguists.
vague language (1, 2)	Expressions common in spoken language that intentionally make a communication or an idea vaguer. For example: *sort of, like,* etc.
voiced (2)	Pronunciation term. Sounds in English can be either voiced (made with a vibration of the vocal chords) or **voiceless**/unvoiced. When you whisper, everything you say is voiceless.
voiceless (2)	Pronunciation term. See: **voiced**.
weak form (2)	Pronunciation term. A weak form is a syllable that is not stressed in a word or sentence, and often includes a 'schwa' sound (/ə/), at least in native speaker varieties of English.
word class (2)	See: **part of speech**.
word stress (2)	Pronunciation term. In words of two or more syllables in English, one syllable typically has more stress than the others. Identifying word stress means finding this syllable.
younger learners (B, 3, A)	Child or teenager language learners. Learners aged 16 or under are usually considered to be younger learners.

References

Anderson, J. (2004) *Teamwork: Interactive tasks to get students talking.* Addlestone, UK: Delta Publishing.

Anderson, J. (2006) *Role plays for today.* Peaslake, UK: Delta Publishing.

Anderson, J. (2014) *Speaking games.* Peaslake, UK: Delta Publishing.

Anderson, J. (2017) 'A potted history of PPP with the help of ELT Journal'. *ELT Journal,* 71 (2).

Anderson, J. R. (1983) *The architecture of cognition.* Cambridge, MA: Harvard University Press.

Biber, D., Finnigan, E., Johansson, S., Conrad, S. and Leech, G. (1999) *Longman grammar of spoken and written English.* Harlow: Pearson.

Brookfield, S. D. (1990) *The skilful teacher.* San Francisco: Jossey Bass.

Butzkamm, W. and Caldwell, J. (2009) *The bilingual reform: A paradigm shift in foreign language teaching.* Tubingen: Narr Studienbücher.

Byrne, D. (1976) *Teaching oral English.* London: Longman.

Byrne, D. (1986) *Teaching oral English.* 2nd ed. London: Longman.

Cameron, L. and Larsen-Freeman, D. (2007) 'Complex systems and applied linguistics'. *International Journal of Applied Linguistics,* 17 (2), pp. 226-240.

Carson, J. G. and Longhini, A. (2002) 'Focusing on learning styles and strategies: A diary study in an immersion setting'. *Language Learning* 52 (2) pp. 401-438.

Carter, R. and McCarthy, M. (2006) *Cambridge grammar of English: a comprehensive guide: Spoken and written English grammar and usage.* Cambridge: Cambridge University Press.

Chapman, G., Cleese, J., Gilliam, T., Idle, E., Jones, T. and Palin, M. (1989) 'The dead parrot sketch', in Wilmut, R., (ed.), The complete Monty Python's Flying Circus: All the words, volume one. New York: Pantheon Books.

Cheung, Y. L. (2002) 'The attitude of university students in Hong Kong towards native and non-native teachers of English'. Unpublished master's thesis. Chinese University of Hong Kong, People's Republic of China.

Coffield, F., Moseley, D., Hall, E. and Ecclestone, K. (2004) *Learning styles and pedagogy in post-16 learning: a systematic and critical review.* London: Learning and Skills Research Centre, Learning and Skills Development Agency.

Cook, G. (2010) *Translation in language teaching: an argument for reassessment.* Oxford: Oxford University Press.

Corder, S. P. (1967) 'The significance of learners' errors'. *International Review of Applied Linguistics,* 5, pp. 161-169.

Coyle, D., Hood, P. and Marsh, D. (2010) *CLIL: Content and language integrated learning.* Cambridge: Cambridge University Press.

Crystal, D. (2009) *Just a phrase I'm going through: My life in language.* London: Routledge.

Deci, E. L. and Ryan, R. M. (1985) *Intrinsic motivation and self-determination in human behavior.* 3rd ed. New York: Plenum Press.

Dörnyei, Z. and Skehan, P. (2003) 'Individual differences in second language learning', in Doughty, C. and Long, M. (eds.), *The handbook of second language acquisition,* pp. 589-630. Malden, MA: Blackwell.

Dörnyei, Z. and Csizér, K. (1998) 'Ten commandments for motivating language learners: Results of an empirical study'. *Language Teaching Research,* 2 (3), pp. 203-229.

Dörnyei, Z. (1998) 'Motivation in second and foreign language learning'. *Language Teaching,* 31 (3), pp. 117-135.

Dörnyei, Z. (2008) 'New ways of motivating foreign language learners: Generating vision.' Links, 38, pp. 3-4.

Ellis, N. C. and Larsen-Freeman, D. (2006) 'Language emergence: Implications for applied linguistics – introduction to the special issue'. *Applied Linguistics,* 27 (4), pp. 558-589.

Ellis, R. and Shintani, N. (2014) *Exploring language pedagogy through second language acquisition research.* Abingdon, UK: Routledge.

Ellis, R. (2008) 'Principles of instructed second language acquisition'. *CAL Digest*. Washington, DC: Centre for Applied Linguistics.

Fitts, P. M. (1964) 'Perceptual-motor skills learning', in Melton, A. W. (ed.), *Categories of human learning*, pp. 243-285. New York: Academic Press.

Foster, J. (2007) *The Poetry Chest*. Oxford: Oxford University Press.

Freeman, D. (1989) 'Teacher training, development, and decision making: A model of teaching and related strategies for language teacher education'. *TESOL Quarterly*, 23 (1), pp. 27-45.

Gardner, R. and Lambert, W. E. (1972) *Attitudes and motivation in second language learning*. 6th ed. Rowley, MA: Newbury House.

Graham, C. (2000) *Jazz chants old and new*. Oxford: Oxford University Press.

Harmer, J. (1998) *How to teach English*. Harlow, UK: Pearson.

Harmer, J. (2007) *The practice of English language teaching*. 4th ed. Harlow, UK: Pearson.

Harris, B. 2015. 'Where are we now? Current teaching paradigms in pre-service training'. Paper presented at the 49th International IATEFL Annual Conference, Manchester, UK.

Hattie, J. (2009) *Visible learning: A synthesis of over 800 Meta-Analyses relating to achievement*. Abingdon: Routledge.

Hymes, D. H. (1972) 'On communicative competence', in Pride, J. B. and Holmes J. (eds.), *Sociolinguistics: Selected Readings*, pp. 269-293. Harmondsworth: Penguin,

Jenkins, J. (2000) *The phonology of English as an international language: New models, new norms, new goals*. 2nd ed. Oxford: Oxford University Press.

Kassabgy, O., Boraie, D. and Schmidt, R. (2001) 'Values, rewards, and job satisfaction in ESL/EFL', in Dörnyei, Z. and Schmidt, R. (eds.), *Motivation and second language acquisition*, pp. 213-237. Honolulu, Hawaii: University of Hawaii Press.

Kumaravadivelu, B. (2003) *Beyond methods: Macrostrategies for language teaching*. New Haven: Yale University Press.

Lantolf, J. P. and Thorne, S. L. (2007) 'Sociocultural theory and second language learning', in VanPatten, P. and Williams, J. (eds.), *Theories in second language acquisition*, pp. 201-224. Mahwah, NJ: Lawrence Erlbaum Associates.

Lee, E. and Lew, L. (2001) 'Diary studies: The voices of nonnative English speakers in a master of arts program in teaching English to speakers of other languages'. *CATESOL Journal*, 13 (1), pp. 135-149.

Leech, G., Cruickshank, B. and Ivanic, R. (2001) *An A-Z of English grammar and usage*. Harlow, UK: Pearson.

Lewis, M. (1993) *The lexical approach: The state of ELT and a way forward*. Hove, UK: Language Teaching Publications.

Lewis, M. (1997) *Implementing the lexical approach: Putting theory into practice*. Hove, UK: Language Teaching Publications.

Lightbown, P. M. and Spada, N. (2013) *How languages are learned*, 4th ed. Oxford: Oxford University Press.

Lipovsky, C. and Mahboob, A. (2010) 'Appraisal of native and non-native English speaking teachers', in Mahboob, A. (ed.), *The NNEST lens: Nonnative English speakers in TESOL*, pp. 154-179. Newcastle-upon-Tyne, UK: Cambridge Scholars Publishing.

Liskin-Gasparro, J. E. (1982) ETS *Oral Proficiency Testing Manual*. Princeton, NJ: Educational Testing Service.

MacAndrew, R. and Martinez, R. (2003) *Instant discussions*. UK: Thomson Heinle.

Mahboob, A. (2010) *The NNEST lens: Nonnative English speakers in TESOL*. Newcastle-upon-Tyne, UK: Cambridge Scholars Publishing.

Mahboob, A. and Golden, R. (2013) 'Looking for native speakers of English: discrimination in English language teaching job advertisements'. *Voices in Asia Journal*, 1 (1), pp. 72-81.

Medgyes, P. (1994) *The non-native teacher*. Oxford: Macmillan.

Murphy, R. (2012) *English grammar in use*. 4th ed. Cambridge: Cambridge University Press.

Oxford, R. (1992) 'Research on second language learning strategies'. *Annual Review of Applied Linguistics*, 13, pp. 174-187.

Oxford, R. (2003) 'Language learning styles and strategies: Concepts and relationships'. *International Review of Applied Linguistics in Language Teaching*, 41, pp. 271-278.

Oxford, R. (2011) *Teaching and researching language learning strategies*. Harlow, UK: Pearson.

Oxford, R. L. (1990) *Language learning strategies: What every teacher should know*. Boston, MA: Heinle & Heinle.

Parrott, M. (2010) *Grammar for English language teachers*. 2nd ed. Cambridge: Cambridge University Press.

Pashler, H., McDaniel, M., Rohrer, D. and Bjork, R. (2008) 'Learning styles: Concepts and evidence'. *Psychological Science in the Public Interest*, 9, pp. 105-119.

Redman, S. and Ellis, R. (1990-2014) *A way with words series*. Cambridge: Cambridge University Press.

Richards, J. C. and Rodgers, T. S. (2014) *Approaches and methods in language teaching*. Cambridge: Cambridge University Press.

Roach, P. J. (1991) *English phonetics and phonology*. Cambridge: Cambridge University Press.

Schumann, F. and Schumann, J. (1977) 'Diary of a language learner: an introspective study of second language learning', in Brown, H., Yorio, C. and Crymes, R. (eds.), *On TESOL '77*. Washington D.C.: TESOL.

Scrivener, J. (1994) *Learning teaching*. Oxford: Macmillan.

Scrivener, J. (2011) *Learning teaching*. 3rd ed. Oxford: Macmillan.

Seidlhofer, B. (2011) *Understanding English as a lingua franca*. Oxford: Oxford University Press.

Selinker, L. (1972) 'Interlanguage'. *International Review of Applied Linguistics,* 10, pp. 209-231.

Seymour, D. and Popova, M. (2003) *700 classroom activities: Conversation, functions, grammar, vocabulary*. 2nd ed. Oxford: Macmillan.

Smith, R. (2008) 'Key concepts in ELT: Learner autonomy'. *ELT Journal*, 62 (4) pp. 395-397.

Swan, M. (2005a) *Practical English usage*. 3rd ed. Oxford: Oxford University Press.

Swan, M. (2005b) 'Legislation by hypothesis: The case of task-based instruction'. *Applied Linguistics*, 26 (3), pp. 376-401.

Swan, M. and Smith, B. (2001) *Learner English*. 2nd ed. Cambridge: Cambridge University Press.

Thornbury, S. (2000) 'A dogma for EFL' *IATEFL Issues*, 153, p. 2.

Trinity College London. (2016) *Certificate in Teaching English to Speakers of Other Languages (CertTESOL): Syllabus – from January 2016*. London: Trinity College London.

Underhill, A. (1994) *Sound foundations*. Oxford: Macmillan.

Underhill, A. (2005) *Sound foundations*. 2nd ed. Oxford: Macmillan.

Villegas-Reimers, E. (2003) *Teacher professional development: An international review of the literature*. Paris: International Institute for Educational Planning/ UNESCO.

Vivian Cook (1995) Multi-competence and the learning of many languages. *Language, Culture and Curriculum,* 8 (2), pp. 93-98.

Watcyn-Jones, P. (1995) *Grammar games and activities for teachers*. London: Penguin.

Widdowson, H. (1978) *Teaching language as communication*. Oxford: Oxford University Press.

Widdowson, H. (1994) 'The Ownership of English'. *TESOL Quarterly*, 28 (2), pp. 377-389.

Widdowson, H. G. (1998) 'Context, community and authentic language'. *TESOL Quarterly*, 32 (4), pp. 705-716.

Wilkins, D. (1972) *Linguistics in language teaching*. London: Edward Arnold.

Wilkins, D. A. (1976) *Notional Syllabuses: A taxonomy and its relevance to foreign language curriculum development*. Oxford: Oxford University Press.

Willis, J. (1996) *A framework for task-based learning*. Harlow: Addison Wesley Longman.

Wu, A., Liang, J. and Csepelyi, T. (2010) 'Coping strategies for NNES teachers' development', in Mahboob, A. (ed.), *The NNEST lens: Nonnative English speakers in TESOL*, pp. 202-221. Newcastle-upon-Tyne, UK: Cambridge Scholars Publishing.

Yazdandoost, Z., Amalsaleh, E. and Kafipour, R. (2014) 'The relationship among collocation knowledge and listening, speaking, reading and writing proficiency of Iranian EFL learners'. *Language, Individual & Society,* 8, pp. 408-419.

Index

Words in italics are explained in the glossary. Page references in bold provide key information: